Beneath the Second Sun

Revisiting New England: The New Regionalism

SERIES EDITORS

Lisa McFarlane, *University of New Hampshire*
Dona Brown, *University of Vermont*
Stephen Nissenbaum, *University of Massachusetts at Amherst*
David H. Watters, *University of New Hampshire*

This series presents fresh discussions of the distinctiveness of New England culture. The editors seek manuscripts examining the history of New England regionalism; the way its culture came to represent American national culture as a whole; the interaction between that "official" New England culture and the people who lived in the region; and local, subregional, or even biographical subjects as microcosms that explicitly open up and consider larger issues. The series welcomes new theoretical and historical perspectives and is designed to cross disciplinary boundaries and appeal to a wide audience.

Richard Archer, *Fissures in the Rock: New England in the Seventeenth Century*

Nancy L. Gallagher, *Breeding Better Vermonters: The Eugenics Project in Vermont*

Sidney V. James, *The Colonial Metamorphoses in Rhode Island: A Study of Institutions in Change*

Diana Muir, *Reflections in Bullough's Pond: Economy and Ecosystem in New England*

James C. O'Connell, *Becoming Cape Cod: Creating a Seaside Resort*

Christopher J. Lenney, *Sightseeking: Clues to the Landscape History of New England*

Priscilla Paton, *Abandoned New England: Landscape in the Works of Homer, Frost, Hopper, Wyeth, and Bishop*

Adam Sweeting, *Beneath the Second Sun: A Cultural History of Indian Summer*

Beneath the Second Sun

A Cultural History of Indian Summer

Adam Sweeting

University of New Hampshire

Published by University Press of New England   Hanover and London

University of New Hampshire

Published by University Press of New England, 37 Lafayette St., Lebanon, NH 03766

© 2003 by Adam Sweeting

Printed in the United States of America

5 4 3 2 1

The author gratefully acknowledges permission to quote from the following previously published sources:

The many Emily Dickinson poems quoted in this book are reprinted by permission of Harvard University Press and the Trustees of Amherst College from *The Poems of Emily Dickinson*, Ralph W. Franklin, ed., Cambridge, Mass.: The Belknap Press of Harvard University Press, Copyright © 1998 by the President and Fellows of Harvard College. Copyright © 1951, 1955, 1979 by the President and Fellows of Harvard College.

"Vermont: Indian Summer," copyright 1953, renewed © 1981 by Philip Booth, from *Relations: New and Selected Poems* by Philip Booth. Used by permission of Viking Penguin, a division of Penguin Group (USA).

"Indian Summer" from *Lucking For Luck*, by Maxine Kumin. Copyright © 1992 by Maxine Kumin. Used by permission of W. W. Norton & Company, Inc.

"Indian Summer," by Al Dubin and Victor Herbert. © 1919, 1939 (Copyrights Renewed) Warner Bros. Inc. All Rights Reserved. Used by Permission. WARNER BROS. PUBLICATIONS U.S. INC., Miami, Florida 33014.

Passages from the Henry David Thoreau, *Journal*, are reprinted with the permission of Princeton University Press.

Library of Congress Cataloging-in-Publication Data

Sweeting, Adam W., 1963–
   Beneath the second sun : a cultural history of Indian summer / Adam Sweeting.—1st ed.
      p. cm.—(Revisiting New England)
      ISBN 1-58465-314-0 (cloth : alk. paper)
  1. American literature—New England—History and criticism. 2. Thoreau, Henry David, 1817–1862—Knowledge—New England. 3. Dickinson, Emily, 1830–1886—Knowledge—New England. 4. New England—Climate—History—19th century. 5. Autumn—New England—History—19th century. 6. Summer—New England—History—19th century. 7. Indians of North America—New England. 8. New England—In literature. 9. Weather in literature. 10. Indians in literature. 11. Autumn in literature. 12. Summer in literature.
I. Title. II. Series.
   PS243 .S94 2003
   810.9'33—dc21   2003004352

To Erica Mallory Foster, with love and thanks

Contents

Illustrations

Acknowledgments

I am doubly fortunate. The beauties of my subject always made my efforts to understand them seem like undeserved fun. One can't help but enjoy writing about Indian summer. But I am fortunate as well to have benefited from the help and support of many colleagues and friends. I am especially grateful for the unwavering friendship and assistance offered by Natalie McKnight, Chair of the Division of Humanities and Rhetoric, and Linda Wells, Dean of the College of General Studies at Boston University. They have supported this project from the start and I owe them both a lasting gratitude. The interdisciplinary environment of the College of General Studies also assures that I am in daily contact with scholars whose expertise spans the university curriculum. Several scholars have helped in important ways: Ted Davis shared his vast ornithological knowledge; Chris Fahy provided steady reminders of the contours of nineteenth-century American culture; and Joellen Masters, a scholar of Victorian literature, helped me understand exactly what I was trying to say after she read an early draft of the introduction.

I thank many others who helped along the way. Kent Ryden read drafts of chapters 1 through 4 and helped steer me toward a clearer sense of Indian summer's place in American culture. His comments could not have been more helpful. Joseph Bruchac and Barry Keim patiently answered my several phone and email questions. Stephen Nissenbaum, Dona Brown, and the staff of University Press of New England cheerfully supported this project through its various stages. I have also learned a great deal about the overlap of natural and cultural phenomena from my colleagues in the Association for the Study of Literature and Environment and the New England American Studies Association. In ways they might not recognize, others urged me to pursue beautifully complex subjects such as the one this book describes: Laura Poston, Sonya Friedman, Jack Holly, Jerry Haffner, Walter Wright, Gary Overvold, Paul Baker, and Kenneth Silverman.

A large portion of chapter 4 and portions of chapter 1 appeared in *Colby Quarterly* 39 (March 2003). I am grateful to Wes McNair, who edited the journal's special edition on New England writing, for inviting me to contribute and for his patience with my many delays. Thanks also to *Colby Quarterly* for granting me permission to reprint portions of the article here.

Finally, my most heartfelt thanks go to my family. Ethan and Sarah— one born in winter and the other in spring—are as wondrously beautiful as an Indian summer day. And Erica, to whom I dedicate this book, announces her loving presence in the first sentence of the introduction.

Beneath the Second Sun

Introduction

I have been equally charmed and fascinated by the season Indian summer since the late October afternoon that I married my wife. The setting could not have been more glorious. Cape Cod always appears lovely, but this particular afternoon possessed a crystalline beauty that perfectly complemented the occasion. From Provincetown to Plymouth, the Cape was blessed with warm, dry air. I remember thinking that the clouds—puffy and small—had stopped moving. They simply stood there, high above the equally still earth. The trees, too, contributed to the sense of enveloped calm. Each of the few remaining leaves barely hung to its branch, hovering between a perch in the air and resting place on the ground. They seemed at once alive and dead, Janus-like figures that looked to two worlds at once. It was, I was told again and again, a perfect Indian summer day, one of the joys of the New England landscape that I (a transplanted New Yorker) had both literally and figuratively married. Why and how this sort of weather should become emblematic of the New England climate is the subject of this book.

The following pages trace the cultural history of Indian summer, from its sudden appearance in late-eighteenth-century weather discourse to contemporary marketing campaigns that advertise the season as the best time to come look at the leaves. The project carves out for analysis that interlude of sudden warmth that briefly interrupts the gradual drop in temperatures characteristic of autumn. I focus primarily, although not exclusively, on nineteenth-century New England. In no other time or place was the season so frequently painted or described. Writers as varied in talent and temperament as Lydia Sigourney, Henry David Thoreau, Henry Wadsworth

Longfellow, and Emily Dickinson all wrote on the subject. In their work, as well as that of several less well known contemporaries, Indian summer played an important and overlooked role in the region's efforts to forge an identity specific and separate from the rest of the nation. To be sure, several figures outside of New England contributed (and continue to contribute) to the cultural history of the season, and their efforts will not be ignored. The earliest references to my subject, for example, occurred in the trans-Allegheny West in the post-Revolutionary decades and then moved rapidly west through the Ohio and Mississippi Valleys. But ever since Indian summer weather entered New England writing around 1820, the season and the region have been indelibly linked. For perhaps a week in early November, New England seems most New England.

The amorphous and unpredictable quality of Indian summer differentiates it from the four commonly recognized seasons. Winter, spring, summer, and fall are natural events—they occur whether or not individuals or cultures observe them. As the literary critic Lawrence Buell notes, Romantic poets such as Shelley and Keats never "doubted for a minute in their respective odes 'To the West Wind' and 'Autumn' that 'autumn' referred to a solid fact of natural history."[1] If we think of them at all, we usually consider the conventional seasons as the temporal settings through which human history unfolds. They seem merely there: time-bound natural facts that contain timeless eternal truths. Indian summer, on the other hand, defies our ability to read the skies. Of all the commonly recognized times of year, my subject stands the furthest removed from the movements of heavenly bodies. We might, for example, write a poem about fall (as many poets have done), but we can never disentangle autumn from its connection to the sun. It arrives each year at a specific moment in time, linking all poetry to the season to a measurable natural fact. Similarly, while spring may poetically suggest feelings of rebirth or youth, only at the precise moment of the vernal equinox can the season truly be said to begin. But with Indian summer we are left to our own intuitive devices. Its poetry occupies an aesthetic realm defined by our linguistic and cultural choices. Without looking to the sky for guidance we must rely on our sense that something about the weather has changed.

Throughout the book I argue that Indian summer occupies an unusual place in our sense of the calendrical cycle. While some commentators have dubbed it "the fifth season" or "the season within a season," I argue that it must also be understood as a form of weather. Consequently, I refer to Indian summer weather *and* Indian summer the season. Like rain and snow, its arrival and duration varies. In claiming for the warm days of fall the same meteorological and cultural significance that we might identify with a January blizzard, I aim to place discussions of meteorology and literature in dialogue with each other. As we will see, Indian summer teases out and examines those places where writing and talking about the weather—the "logos of meteors," in the words of the critic Arden Reed— dissolves traditional disciplinary boundaries.[2]

Sometimes such talk tries to explain and contain the weather through the discourse of science; at other times metaphors and tropes seem the best way to understand such an amorphous experience as the weather. Meteorological patterns such as Indian summer never stand in one place at one time; rather, they ebb and flow across the landscape in packets of energy that defy the predictions of the forecaster. Nor can the weather be contained. It seems at once a measurable statistical unit—and hence a subject of meteorology—and a diffuse collection of possible metaphors. With its mixture of hot and cold seasons and its lack of temporal speci- ficity, Indian summer offers the perfect subject for the exploration of how discourse about the weather functions in the works of literary naturalists, artists, and poets.

Contemporary meteorologists attribute the sudden burst of autumnal mildness to the movement of an anticyclone, a wind pattern that rotates clockwise around a zone of high barometric pressure. As these systems travel out of Canada in the fall, cold northwest winds bring a chill to the American Northeast, giving rise to the impression that the autumnal cool has settled in for a long stay. Frosts frequently occur under such conditions. But occasionally (and not every year) a high-pressure zone stalls off the Atlantic coast. As this happens, the clockwise rotation of the anticyclone pulls in warmer air from the south and southwest. Temporarily blocked by the stalled high, the stagnant warm air overlies the colder surface temper- atures, briefly halting the general cooling process that develops over the course of a typical fall. In New England, the average daytime temperature, which normally starts to decrease in late July, suddenly spikes upward to create a temporary interlude of mild, almost summerlike days.[3] Stunning in its beauty, the result is a period within the fall that clarifies the larger season precisely because conditions seem to have been sent to us from some other time.

Without ignoring scientific explanations (indeed, the book explores sev- eral) I have adopted an approach different from the one informing the previous paragraph. In recent years scholars and critics have argued that seemingly natural categories such as race and gender emerge from the complex interaction of social forces and history. They function, as the much-used phrase suggests, as social constructions, products of culture as much as—if not more than—biology. This is not the time or place to explore the implications of these critical developments other than to acknowledge that no serious student of the humanities or social sciences can ignore them. To the list of social constructions I would add the weather, a claim for which Indian summer offers perhaps the strongest evidence. Far from a purely natural event, the season offers itself as the preeminent case of invented weather. Its invention springs, not so much from the natural evolution of meteorological forces, but from the contingencies of late-eighteenth- and early-nineteenth-century American life. Like poetry and prose, or buildings and cities, Indian summer can be researched, discussed, and understood as a cultural artifact. Like the reception of a poem, which deviates as new reading practices and critical strategies emerge, Indian summer contains not only the seeds of its own history but continuously renegotiates its place in the day-to-day life of the present. Indeed, as the subsequent chapters reveal, an Indian summer often occurs precisely because certain cultural circumstances have created the very conditions that enable the season to exist. Culture, I argue, can construct weather.

A few words concerning my methodology and materials may be in order. Although the chapters follow a rough chronological path, my interest lies in cultural patterns rather than historical detail. In chapters 1, 2, and 3 I examine the available record to explore how and why Indian summer weather emerged when it did. Accordingly, I discuss those cultural sites where the season first entered the weather vernacular. In chapter 4 I turn to New England to consider why Indian summer resonated so deeply among the region's nineteenth-century writers. In chapters 5 and 6 I narrow my focus to consider how two canonical figures, Henry David Thoreau and Emily Dickinson, utilized Indian summer imagery to map their complex visions of the relationship between the natural world and the words we employ to describe it. Thoreau and Dickinson, I argue, saw meteorological and emotional complexities in the season to which most of their contemporaries remained blind.

Despite this outline, each chapter ranges widely across the centuries in search of those places where Indian summer illuminates broader cultural concerns. Like Indian summer itself, my materials are necessarily diffuse.

I draw on poetry, folklore, meteorological science, and natural history writing to address the season's delicate stance between the sensual and the linguistic experience of the natural world. As a season that lacks temporal and scientific specificity, it requires our words to give it shape.

Although I do not present a strict historical account, my investigation into the cultural history of Indian summer grew out of my interest in an etymological oddity: While only a small handful of references to the season prior to 1800 survive, by 1820 the term was ubiquitous in the nation's meteorological talk.[4] Having sprung from apparently nowhere, Indian summer terminology was now applied to virtually every aspect of American cultural life. Wherever we turn—poetry, painting, horticulture, even music—we find the season displaying both its actual and metaphoric face. How and why that happened informs each of the chapters that follow. Eventually, of course, the season settled into a consistent set of imaginative uses, several of which continue to be employed today. Because of its idyllic conditions and premonitions of pending death—we all know the beauty will not last— Indian summer provided a climatological backdrop for the rise of American sentimental poetry during the 1820s. Twenty years later, the same conditions encouraged Thoreau's transcendental muse, a subject to which I devote all of chapter 5.

Nineteenth-century Indian summer also came to symbolize wizened understanding, a period of second (and smarter) youth that follows a hard-won maturity. Seasons, of course, lend themselves to literary depictions of the stages that comprise human life. The conventions are well known. Spring implies youth, while summer ushers in young adulthood; autumn in turn brings maturity, while winter signals old age and death. Indian summer allows a more nuanced reading of the inevitable advance of years. Because plants and shrubs briefly rebound to life, it invites writers to fuse images of youthful exuberance with the seasoned understanding of the mature. We see this perhaps most obviously in William Dean Howells's 1886 novel *Indian Summer*. Its hero, a forty-one-year-old man troubled by his flirtations with a woman barely past twenty, eventually settles down and accepts the serenity of middle age. Having come dangerously close to tapping into the erotic passions of spring, he instead acquires an ennobling calm reminiscent of the warm light of an Indian summer sky.

The flip side to such newfound stability would be the allegedly unpredictable natures that contribute to an equally strong Indian summer tradition. Grace Metalious's controversial 1956 novel *Peyton Place* does this most explicitly. Set in a fictional northern New England town, the novel opens with a startling statement: "Indian Summer is a woman." Whereas Howells associates the season with a masculine recognition of limits, Metalious evokes an erotic and distinctly feminized time of year: "Ripe, hotly passionate, but fickle, she comes and goes as she pleases so that one is never sure whether she will come at all, nor for how long she will stay."[5] For her, Indian summer resembles Peyton Place itself: dark, full of secrets, and irresistible to readers—a seasonal femme fatale.

Metalious's opening line regarding Indian summer's evocative power to deceive—first it is cool, then hot, then frigid—recalls one reason why the season may carry the name that it does. Indian summer entered the weather vernacular during the late eighteenth and early nineteenth centuries, a period when many white Americans feared Indians for their supposedly cunning ways. As we will see in chapter 3, one popular nineteenth-century explanation for the origin of the term "Indian summer" traced its derivation to the fear among white settlers that the gentle weather characteristic of the season offered Indians the best opportunity to stage surprise attacks. An interlude remarkable for its beauty, Indian summer also contains no small amount of cultural mistrust.

The stark beauty of Indian summer has also made the season a particular favorite of American poets. Starting in the 1820s and continuing today, the season has been described in several dozen poems, ranging from the sentimental to the terrifying. Popular nineteenth-century poets such as William Cullen Bryant, Henry Wadsworth Longfellow, and Lucy Larcom wrote verse that while not always explicitly devoted to the season, relied on readers' familiarity with its dominant images. Hardly a year went by in the second half of the century without a major literary magazine such as *Harper's*, *The Atlantic*, or *Scribner's* publishing at least one Indian summer poem. Typically, nineteenth-century poets wrapped the season in sentimental garb; they stressed second springs and flowers reinvigorated with life. Thus, in the late 1830s the Rhode Island poet Sarah H. Whitman described "A Day of the Indian Summer" as a last opportunity to retrace "each sweet, summer haunt / And sylvan pathway," a period tinged with "the saffron stars / Of the witch hazel" that has suddenly come into bloom.[6] In the twentieth century, poets such as Vachel Lindsay, Maxine Kumin, and Philip Booth found a sense of temporal dislocation in Indian summer that their earlier counterparts typically did not. In a poem such as Booth's 1953 "Vermont: Indian Summer," for instance, the season functions as a time out of time, at once a specific moment of the year but also an interruption of the seasonal flow:

> Unseasonable
> as bees in April,
> rime in May,
> or Orion high
> in June,
> > days lost
> somewhere in August,
> green days, dun,
> return at noon
> as numb-winged wasps
> swim in the lapse
> of weather

On such days, Booth continues, "the sun / and weathervane / are still." If we are not careful, we may become "dazzled" like the wasps that "climb numb in the lapse of weather," becoming "lost / in what cannot last."[7]

No poet, however, thought more seriously about the implications of Indian summer than Emily Dickinson, whose work anchors the discussion of darker Indian summer visions outlined in chapter 6. Without once naming the season in a poem (although she does so in her letters) Dickinson nonetheless captures its tense stand between the warmth of summer and the winter coldness to come. For her, the season's arrival often signals an ominous turn of events, a late-year turn made all the more problematic for its repetition of the first summer's promise of life:

> Summer has two Beginnings –
> Beginning once in June –
> Beginning in October
> Affectingly again –
>
> Without, perhaps, the Riot
> But graphicer for Grace –
> As finer is a going
> Than a remaining Face –
> Departing then – forever –
> Forever – until May –
> Forever is deciduous –
> Except to those who die –
> > > (F 1457)[8]

In nearly a dozen related poems, Dickinson drew on many of the conventional and sentimental figures—blooming flowers, returning birds, sylvan paths—but she added new layers of complexity to our desire to stand "Beneath the second sun," the title of my book and the second line of one of her more chilling poems. More than any other poet, Dickinson stressed Indian summer's potential to unnerve our seasonal rhythms. She saw in ways that her contemporaries did not a meteorological arrow shot from apparently nowhere, one that punctures and rips open our conception of the fall.

While I aim to uncover the history of the season, I do not want to lose sight of Indian summer's capacity to make us marvel at how splendid the weather can be. It is "the moment of miraculous restoration," writes the poet Donald Hall, "Summer's curtain call or triumphant final tour."[9] As we swap sweaters for shirtsleeves, we cannot help but notice the beauty that surrounds us. Aside from pleasant warmth, Indian summer also brings the angular light cast by the low autumnal sun. Bathed in such a glow, objects appear sharper, as if contained within clearly defined frames, even as the season itself remains unbounded and undefined. Occasionally, a soft haze settles over the landscape as the warm air traps atmospheric dust and smoke. As the sun's warm rays pass through the haze, the landscape stands calm and still. Because they seem imbued with mystical light, such gentle scenes attracted nineteenth-century luminist painters such as Sanford Gifford and Worthington Whittredge. In their canvases, the landscapes created by Indian summer seem frozen in time; they invite viewers to stop and take a look. We see better on such days. In rural areas, flowers and shrubs return to life, adding new rounds of color to the fall. In cities we walk with an extra bounce in our steps. And if we pay close attention, as Thoreau did one Indian summer day in 1852, the arresting calm enables us to become more fully embedded within the sonic texture of the season. During Indian summer, he wrote in his *Journal*, "there is a certain resonance and elasticity in the air that makes the least sound melodious as in spring."[10]

Ralph Waldo Emerson caught something of that splendor when he noted that the "tempered light of woods" during Indian summer "is like a perpetual morning, and is stimulating and heroic." The "stems of pines, hemlocks, and oaks almost gleam like iron on the excited eye." For Emerson, such days secured his transcendental belief in the correspondence between man's symbol-making power and nature. During Indian summer, he claimed, previously "incommunicable trees begin to persuade us to live with them, and quit our life of solemn trifles."[11] Thoreau agreed, although, as we shall see in chapter 5, he worked to distance his mature Indian summer journal entries from his youthful Emersonian faith in the direct link between spiritual truths and natural facts. "These are the finest days of the year," he wrote on October 10, 1856. The soft "note of the chickadee is now often heard in the yards, and the very Indian summer itself is a similar renewal of the year."[12] For Thoreau, the lessons of the season were clear: Life continued, nature never ceased, change was the way of the world.

For all its poetic potential, Indian summer remains a difficult term to define. This book will not settle the confusion. According to the American Meteorological Society's *Glossary of Weather and Climate*, Indian summer is "a time interval, in mid or late autumn, of unseasonably warm weather, generally clear skies, sunny but hazy days and cool nights." In New England, the same publication continues, "at least one killing frost and preferably a substantial period of cooling weather must precede that warm spell in order for it to be a considered a true Indian Summer," a specific requirement not made for any other region of the country.[13] Despite this contention, the definition of Indian summer has only recently received such an official imprimatur. Nineteenth-century commentators, on whom this book primarily focuses, defined the term in many ways—some, such as the natural history essayist Wilson Flagg, insisting on the necessity of frost, others, most notably Thoreau, merely on a sudden burst of warmth.[14] For the most part, we have come to identify Indian summer with a few warm days in the fall, usually (though not always) enjoyed in early November. Because I am primarily interested in the ways the season has been imagined and described, I have adopted this somewhat loose definition. As Thoreau once remarked of the cause of autumn's colors, "I am more interested in the rosy cheek than I am to know what particular diet the maiden fed on."[15] I, too, am intrigued less by precisely what Indian summer *is* than in the broad array of cultural practices that the season can help illuminate.

The history of the term "Indian summer" is equally difficult to pin down. I discuss the various theories in chapter 3, but I should warn readers at the start that this book shies away from a precise historical account regarding the origins of my subject. That etymology has been lost in the tangled and tortured history of white America's relationship with the indigenous peoples for whom the season is so enigmatically named. I recall as a child hearing many different explanations for why a warm spell in the fall bears the name Indian summer. I have also read dozens of conflicting theories in the course of my research. But precisely where, when, and how warm autumnal weather and Indians became etymologically linked will never be firmly established, a fact for which I am grateful. For instead of provable origins or firsts, we have legends, myths, and conjectures, the very stuff of the symbol-building potential that makes Indian summer such a compelling time of year. As Emerson suggested in *Nature*, "All the facts in natural history taken by themselves have no value, but are barren, like a single sex. But marry it to human history, and it is full of life."[16] And so it is with Indian summer. Its buried origins and loose definitions make it an ideal subject for poets, artists, essayists, and cultural histories such as the one I undertake in this book.

What little scholarly attention has been paid to the season tends to focus on the sources of the term. Unfortunately, most such attempts to track down the "true" source of Indian summer read like rummages through an antiquarian's musty closet. They are long on facts, but short on understanding. The best such work was written a century ago by Albert Matthews, a Boston-based lexicographer and historical sleuth. In an extraordinarily learned 1902 article in the *Monthly Weather Review*, Matthews identified dozens of Indian summer references that began in the late eighteenth century and increased in number as the nineteenth century progressed. No one who writes about Indian summer can ignore Matthews's effort to locate the oldest surviving references to the season; I have found others, but I am heavily indebted to his labors.[17]

Still, I would like this book to tilt discussions of Indian summer away from sources and origins. Far more interesting than finding its exact definition, I would suggest, is an understanding of how and why Indian summer has been imaginatively constructed (and restructured) over the years. To that end, I offer the following chapters as a poetic meteorology of the season.

As I make clear, Indian summer has served a number of complex—and often contradictory—functions during the roughly two hundred years that the phrase has been in documented existence. Throughout its history it has occupied a cultural space somewhere between our sensual knowledge of the natural world and our linguistic capacity to name and define. It has been a sentimental touchstone and a transcendental icon, a meteorologist's whipping boy and a poet's best friend. But for all its complexities, Indian summer remains a startlingly beautiful time of year. It is that sense of the complexly beautiful that this book works to uncover.

The Birth of a Season: Indian Summer Before 1820

It is for man that the seasons and all their fruits exist.
—Henry David Thoreau[1]

I begin with a history of Indian summer prior to 1820, not to locate its definitive origins but to map out where and why our conception of the season began to take shape. Although theories abound, no one can claim with certainty why a warm spell in the fall first received the name Indian summer. Indeed, no amount of sleuthing has elevated the precise history of the term from a matter of speculation into the realm of fact.

In subsequent chapters I address New England's love affair with Indian summer, a passion that did not begin in earnest until the 1820s. But first, we must explore, to the extent that the limited historical record will allow, how the season initially penetrated American weather consciousness. As we will see in chapter 3, evidence collected in the nineteenth and early twentieth centuries suggests that Ojibwa and Penobscot Indians may have had oral traditions of what we now call Indian summer. The earliest written Anglo/American references to the season indicate that it entered white discussions about the weather in the second half of the eighteenth century; then, between 1790 and 1820, the season shows up in accounts of the weather in the Ohio River Valley and regions just west of the Alleghenies in what is now western Pennsylvania, Ohio, and Kentucky. Only after 1820 do we see Indian summer celebrations consistently tied to New England. And yet, I must remain cautious in making any sort of assertion about Indian summer's early history, as only a handful of references to the season prior to 1820 survive. Those that do, reveal a purely descriptive term without the rich metaphoric language that later writers brought to the season. How and why poets, artists, and travel writers first recognized the season and then aestheticized the initial descriptive language informs the discussion in this and the subsequent chapter.

While the origin of the term "Indian summer" remains a matter of dispute, sudden outbreaks of autumnal heat had been celebrated in Europe long before the colonization of the Americas. One common phrase for such weather is "halcyon days," a term often used to describe happy or serene periods in one's life. The name derives from the mating season of the halcyon, a Greek mythological bird that each year protects its nests near the sea by influencing the gods into briefly halting all storms and dangerous winds. In Rome, Pliny the Elder noted that for "six days before the shortest day and six days after it the sea calms down for the breeding of the halcyons, from which these days derive their names."[2] Eventually, the term lost its connection to the legendary bird to stand, as in Whitman's late poem "Halcyon Days," for hard-earned moments of repose.

> As the days take on a mellower light and the apple at last hangs
>   really finish'd and indolent-ripe on the tree,
> Then for the teeming quietest, happiest day of all!
> The brooding and blissful halcyon days!

Included in the "Sands at Seventy" section of *Leaves of Grass*, Whitman's brief poem evokes fall's full bloom. The apples have ripened and hang indolently from the tree. It is a classic Indian summer scene, one that Whitman, who typically gravitated to the American idiom, here uncharacteristically ascribes to the ancient Greek halcyon.

A less well known precursor to Indian summer is the "summer of St. Demetrius," an important marker on the Greek Orthodox calendar. Named for an early-fourth-century martyr, Demetrius' October 26 celebration coincides with an anticipated spell of autumnal warmth during which rural communities hope to rejoice in the fruits of their harvest amid an interval of glorious weather. French farmers called a similar interlude "St. Martin's summer" in honor of the fourth-century cleric whose November 11 feast day often saw a return of July-like conditions.[3] Briefly a popular season among European authors—both the novelist Raphael Sabatini and the poet Robert Louis Stevenson wrote works carrying its name—St. Martin's summer has occasionally attracted the attention of American artists and poets as well. In an 1879 poem, for instance, John Greenleaf Whittier, whose

Indian summer visions I consider in chapter 4, describes St. Martin's summer as the ideal meeting ground between summer and winter, a meteorological truce that provides "A soft, consenting atmosphere."[4]

Shakespeare mentions two seasons similar to Indian summer in part I of *Henry VI*. Set during the War of the Roses, the play features a promiscuous Joan of Arc who briefly tricks her enemies by wearing male military attire, much as the various legendary seasons might trick us into believing that summer has returned. As Joan assumes control of her troops, she warns her opponents to "Expect Saint Martin's Summer, halcyon days." Such a burst of warmth, she imagines, will signal the imminent defeat of English invaders and the return of French sovereignty over her native land. He refers to still another annual warm spell in part I of *Henry IV* when Prince Hall bids adieu to Falstaff by noting the apparent increase in temperatures that many believe occurs on or near the November 1 celebration of All Saints' Day. "Farewell, thou later spring! Farewell, All-hallown summer."[5] Like the other European antecedents to Indian summer, these Shakespearean seasons unfold exactly as their American counterpart does. They interrupt the gradual fall cooling with a brief but intense period of beauty and calm while also warning us to prepare for the inevitable cold to come.

Indian summer represents a late addition to this catalogue of autumnal warmth. Its entrance into American weather discussions occurred well after Europeans came to the New World. As Albert Matthews noted in his exhaustive survey of early Indian summer references, no document from the colonial era containing the term has been found. Nor do we have colonial-era records of any of the other legendary warm spells, even though colonists certainly had access to such legends, most notably through Shakespeare. One searches in vain through the works of early chroniclers such as William Bradford and John Winthrop for allusions to weather that even resembles Indian summer. A similar silence marks classic eighteenth-century works of natural history such as Robert Beverley's 1705 *History and Present State of Virginia* and William Bartram's *Travels*. Both Bartram and Beverley describe the kinds of weather that typically prevail in any given season, but they make no reference to an annual warm spell in the fall. Nor does Thomas Jefferson, who otherwise discusses the dates and ferocity of autumnal frosts in his 1785 *Notes on the State of Virginia*. But like his fellow eighteenth-century naturalists, Jefferson did not place these events within an anticipated progression of cool to warm to cold, the very progression that defines an Indian summer.[6]

The closest New World approximation to Indian summer I have found prior to the American Revolution occurs in a passing reference to weather in the Hudson Valley made by the Swedish naturalist Petr Kalm. During a visit to Albany in 1751 Kalm noted that "it was considered a certain sign" in the fall that following "two or three days" of warm southwest wind— the same breeze that modern meteorologists tell us carries Indian summer's warm air—"a clear and cold atmosphere" would descend.[7] Without naming this weather pattern, he suggested that a warm spell could be expected each fall. But aside from Kalm's description of Albany, no one reported an annual period of warmth just before the onslaught of winter's chill. A season we now assume annually visits the landscape simply did not register in colonial meteorological consciousness.

The Early Record

According to the *Oxford English Dictionary* the oldest reference to Indian summer occurs in an essay written in the late 1770s by J. Hector St. John de Crevecoeur, the French-born author of the landmark *Letters of an American Farmer* (1782).[8] I have found no evidence to dispute this assertion. Crevecoeur describes the arrival of Indian summer in "A Snowstorm as it affects the American Farmer," an essay that he first wrote in English but that saw its initial publication in French. Writing near the end of his ten-year residence in Orange County, New York, and just before his royalist sympathies during the Revolutionary War will send him scurrying back to France, Crevecoeur remarks that only after "those few Moderate days" of Indian summer have passed will American farmers reckon "winter to be-gin." Thus, as fall progresses,

Great rains at last replenish the springs, the brooks, the swamp and impregnate the earth. Then a severe frost succeeds which prepares it to receive the voluminous coat of snow which is soon to follow; though it is often preceded by a short interval of smoke and mildness, called the Indian Summer. This is in general the invariable rule: winter is not said properly to begin until those few moderate days & the raising of the water has announced it to Man.[9]

The tone suggests a phrase of recent though accepted vintage. On the one hand, the season apparently had a history before Crevecoeur, as he calls its arrival "the invariable rule." At the same time, he also seems intent on explaining a weather pattern unfamiliar to potential readers, as if the term has only recently begun to circulate. Whatever the case, with this brief reference, occupying just a few sentences in an essay devoted to American agricultural habits, Indian summer enters the historic record.

Few contemporary readers would have encountered the season's literary debut, however. Though Crevecoeur wrote these lines at the height of the American Revolution (probably 1778), the essay remained unavailable in the United States until the 1920s. He wrote the snowstorm essay during the same period that he was gathering material for *Letters of an American Farmer*, his soon-to-be-famous book. But Crevecoeur's uncomfortable political stance (a Frenchman in America under suspicion for holding sympathies for the English crown) led him to return to France, where he remained for the duration of the war. Upon arriving in Europe, he turned his attention to the justifiably renowned *Letters*, a genre-defying blend of history, fiction, and autobiography that belongs on any list of classic early-American writing. The book's success in France led its author in 1788 to translate and publish his remaining manuscript notes, including the snowstorm essay and its brief depiction of Indian summer in America.[10] The historical irony would no doubt have appealed to Crevecoeur's cross-cultural sensibilities: Though originally contained in the author's English-language manuscript, the term "Indian summer"—which describes one of America's meteorological glories—was first published in French.

Despite the paucity of American readers, Crevecoeur lists three features found in the hundreds of Indian summer descriptions to come. First, like nearly all nineteenth-century commentators, he notes the presence of atmospheric smoke, a quality (as we will see in the following chapter) that became a staple of discussions of the season. Though we today tend to celebrate the clarity of an Indian summer sky, nearly every description of the season prior to 1900 mentions the presence of some form of smoke or mist. Emily Dickinson, for example, believed the season allowed for a "Communion in the Haze" (F 122). Second, Crevecoeur claims that the sudden burst of unseasonable warmth reliably predicts the approach of winter's cold. For farmers, the interlude represents a signal to hurry up and complete their outdoor chores: "The man of foresight neglects nothing," he writes later in the same passage. And third, he places the season after the death of frostbitten leaves. Nineteenth-century authors occasionally placed Indian summer as early as September, when summer's heat had barely expired, while others dragged the season into January, perhaps confusing it with that month's much celebrated thaw. Most, however, followed Crevecoeur's lead by identifying Indian summer as an autumnal rite that follows hard upon a killing frost.

In the twenty years after Crevecoeur's brief description, the record grows thin. The accounts of two military men from the 1790s indicate that the term "Indian summer" was used in American Army camps in the old Northwest Territory, the vast triangular swath encompassing present-day Ohio, Indiana, Michigan, Wisconsin, and Illinois that England ceded to the United States at the close of the Revolutionary War. In the first, General Josiah Harmar in 1790 several times recorded that the "fine weather" of Indian summer was at hand. That fall, near the start of what proved to be a ten-year struggle for control of the region, Harmar led an expedition against the Miami Indians in southern Ohio and Indiana. The campaign proved disastrous for the Americans, briefly tilting the balance of power in favor of the Indians. Disorganized and badly beaten, Harmar and his men conducted a hasty retreat to Cincinnati. But before they reached their base, the troops, whom Harmar had recruited primarily from Ohio Valley towns in Kentucky, directed a reign of terror against Indian encampments. During the week of October 14, a period Harmar consistently described as Indian summer, they destroyed five villages and burned twenty thousand bushels of corn. Harmar announced the simultaneous presence of Indian summer weather and violence toward Indians throughout his journal: "Fine weather – Indian Summer," he wrote on October 23. "Having completed the destruction of the Maumee towns, as they are called, we took up our line of march this morning from the ruins."[11]

A similar brief reference to the season occurs in the 1794 journal of Major Ebenezer Denny, Harmar's friend and onetime aid. Denny, whose diary remains a central document in the history of Indian wars in Ohio and Pennsylvania, had as much firsthand experience with the conflicts between whites and Native Americans as any military figure of his time. An officer under Washington at the Battle of Yorktown, he also published an English/ Delaware dictionary that both sides used during treaty negotiations. After serving in Harmar's campaign, Denny received a commission to defend northwestern Pennsylvania against a united front of Iroquois and Miami. Tensions ran extremely high that fall, as the local Indians, many of whom had allied themselves with the British during the Revolutionary War, threatened to drive the Americans from the region. As both sides prepared for war, Denny simply noted the presence of "Pleasant Weather. The Indian Summer here," a simple matter-of-fact statement that belied the violence that loomed.[12]

These scattered and isolated references do not reveal why a warm spell in the fall was named for Indians, though the centrality of Indian warfare in the Harmar and Denny journals is suggestive of a possible etymological link between Indian summer and white/native hostilities (I explore this possibility in detail in chapter 3). Nevertheless, the brevity of these statements indicates that Indian summer was an accepted part of military camp life of the 1790s. They offer little by way of elaboration and nothing of the aesthetic charm the season would soon accrue. We certainly cannot tell from such brief remarks where Denny and Harmar first learned about Indian summer. But their casual tone at the very least suggests that Indian summer weather was readily understood as the eighteenth century drew to a close. A mundane term that did not aim to inspire, there was little need to elaborate on the season's poetic potential.

The English Connection

The one thing we can say for certain about the early history of Indian summer concerns how and by whom the term was first consistently introduced to the reading public. It is one of the great oddities of pre-1820 discussions of Indian summer—a season so beloved by Americans—that English travel-book authors took the lead in assuring its place in the printed record. Written primarily for consumption by readers back home, the travel books addressed a growing English curiosity about American life, especially in the newly opening regions of the West. That curiosity, in turn, led many Britons to consider immigrating to the New World. To satisfy this sudden market, publishers rushed to print practical guidebooks detailing the prospects awaiting would-be settlers should they choose to stake claims in the American West.[13]

Although English writers eventually embraced the season as their own, the earliest guidebooks did not paint an especially flattering portrait of the young country and its Indian summer. American boastfulness, a trait that nearly every guidebook writer commented upon, especially annoyed the English writers. "Every American considers that it is impossible for a foreigner to teach him anything," complained one disgruntled early-nineteenth-century visitor.[14] Boasts concerning the apparent healthfulness of the climate particularly upset English visitors, many of whom believed America's weather extremes posed dangers to constitutions accustomed to England's less drastic temperature shifts. For them, the high praise that western Americans bestowed on Indian summer weather—even if they did not put that praise into print—did little to alleviate the fear that sudden increases in heat could injure an Englishman's health.

The Irish-born adventurer Thomas Ashe was among the first to ridicule the American tendency to view the autumnal "second summer" in overly positive terms. Ashe, whose checkered career included stints in the British Navy as well as a brief interlude as an aide to Thomas Jefferson, came to Kentucky in 1805 hoping to make a profit from the sale of mammoth bones unearthed along the banks of the Ohio River. Partly out of frustration that this improbable venture left him broke, Ashe's published account of the journey condemns the morals and manners of the residents of the river towns he visited along the way. Among the customs he singled out for condemnation was the local praise for the "second summer." With barely contained disdain, he mocked the local belief "that Kentucky *must* be healthy, that enjoying such a climate, it cannot be otherwise, and that no country of the globe can boast of such salubrity and such an atmosphere."[15] Such boastfulness, Ashe reasoned, confirmed the backwardness of the new country's backwoodsmen, who, with little education or culture to speak of, could only brag about the weather.

If Ashe gently (and occasionally not so gently) mocked his subjects, William Faux, an English farmer investigating conditions on the Illinois prairie, broadly condemned the season so many Americans apparently enjoyed. Faux had harsh words for every part of the country; New Englanders, he claimed, practiced "a dull and insipid" religion while southerners mistreated their slaves, a point he made with particular vigor. But he directed his ire most consistently toward Americans who lived in the West, finding them besotted, violent, and insufficiently churched. The frequent fires during the dry western Indian summer were one reason the region inspired such disdain. As with Ashe, we have with Faux only a British response to the American Indian summer, but his vituperation suggests that the season got under his skin. His 163-word sentence-long account of one conflagration is rendered in apocalyptic terms.

The season, called the Indian Summer, which here commences in October, by a dark blue hazy atmosphere, is caused by millions of acres, for thousands of miles round, being in a wide-spreading, flaming, blazing, smoking fire, rising up through wood and prairie, hill and dale, to the tops of low shrubs and high trees, which are kindled by the coarse thick, long prairie grass and dying leaves, at every point of the compass, and far beyond the foot of civilization, darkening the air, heavens and earth, over the whole extent of the northern and southern continent, from the Atlantic to the Pacific, and in neighborhoods contiguous to the all devouring conflagration, filling the whole horizon with yellow, palpable, tangible smoke, ashes, and vapor, which effect the eyes of man and beast, and obscure the sun, moon, and stars, for many days, or until the winter rains descend to quench the fire and purge the thick ropy air, which is seen, tasted and felt.

The entire experience, he adds, "partakes of the vulgar idea of the infernal." To make matters worse, though the fires had previously been set by Indians, they are now lighted "by the White Hunters" who reign over the land.[16]

Such a cross-continental blaze seems comically implausible, so much so that one wonders whether Faux's absurdly large blaze and ferocious storms of dust might best be classified as some sort of frontier tale run amok. In a 1989 study of the American tall tale, Henry B. Wonham argues that such tales flourished in frontier districts of the late eighteenth and early nineteenth centuries, the very places visited by Faux and his traveling English brethren. Tall tales often "originate in actual facts," Wonham claims, only to become embellished through frequent retelling for comic purposes. Such a tale is "neither purely true nor purely fantastic but depends for its effect upon the listener's ability to perceive its relation to both fact and fantasy."[17] Faux seems to have lacked this ability, as his conflagration, which has a basis in fact, becomes in his apocalyptic rendering a credulity-straining inferno.

That at least some Americans would try to humorously turn the tables on English criticisms of Indian summer is evidenced by James Kirke Paulding's efforts to satirize English visitors who mocked the season. An active participant in the so-called paper wars, a transatlantic skirmish between magazine editors that peaked around 1820, Paulding (1778–1860) took special umbrage at any negative comment uttered about the United States. In *John Bull in America* (1825), a sharply satirical work written in retaliation against English denunciations of frontier manners and drunkenness, he adopted the travel book genre to mock English visitors he believed were both nasty and easily fooled. The tone is not subtle. With his tongue firmly planted in cheek, Paulding skewered early English descriptions of Indian summer. When, for example, the narrator enters the prairie town of Communipaw, he encounters an "immense number of fat fellows" wasting away the afternoon alternately spitting and smoking their pipes. The American passion for tobacco, Bull reasons, leads to an annual display of horrid Indian summer smoke. Indeed, "such is the extent of this practice of smoking tobacco, that at a certain time of year, during the autumn, when people of the country have finished gathering in the products of their fields, and their leisure time comes, they commence a smoking festival, in which every man, woman, and child partakes." That season, he adds, "is called the Indian summer." Each year, for "five or six weeks," the atmosphere becomes impenetrably hazy and obscure. The locals "pretend to ascribe" the smoke "to the Indian custom of burning the long grass of the immense Prairies in the west." The narrator, however, assures his readers—rhetorically positioned as comfortable English men and women—that the true cause lies in the continuous exhalations from backwoods pipes, a scene sure to repulse anyone who considered himself polite.[18]

The Climates of Early Indian Summer

No topic generated more attention in the transatlantic sparring over the pre-1820 Indian summer than the season's assumed potential to injure one's health. An interlude marked by drastic swings in temperature, Indian summer came under early medical suspicion by those who believed that America's weather extremes could harm Europeans accustomed to less dramatic shifts in temperature and barometric pressure. Although most American doctors could not trace temperature extremes any greater than those experienced in Europe, scientists on both sides of the Atlantic generally assumed that climate played a central role in both physical and moral health, a belief that led many to assume the new nation's growth would be limited by apparently wild temperature swings. The great Swedish naturalist Petr Kalm, for example, remarked in 1750 that because temperature swings increased during the eighteenth century, Americans were "more unhealthy at present than they were formerly."[19] The American climate, Kalm insisted, assured a nation burdened by poor health.

Sudden late-year sudden increases in heat, which always mark an Indian summer, particularly frightened urban residents of the 1790s. Outbreaks of yellow fever, which one Baltimore physician called America's "great outlet from life to grave," typically began during the warmth of late summer and ended only when the temperatures grew cool in the fall.[20] During the dreadful 1793 outbreak in Philadelphia (which killed 10 percent of the population), the rate of new infections finally slowed when temperatures cooled in early October, only to go back up again when the weather suddenly turned warm on the fifteenth. Unfortunately, one form of legendary autumnal weather that may bear some etymological connection to Indian summer apparently did not make its expected appearance in Philadelphia that fall. According to an English traveler visiting at the height of the epidemic, in late September Philadelphians typically awaited the arrival of cold northwest winds, which "the Indians call *half* winter." Brisk autumnal winds, many physicians argued, could cleanse the air of infectious agents that built up during the stagnant summer months. Tragically, the traveler added, Philadelphia had "no half winter in the year 1793."[21] Although they misunderstood the causal relationship between climate and health, Philadelphians of the day recognized that so long as the temperatures remained warm in the fall, the decimation wrought by Indian summer would continue.

The fear that Indian summer might prove injurious to health resembles the concern caused by another legendary weather pattern, the dog days. During this interlude, all sorts of ill health and intemperate behavior supposedly erupt. In the face of the heat, we become—the phrase goes—"sick as a dog." Like Indian summer, the dog days have no official dates (the claims of almanac writers notwithstanding). Most people assume that they begin with the rise of Canis Major, the Dog Star, just after the summer solstice. But as Eleanor Long has shown in her study of the folklore behind this weather, the term "dog day" may have originated from ancient customs linking dogs with disease rather than any astrological event (thus, the hair of a dog supposedly heals the bite of that very same dog, a remedy that any hangover sufferer knows to be false). As with Indian summer, the heat of the dog days may not be the immediate *cause* of ill health, but certain conditions typical of such spells—the tendency for food to spoil, for example—periodically allow them to become the *occasion* when either dogs or people become sick and mad.[22]

Because suspicions of late-year warmth remained high, several American doctors turned to Indian summer to demonstrate that poor health bore no direct relationship to climate, a position that placed them directly (and correctly) at odds with Benjamin Rush, the country's most celebrated physician. In a June 1798 article exploring possible correlations between high temperatures and the incidence of disease, Dr. Mason Cogswell charted fluctuations in Hartford, Connecticut, during the previous December. The month, he noted, had been "uniformly cold," while in January "the weather softened considerably." Local residents, he continued, "assumed that the Indian Summer was approaching." Happily, the changes caused no undue harm; other than "a few strongly marked pleurisies," the city's health had not been compromised. Cogswell's 1798 report, which includes the earliest reference to Indian summer in New England that I have seen, also points to the season's slippery definitions. By placing Indian summer in January, he implied that any sudden warm spell in the midst of cold weather could carry the name. For the medical community, however, the big news was that violent swings in temperature by themselves did not injure the health of urban dwellers. Any lingering doubts were addressed ten years later when Dr. Shadrach Ricketson proclaimed in the same journal in which Cogswell wrote that "the dry smoky weather long known in the country as Indian Summer" had not ushered in a period of poor health in his home city of New York (note the use of the phrase "long known").[23] Like Cogswell, Ricketson argued that the sudden changes involved in the arrival and departure of Indian summer should not cause alarm.

Nevertheless, questions concerning Indian summer's possible effect on health continued to trouble some visitors to the American West, much to the consternation of the local population. In 1815, for example, Cincinnati's Dr. Peter Drake satirically remarked the "effect of this peculiar atmosphere on hypochondriacs is similar to that produced by the November fogs of Great Britain."[24] It produced worries, that is, where none need exist. But still, the fears persisted. As late as 1832, the English commentator Frances Trollope found the sudden heat dangerously oppressive. In a decision she quickly came to regret, Trollope had immigrated to Drake's Cincinnati in the late 1820s to open a merchant house in the quickly growing town. Her two-year stay, after which she wrote the much quoted *Domestic Manners of the Americans*, proved unhappy and economically disastrous. She liked little that she saw in Cincinnati, and the book detailing her stay predictably angered its residents. Among many other complaints, the city's Indian summer heat irked her considerably. The season's temperature surge, she claimed, "sufficiently accounts for the sickliness of the American autumn. The effect of it is extremely distressing to the nerves." Such fierce autumnal warmth, she added, "was infinitely more disagreeable than the glowing heat of the dog days" of summer.[25] Without so much as a gesture toward the season's potential charm, Trollope dismissed its heat as an ungodly assault on the equilibrium she had developed while growing up amid the more predictable temperature changes that accompany the English seasonal round.

Describing Beauty

Yet for all descriptive skill, Mrs. Trollope spoke too late when it came to Indian summer. By the time she issued her public displeasure with the season in 1832, English *and* American writers had been describing its charms for more than a decade. Cranks like Faux aside, by 1820 the season had become the lovely time of year we now assume it to be. And once again, British travelers into the American West took the lead, making that part of the world the first to give rise to a consistent vocabulary of Indian summer beauty, a vocabulary, ironically enough, that often began in a fit of speechlessness as the visitors struggled for words to describe what they saw.

The Indian summer depictions offered by the travel writer Adlard Welby exemplify the early approach to the season's charms. Like many of his compatriots, Welby believed the opening frontier would prove inhospitable for English settlers. A "rough untutored set of savages," he said of the native inhabitants, has been succeeded by "another race of little less than savages—clothed savages."[26] But unlike the others we have seen, Welby was taken aback by what he saw one Indian summer day in 1819 near the remote outpost of Vincennes, Indiana. Amazed by the light and warmth, he searched for words.

This season is called here the Indian summer, and indeed the agreeable temperature of the air, the beauty of the day, and the variety of forest scenery I could much wish to describe though vain would be the attempt. Let the reader imagine the finest autumnal day in England, and suppose an unvaried succession of such days, as far from oppressive heat as from cold; let him then cull from our woods every tint of autumn's foliage, heighten every colour in imagination, and add more; then perhaps he may have a faint idea of the Indian summer season.[27]

Two years earlier, Henry Bradshaw Fearon, still another British writer critical of the American frontier, found the words that Welby lacked to offer a succinct appraisal of a similar scene. Until now, he claimed, "I never knew what really fine weather was."[28]

By far the most eloquent example of the early British celebration of America's Indian summer appears in the published journal of the naturalist John Bradbury. More than anyone's we have yet considered, his praise of the season marks its transformation from the utilitarian to the aesthetic. A self-taught student of insects and plants, Bradbury was hired by the Botanical Society of Liverpool in 1809 to conduct a survey of plant life in the American South in preparation for the society's plan to lay claim to productive cotton fields in the region. Perhaps at the instigation of his friend Thomas Jefferson, with whom he conducted a lively correspondence, the naturalist abandoned his commission and instead joined John Jacob Astor's

1810 fur expedition up the Missouri River. Along the way he collected natural history materials for his splendidly written (and unjustifiably obscure) *Travels in the Interior of America in the Years 1809, 1810, and 1811.* Among many notable passages, the book offers the oldest surviving extended effort to capture the visual beauty of Indian summer.

Bradbury begins his remarks on the Indian summer weather near St. Louis with the same matter-of-fact tone utilized by Crevecoeur, as if he, too, simply wants to explain an unfamiliar regional weather pattern. But Bradbury, who alone among the British authors we have been considering did not view American manners with disdain, soon turns to a painterly language noticeable for its stress on the quiet, almost silent, majesty of the Indian summer sky. The light haze, he writes, "gives to the sun a red appearance and takes way the glare of light, so that all the day, except a few hours about noon, he may be looked at with the naked eye without pain." At such moments, "the air is perfectly quiescent and all is stillness, as if nature, after her long exertions during the summer, were now at rest."[29] Nearly fifty years later, Thoreau also celebrated the quiet of an Indian summer afternoon while basking along a river so calm that it "gleams like liquid gossamer in the sun."[30] But in Bradbury, an English naturalist standing on the banks of the Missouri before Thoreau was born, we find Indian summer for the first time causing someone to stop in his tracks.

Why England?

The question remains, however, as to why British rather than American writers first grabbed hold of this New World weather pattern. Part of the answer lies in the social and educational differences between American settlers and their English visitors. As the historian Gregory Nobles reminds us in his appraisal of scholarship of the old Northwest Territory, "much of the written evidence that survives comes from members of the elite, whose observations of backcountry society contain an obvious bias."[31] Even without such differences, new settlements often discourage the kind of writing that Bradbury employed, as day-to-day struggles allow for little more than a utilitarian interest in the weather. Clearly, a number of such reports indicate that western Americans commonly used the term "Indian summer" as the nineteenth century dawned, and I suspect that some archive will eventually produce a diary entry or letter in which ordinary residents recorded their impressions of Indian summer weather. For the most part, however, the locals left the task of placing the season on the page to their literary-minded English visitors.

Closer connections to European interludes such as St. Martin's summer may have allowed the British travelers to understand and name such weather in ways that their American hosts could not. And yet, the English awareness of Indian summer seems less a matter of cultural continuity than an early example of visitors or immigrants revealing to Americans those aspects of their culture to which Americans themselves had hitherto been blind. The naturalist Susan Fenimore Cooper once suggested that had "the same soft atmosphere of the Indian Summer warmed the woods of Windsor, year after year, while Geoffrey Chaucer roamed among their glades, the English would have had a word or phrase to express the charm of such days, before they borrowed one from another country."[32] As we have seen, the English had long enjoyed spurts of autumnal warmth, but Cooper's remarks nonetheless indicate that British observers saw something special in this weather that they did not see at home. Such a pattern, in which visitors capture the nuances of American customs better than Americans do, has enjoyed a rich tradition in transatlantic cultural relations. More than 150 years after Bradbury wrote, English musicians reenergized the American-created rock 'n' roll, thus refilling the nation's ears with its own raucous beat. And so it was with Indian summer, a season whose name and physical characteristics suggest an American origin that nonetheless went largely uncelebrated in print until the arrival of foreign pens.

One consequence of the early English interest in the season (as an object of either praise or fear) was that the term quickly spread throughout British letters, leading Cooper to proclaim, "we now see frequent allusions to the Indian Summer by Englishmen." An 1830 biographical essay by Thomas De Quincey, for example, describes the "Indian Summer" that "crept stealthily" over the eighty-year-old Richard Bentley, the brilliant but controversial seventeenth-century Cambridge classicist. American writers, most notably Howells, later adopted Indian summer as the preeminent natural emblem of wizened maturity, but De Quincey seems to have been the first to publicly draw the connection. English novelists also adopted the season when depicting their own terrains. In her 1849 novel *Shirley*, for instance, Charlotte Brontë describes the picturesque Indian summer light "that mellowed the pasture far and wide." And in 1857, the American landscape painter Jasper Cropsey went to London to paint *Indian Summer Morning in the White Mountains*, one of the most splendid paintings ever done of the season. Conceived and executed entirely with the London art

1. Jasper Cropsey, *An Indian Summer Morning in the White Mountains* (1857). The Currier Gallery of Art, Manchester, New Hampshire. Museum Purchase: Currier Funds, 1962.17.

market in mind, Cropsey's painting remained in England for a century (figure 1). By century's end, English acceptance of Indian summer was so complete that Queen Victoria's eightieth birthday was greeted by the poet laureate's wish that Her Majesty's "Indian Summer days" would long "linger in the land you love so well."[33]

I could continue to list examples, but they would only underscore the point that in overcoming the traditional antipathy that educated Britons of the first half of the nineteenth century held toward American terms, these writers helped establish this new meteorological terminology on both sides of the Atlantic. In so doing, they made Indian summer one of the earliest American phrases to supplant long-standing local linguistic tradition. Where Shakespeare spoke of Saint Martin's summer, his literary descendants applied the term "Indian" to their late-year bouts of warmth.

But for all the English efforts to adopt Indian summer weather as their own, the season remained (and remains) indelibly linked with the American climate. Its dominant imagery, its colors, and especially its name were drawn from the landscapes of the New World, factors that led American writers to take up Indian summer with enthusiasm in the post-1820 decades. To be sure, the same boastfulness to which the English visitors objected partially fueled literary America's embrace of the season. Indeed, in the surge of nationalism that followed the War of 1812, Americans were eager to celebrate their climate as never before. But nationalism alone does not account for the rapid growth in writing about Indian summer in the United States. As we will see, a series of related developments in American culture after 1820 led to the quick dissemination of Indian summer literature in the country that gave rise to the season.

Thoreau once said, "we ordinarily do not see what is before us, but what our prejudices presume to be there" (X: 107). We see what we are prepared to see. To hike in the woods after learning about certain local plants virtually assures that we will see them along the path. The same holds true for Indian summer weather. Once the season had been consistently recognized in print, it could be seen as a broadly national phenomenon that extended beyond the few scattered references in the West. It became an object of aesthetic contemplation, which in turn set the conditions for the Northeast's regional embrace of annual autumnal warmth.

By 1820 more than forty years had passed since Crevecoeur's practical description of the season, while three decades had lapsed since Harmar's and Denny's Indian summer military campaigns. Meanwhile, the English had been gradually building a literary tradition around Indian summer since the start of the nineteenth century. But it required a host of changes in American popular culture before the season could truly shine. Pride in local scenery, the first strands of Romanticism, and the rise of sentimental writing all contributed to the transformation of this once obscure western weather pattern into a subject of broad national concern. I will argue in the next chapter that Americans, particularly the middle-class readers and writers who encountered Indian summer in eastern newspapers and magazines, learned to view the season as the decades unfolded. As cultural conditions changed, they became acclimated to a season that had hovered at the meteorological margins. We turn now to that learning process.

2

Science and Sentiment: Indian Summer in Nineteenth-Century Popular Culture

The things which are dear to men at this hour are so on account of the ideas which have emerged on their mental horizon, and which cause the present order of things, as a tree bears its apples.
—Ralph Waldo Emerson[1]

Having circulated through the sparsely populated West of the early 1800s, Indian summer achieved iconic status in the American Northeast in the four decades preceding the Civil War. Celebrations and discussions of the season spanned the spectrum of popular publications. Metropolitan newspapers frequently published essays and poems on the subject, as did more specialized journals such as those catering to the agricultural and scientific communities. Indeed, the season appeared in virtually every literary format associated with the era. Almanacs, magazines, domestic novels, and tourist gazetteers all found room for Indian summer after 1820. And while the specific context of each new depiction varied from publication to publication, nearly all presented the season as the crown jewel of the calendrical cycle. This chapter examines how and why a season with such a thinly documented past penetrated so quickly and so deeply into popular conceptions of American weather. It will suggest that middle-class readers and writers in the antebellum urban Northeast jointly created the cultural conditions that enabled Indian summer weather to reign over the land.

Cultural changes often reveal hitherto unrecognized natural phenomena. Legend holds, for example, that Petrarch's "Ascent of Mount Ventoux" introduced readers to the beauty of mountain vistas. In attaining the peak, he created the view.[2] The nineteenth century witnessed similar creations. In his recent study of the Grand Canyon, the historian Stephen J. Pyne describes how sixteenth-century Spanish explorers traveling north from Mexico had little to say about the canyon. Unsuccessful in their quest for gold and unable to reach the bottom, they turned away in disappointment without a word for the view we now consider stunning. Throughout the eighteenth century explorers circumvented the canyon but made no mention of its aesthetic grandeur. Those who did comment typically described a problematic eyesore that impeded movement across the land. The canyon we see as grand came into being in the nineteenth century, a transformation driven by the confluence of poetry, politics, and war. Fueled by Romantic-era interest in natural grandeur and concomitant American claims of Manifest Destiny, the canyon joined the list of the nation's scenic wonders.[3] An analogous pattern propelled the Indian summer of the American Northeast into nineteenth-century conceptions of meteorological splendor. A weather pattern that had either escaped the notice of earlier residents or been feared for its presumed deleterious effects on health became a hallmark of the young country's natural beauties.

Such a claim does not imply that nineteenth-century Americans invented Indian summer simply to serve purely cultural needs. The name "Indian summer" emerges from human culture, but the weather pattern itself originates in the movement of trade winds and naturally occurring shifts in the production of heat. We will of course never fully disentangle the complex weave that nature and culture presents, so it remains difficult, if not impossible, to determine just how much Indian summer weather owes its existence to the activities of man. As early as 1864, the Vermont-born geographer George Perkins Marsh argued that wide-scale deforestation, which peaked in the Northeast around 1850, caused temperatures to fluctuate dramatically—a fact of human history that may have contributed to the presumably natural spike in heat that characterizes an Indian summer day. On the other hand, as we will see at the end of this chapter, others pointed to the same pattern of forest clearing to argue that the intensity of Indian summer had been *lessened* rather than heightened by the activities of man.[4] For the most part, we can reasonably assume that temperatures naturally increased during some intervals nearly every fall, bringing with them renewed summerlike energies to certain flora and fauna that had only recently prepared themselves for the coming cold. In other words, the weather of Indian summer remained fairly constant throughout the eighteenth and nineteenth centuries. What changed were the conditions of viewing and describing its arrival.

Indian summer entered the American weather vernacular during the same decades that gave rise to several other beloved late-year traditions. In the 1810s and 1820s, for example, Santa Claus and decorated trees became domestic signposts for a holiday that in the eighteenth century had inspired carnival-like antics quite different from the family-centered holiday we have come to enjoy. Whereas the early nineteenth century witnessed the entrance of the red-suited jolly Saint Nick, public drunkenness and general misrule had often marked earlier nativity feasts. As Stephen Nissenbaum has shown, a new child-centered and domestic holiday replaced older rituals that had brought gangs of young men into the streets.[5] Twenty years later, Thanksgiving also assumed its modern form, largely through the efforts of the magazine editor Sarah Josepha Hale. In the 1830s and 1840s, Hale's *Godey's Lady's Book* helped transform Thanksgiving from a regional New England holiday into a national celebration of family and Pilgrim ancestors.[6] As young New Englanders were leaving their families and heading west in droves, the national holiday paradoxically established the New England extended family as the primary locus of domestic value. Almost overnight, the customary habits of the day—from the oversize turkeys to the frenzied preholiday rush home—quietly took root as if they had marked the day all along.

The historian Eric Hobsbawm has labeled such customs invented traditions. In Hobsbawm's words, such traditions "attempt to establish continuity with a suitable historic past," whether or not such continuity actually exists. They cover recently constructed customs with a patina of aged charm. The Scotch tradition of wearing kilts, for example, emerged in the late eighteenth century as part of a nationalist campaign aimed toward the construction of a heroic military and cultural past. By century's end, kilts became associated with Scotland's ancient history, even though they were woven first by an English clothier around 1730.[7] Indian summer, I would argue, followed a similar course. I explore the reason behind this process in detail in chapter 4. Here I need simply remark that writers and readers began using the term only to then assume it had existed for an extended period of time. The season seems to have been born old.

The sudden embrace of heretofore unrecognized customs might strike us as little more than opportunistic gimmickry. Recently, however, Gene Bluestein has argued that the study of American folklore needs to be reconfigured as "poplore" to allow for a deeper understanding of popular entertainments. Rather than searching for an elusive authenticity, Bluestein draws attention to the ways by "which creative individuals integrated sources similar to those in older, more traditional cultures with popular or commercial elements."[8] He urges scholars to consider how individuals and groups acting within commercial enterprises can transform the materials at hand to facilitate popular consumption. Rather than viewing the consumerist aspects of, say, Christmas as an affront to the traditional or authentic holiday, such a program would recognize those new aspects as a legitimate popular custom.

The popular and occasionally commercial aspects of Indian summer in the early nineteenth century suggest that, like Christmas, this brief season can be transformed to meet any number of contemporary cultural needs. The rise of tourism in the American Northeast offers a case in point. The season entered the weather vernacular at a crucial moment in the history of American travel. As Dona Brown has noted, middle-class Americans of the first half of the nineteenth century increasingly embarked on domestic excursions modeled on the European grand tour, many of them carrying cheaply published gazetteers in their pockets to help them find the most interesting and scenic routes. Such publications often extended the length of Indian summer well beyond the few days to which we are now accustomed. An 1813 *Gazetteer of New York*, for example, noted that this "peculiar and elegant feature" of autumn "commences usually about the last of October and extends into December." Similarly, an 1823 New Hampshire gazetteer claimed that the state's "singularly bright and beautiful" Indian summer lasted for at least one month. Of course, extending the season over a period of weeks or months allowed ample opportunity for Indian summer visitors to spend their money in the new hotels and stages set up to accommodate seasonal visitors. But just as important, the acceptance of the phrase "Indian summer" also helped establish the rhythms of the tourist trade.[9]

Tourism aside, two sets of convergent forces shaped the depiction of Indian summer in poetry, prose, and the press. The first emerged within an odd confluence of nationalism, sentimentalism, and Romanticism, while the second occupied the overlapping cultural space of nineteenth-century literature and science. In each case, writers who commented on the season drew from available popular sources to create a time of year that earlier generations of eastern Americans had not observed. As celebrations of the season entered the broader culture, poets and other commentators located Indian summer in the nether spaces between emerging aesthetic and scientific realms. No longer a purely descriptive term of the sort we encountered in chapter 1, the versions of Indian summer that emerged in the first half of the century operated between discursive fields. Neither a simple descriptor nor a full-blown metaphor, the newly popular season contained aspects of both.

A Season for Dabblers

The poetic history of Indian summer begins in Philadelphia, the same city that so feared the fever-inducing powers of late-year warmth. But precisely who first brought the season into verse remains obscure. There are two likely candidates. The earliest published poetic invocation of Indian summer that I have seen occurs in a long narrative poem by the Scottish-born ornithologist Alexander Wilson, the author of the landmark *American Ornithology*. In his 1806 "The Foresters," Wilson (still another Briton in our story) described the season near Philadelphia as he prepared for a three-month expedition to Niagara Falls:

> The air was mild, the roads embrowned and dry
> Soft, meek-eyed Indian Summer ruled the sky.
> Such was the season when equipt we stood
> On the green banks of Schuykill's winding flood,
> Bound on a Tour wide northern forests through,
> And bade our parting friends adieu.[10]

As far as I can tell, this represents the first printed poem to mention the season.

A second and slightly less turgid effort with connections to Philadelphia can be found in Philip Freneau's "October's Address," first published in 1815 but probably written in the first years of the nineteenth century. A writer usually remembered for his patriotic verse composed in the aftermath of the Revolutionary War and his editorial work for Philadelphia newspapers of the 1790s, Freneau was also a nature poet of some note who took particular interest in seasonal change. The years separating two such poems correspond with the early history of Indian summer. The first, "The Seasons Moralized" (1785), adopts the conventional trope of linking each season with a stage of life. At no point does Freneau stray from the rigid four-season formula that mapped the progression from childhood to old age against the movement of spring toward winter.[11] "October's Address," however, avoids this well-worn motif to highlight a second, smaller season within the broader fall. Like Crevecoeur before him, Freneau notes that when "Indian summer days appear," one must "Be sure to hail the winter near." Yet the returned warmth also proves deceptive, leading Freneau to label the brief interlude a "deceitful second summer," a sense that Emily Dickinson would later underscore in her several poems about the season.[12]

Despite these modest beginnings, Indian summer became a full-fledged literary subject within ten years of the 1815 appearance of Freneau's poem. The season proved especially fruitful for poets operating within the broad cultural framework of literary sentimentalism. Poets working in this vein either featured nostalgic and mildly sad accounts of a second summer in the fall or presented delicate scenes that draped late-year flowers and shrubs over the processes of death. Few, however, aspired to anything grander than amateurish depictions of the season. Typically, American dabblers working in the tradition of English men of letters wrote the Indian summer poems of the 1820s and 1830s.[13] Written by lawyers and ministers such as William Thompson Bacon and James Dixon, the first wave of Indian summer poetry combined the decorousness of polite literature with folk enthusiasm for the newly celebrated season. As a result, Indian summer emerged as an important civilizing force as well as a beautiful time of year.

The abortive literary career of John G. C. Brainard (1796–1828) perhaps best exemplifies the type of writer that turned Indian summer into literary material in the 1820s. A consumptive Connecticut poet, Brainard left the practice of law in 1822 to edit the Hartford-based *Connecticut Mirror*, a periodical that contained poetry, sketches, and a smattering of news. Though forgotten today, he enjoyed considerable prestige in his time; indeed, his death at age thirty-two was viewed as a significant loss to the nation's literary life. In 1832, for example, John Greenleaf Whittier claimed in his edition of Brainard's *Literary Remains* that the small volume "contains more pure, beautiful poetry than any equal number of pages ever published in this country."[14] Whittier overstated the case considerably; still, Brainard knew enough of the emerging local color of his region to write the first work bearing the title "Indian Summer." The poem is worth quoting in its entirety:

> What is there saddening in the autumn leaves?
> Have they that "green and yellow melancholy"
> That the sweet poet spoke of? Had he seen
> Our variegated woods when first the frost
> Turns into beauty all October's charms –
> When the dread fever quits us – when the storms
> Of the wild equinox, with all its wet,

Has left the land, as the first deluge left it
With a bright bow of many colours hung
Upon the forest tops – he had not sighed.
    The moon stays longest for the hunter now:
The trees cast down their fruitage, and the blithe
And busy squirrel hoards his winter store:
While man enjoys the breeze that sweeps along
The bright, blue sky above him, and that bends
Magnificently all the forest's pride,
Or whispers through the evergreens, and asks,
"What is there saddening in the autumn leaves?"[15]

Although clearly not great verse, these lines capture much that typifies antebellum Indian summer poetry. Having arrived "when the dread fever quits us"—a reference to the feared autumnal heat I discussed in the previous chapter—the frost now works its magic to transform the woods into a glorious bouquet. For a brief moment in time the calendrical cycle seems caught between proceeding on its charted path and stopping in its tracks. The squirrel (and presumably the other animals) prepare for the months ahead, while the human walker in the woods stops to notice the breeze. Through it all, an element of sadness hovers over the scene, as the speaker asks, "What is there saddening in the autumn leaves?"

    Another Indian summer poem by the Connecticut poet William Thompson Bacon similarly reveals the appeal the season held for literary dabblers. A Congregational preacher in Trumbull, Bacon in 1837 published a collection of poems written while a student at Yale. Like Brainard's, Bacon's poetry is derivative; but also like Brainard, he viewed Indian summer as a time that mixes the beautiful with the sad:

The Indian Summer has come again,
With its mellow fruits and its ripened grain;
The sun pours round on the heavy scene
His rays half shorn of their golden sheen
And the birds in the thicks seem too sad to sing
And sad is the sound of the wild winds wing.[16]

    The absence of adequate copyright protection allowed periodical editors, who clearly believed that a sizable audience existed for such poems, to republish Indian summer verses in any of the hundreds of regional newspapers and magazines that helped fuel a decades-long interest in occasional verse. Brainard's poem, for example, first appeared in his 1825 collection and was reprinted in an 1835 number of the Albany-based *Zodiac* and an

1844 issue of *The Farmer's Cabinet*. It appeared yet again in a collection of poems by Connecticut authors and in William Cullen Bryant's edited collection, *Selections from the American Poets* (1860). Likewise, Bacon saw his Indian summer poem (which he first issued in his own 1837 collection) on page 1 of an 1839 number of *The Corsair*, a gossipy New York magazine published by Nathaniel Parker Willis. A similar pattern of repeated publications marks Charles Fenno Hoffman's 1828 "Indian Summer," which appeared in an 1840 collection of New York poetry as well as a later number of *Arthur's Magazine*, a temperance journal issued in Philadelphia.[17]

Such frequent reprinting reveals one of the underlying paradoxes of poetic versions of the season: Though the poems typically celebrated premodern rural scenes, antebellum Indian summer was largely a creation of the modernized urban press. As the historian Ronald J. Zboray has noted, the pre–Civil War urban Northeast witnessed the beginnings of industrialized printing, a development fueled by new technologies such as stereotyping and the cylindrical steam press. At the same time, the growth of railroad networks centralized publishing activity in cities such as Boston, Philadelphia, and New York. As Zboray notes, "the coming of the railroad created geographical biases in literary distribution" that allowed the Northeast to be blanketed with printed material to a degree that other parts of the country were not. At speeds unimaginable just a few decades before, newly spun legends and customs such as Indian summer could thus be printed, distributed, and reprinted with ease.[18] For commentators working in the new mass media of the day, the season arrived in the right place and the right time.

A Season of Regrets

For all their reliance upon modern technologies, Brainard, Bacon, and other early Indian summer poets remained steeped in the strong emotions inspired by sentimental regret. At the risk of gross oversimplification, sentimental writing—which filled the pages of antebellum periodicals—placed the highest cultural value on emotions such as sympathy and affection. Indian summer poets, in turn, fused these emotions with the season's capacity to fuel a meteorologically inspired sense of loss. At such times, nature seems to provide us with just the right equipment for tugs at our more tender side. The process begins by recognizing the beauty of the day. In the late afternoon, quiet fills the air, even in cities such as the one where I sit in October writing this chapter. Throughout the fall, the amount of

2. Worthington Whittredge, *Indian Summer*. Courtesy of Joan Whalen Fine Art, New York.

available sunlight declines noticeably each day, but a visit by Indian summer brings forth a marvelous intensity to those few hours that divide the looming dark. But with that intensity comes a certain melancholic sense born out of our knowledge that the beauty will not last. Though the weather may be glorious for a spell, our ability to hold that glory diminishes with each flip of the calendar page. During Indian summer birds may sing again and crickets may once again chirp, but we know their voices will soon be gone (figure 2).

Anyone who has been a parent of young children can understand how such weather seems infused with regret. I still recall last fall's Indian summer trek with my son out of the city and into the country in search of the perfect Halloween pumpkin. The weather was perfect—warm, sunny, and well beyond the first devastating frost. And yet the experience, which I would not replace for a moment, amounted to an emotional mixed bag. As we passed farm stands rife with apples and late corn, my own childhood drives with my father came to mind. Would my son remember this excursion, I wondered? I tried hard to focus on my parental duties, but waves of nostalgia, the most crippling emotion, carried me from the immediacy of the present to remembered Indian summer journeys from my past. Eventually I surrendered to the moment, allowing the smells of dried leaves and hay to evoke, as only aromas can, my more youthful days. Every jack-o'-lantern from childhood seemed to once again glow. But then the most difficult moment occurred. As my son bounded out of the car, proclaiming one pumpkin after another the best, I understood perhaps as never before the days I could not have back.

As Keats understood, autumn months in general can leave us watching "the last oozings hours by hours" as we prepare physically and spiritually for the winter that lies ahead. Indian summer poems, however, condense that preparation to a brief window in time that focuses our attention on the dead and dying leaves that surround us. The season "is necessarily sad," read one 1853 *Harper's Monthly* article, precisely because "the pilgrim of the year understands that these bright days are the last green points of the pleasant summer along which he has been idly coasting."[19] The poets concurred. Reverend Bacon, for example, lamented that upon the arrival of Indian summer, "The leaves of the briar are dead and dying." James Dixon, still another Connecticut dabbler, similarly found the season remarkable for the sighing "dying swell" of the zephyr's "last farewell." In the end, the brief moments of beauty, "the golden glow of the sun," prove chimerical.[20] Like the laughter of children, they trick us into the momentary belief that all is right with the world.

On the other hand, Indian summer could lighten the fear of death by assuring the deceased an extended period of beautiful repose. Indeed, the poet Lucy Larcom, who first came to prominence as the editor of the *Lowell Offering*, in 1857 proclaimed Indian summer the best season in which to die:

> Oh, to die
> When the sky
> Smiles behind the Indian Summer's hazy veil!
> Thus to glorify decay,

> Going in life's best array,
> Unto groves where death is a forgotten tale![21]

Larcom's sentiments resemble the approach to dying outlined in the nineteenth-century rural cemetery movement. As Calvinism's emphasis on predestination and sin gave way to a lighter theology stressing salvation and grace, a new approach to burying the dead ensued. Nowhere were these developments more pronounced than in the antebellum urban Northeast. Whereas older burial grounds were deliberately left unkempt and in the center of town—in order to warn the living of the tortures lurking on the other side of the grave—landscaped cemeteries such as Boston's Mount Auburn (which opened in 1832) aimed to do just the opposite. Rather than serving as portals to hell, the new cemeteries offered a peaceful resting ground in anticipation of the heavenly bliss to come. Indian summer poems such as Larcom's share a similar set of assumptions. As with the rural cemeteries, such works assume that while the workings of the natural world may occasionally lead to sadness, a divine beneficence ultimately secures a lasting peace. "'Tis a season of deep and quiet thought," James Dixon wrote, "And it brings calm to the breast."[22]

A Romantic and Smoky Time

While remaining firmly sentimental, early Indian summer poetry also helped bridge the gap between eighteenth-century formalism and nineteenth-century Romanticism. The process began amid a growing nationalistic interest in local subject matter, an interest that increased noticeably after the War of 1812 and which led American writers of the 1820s and 1830s to incorporate those aspects of Romantic thought that could best facilitate the celebration of American landscapes and idioms. Typically, the first American writers in this vein retained vestiges of eighteenth-century formalism (which characterized most native writing through 1820) while also making tentative gestures toward the new style, usually by offering highly formulaic praises of nature in America. Both Brainard and Bacon, for example, seem aware of the strains informing early American Romanticism, but they offer only mild celebrations of the wild without drawing epistemological or metaphysical insights from what they observe, as later American Romantics such as Emerson and Thoreau would. Instead, they draw heavily on eighteenth-century neoclassicism to inscribe Indian summer within a set of abstract notions about nature's ways. Written in conventional meter and reliant upon well-worn tropes, their depictions of the season functioned within a poetic tradition that had already run its course.[23] Still, we can see them straddling two poetic modes—celebrating wild nature while putting it into organized form.

We can trace the in-between status of early Indian summer poetry by looking to the season's frequent appearance in poems celebrating the immediate aftermath of the harvest. Farmers' almanacs began listing Indian summer as a regular occurrence around 1810, usually by simply stating that one could expect its arrival in November.[24] By the 1830s, however, magazines such as the *New England Farmer*, the *Boston Cultivator*, and the *Farmer's Cabinet and American Herd-Book* regularly reprinted in their autumn editions sentimental poems about the season. Such poems typically spoke of, for example, the return of "the lost pleasures of the earth" or "the variegated woods" that "the first frosts / Turn in beauty." They offered delightful visions of birds coming back in autumn. While none of these poems amounted to memorable verse, their inclusion in agricultural journals underscores a widespread antebellum interest in the aesthetics of farming life. In the Northeast in particular, farmers were encouraged by horticultural societies to view themselves as cultivated gentlemen interested in science and art rather than as mere cultivators of the soil. As a result, farming periodicals interspersed poems among utilitarian articles on plowing, planting, and fertilizing. A few sentimental lines about Indian summer, read after the labors of the year were complete, could thus link the beauties of the season to the era's recently aestheticized farms.[25] For authors aware of the Romantic strains in the cultural air, such poems allowed for the celebration of the natural while keeping those same celebrations under control.

For many writers, the most conspicuously Romantic aspect of Indian summer was its attendant smoke. For all its warm beauty, nearly every antebellum discussion of the season highlighted this peculiar feature. This was not always the case. Crevecoeur, we recall, noted that a hazy film invariably marked an Indian summer afternoon without finding any especial beauty or romance in its drift across the sky. For him, the seasonal smoke was a simple meteorological fact. In the first half of the nineteenth century, however, this same haze occupied an important new imaginative realm. The literary critic Arden Reed has suggested that the history of eighteenth- and nineteenth-century poetic accounts of the weather underwent a similar transformation. According to Reed, Enlightenment writing tended to downplay the eruption of meteorological oddities in order to describe a rational and orderly world. But in the wake of nineteenth-century English Romanticism, which welcomed the offbeat and strange, weather returned to the literary and artistic stage in the form of clouds, rain, wind, and snow—unpredictable forces and substances that seem too diffuse to completely explain. We see this perhaps most paradigmatically in the sky paintings of Turner and the weather-filled poems of Coleridge and Wordsworth.[26]

The growing Romantic appreciation of Indian summer as the smoky time of year exemplified America's own outbreak of artistic weather. For most commentators the smoke enhanced the Romantic beauty of an antebellum Indian summer day. In his 1821 *Letters on the Eastern States*, for instance, William Tudor noted that during Indian summer "a slight haze, like smoke" created a "vernal softness in the atmosphere." When seen hovering in the season's normally still sky, the gentle mists highlighted rather than obscured the wonderful hues of the fall. Still others described the smoke in picturesque terminology reminiscent of the landscape paintings of Salvator Rosa and Claude Lorrain. The light smoke, they reasoned, helped focus the eyes on the surrounding terrain. Thus, one 1838 magazine article claimed that the "thin veil of mild smoke and haze" helped "Nature hide those defects which she can not otherwise conceal"; it gave "a warmth of tone and coloring to the whole landscape." When the angle of the setting sun was just right, a "ruby gleam" of light and smoke illumined the horizon. Like the sunsets produced by our contemporary smog, which deflects or absorbs the lighter colors of the spectrum, the presence of smoke allows the darker orange rays to pass through and produce what Thoreau called the "glowing, warm brown red in the Indian Summer sun."[27]

Precisely why the fall produced a dusting of smoke nevertheless proved difficult to explain. Suggestions often fell along regional lines. As we saw in the previous chapter, writers in western districts such as Faux generally pointed to the traditional Native American practice of setting fire to the land. Eastern visitors to the West such as Washington Irving similarly attributed the "smoky haze" of Indian summer "to the burning of distant prairies by the Indian hunting parties."[28] Although burning practices varied from region to region, Indians throughout North America used fire to create grasslands, intimidate enemies, and hunt for game. In southern New England burns tended to be small and relatively controlled, as they were intended merely to clear the forest of underbrush; further west they raged across wide swaths of land. The time of Indian fires varied as well, although they were usually set in the fall, when the ground was most susceptible to flame.[29] Yet by the mid–nineteenth century, such practices had been largely curtailed, thus making it unlikely that Indian fires spewed the seasonal smoke once the first wave of white movements across the prairie had come to a close.

New Englanders tended to identify the source of smoke in the drying vegetation of the fall. Vermont's Zadock Thompson, for example, first proposed in 1832 that "the atmosphere possesses a solvent power, by which it is capable of raising and supporting the minute particles of decaying leaves and plants." The field biologist Peter Marchand suggests that this process is consistent with the production of atmospheric aerosols. As vegetation dies and dries at the end of summer, hydrogen and carbon atoms boil off in the form of vapor and combine with other elements in the sky to form aerosols, which Marchand defines as "particles slightly larger than molecules but small enough to remain suspended in the air."[30] Upon the increase in the number and size of aerosols, the entering sunlight is deflected from its course, thereby creating the seasonal haze.

Whatever its source, the smoke that highlighted many an Indian summer sky shares Romantic attributes with other meteorological phenomena. Like fog and mist, smoke can be described as both tangible and ephemeral, as if existing in two states at once—in part real, in part ideal. Snow, too, possesses similar intangible features, as Hawthorne noted in his 1837 sketch "Snow-flakes." Flakes, he suggests, "hover downward with uncertain flight, now almost alighting on the earth, now whirled again aloft into the remote regions of the atmosphere."[31] But eventually snow also accumulates into tangible (and heavy) piles. Indian summer smoke perhaps most closely resembles the vaporous material described in Coleridge's "Frost at Midnight," where, "Unhelped by any wind," the substance "performs its secret ministry."[32] While shifting from one ontological realm to another, the midnight frost straddles the division between one day and the next. Like Indian summer, which itself hovers between winter and fall, the season's smoke seems to exist in two worlds at once. So much so that Indian summer smoke belongs on any list of definitive Romantic-era meteorological effusions.

Eventually, smoky Indian summer scenes were placed into the service of American nationalism. As one poet proclaimed in an 1855 edition of the *Knickerbocker*,

> The Orient basks in brighter skies,
> Italia boasts a softer clime,
> But no land has the gorgeous dyes
> Of our mild Indian Summer time.[33]

But without question, the Hudson River school painter Jasper Cropsey (1823–1900) offered the most evocative nationalistic and Romantic visual depiction of the season in his 1866 painting *Indian Summer* (figure 3). No other artwork more grandly presents the exalted sky and landscape that mid-nineteenth-century Americans came to associate with the season. The work represents Cropsey's second major statement on Indian summer. The first, *Indian Summer Morning in the White Mountains* (1857), places the season in the heart of New England (figure 1). But as the art historian William Talbot points out, in the later work Cropsey instead inserts Indian summer squarely within a broadly national project, a project severely tested by the Civil War that had ended just six months before the artist completed the work. Looking south from a hill near Newburgh, New York, the painting presents the Hudson Valley as an enveloped landscape of domesticated splendor. Two passersby in the lower right have stopped to take a look at the golden colors that surround the grand river and the babbling brook. Nestled securely within the beautiful scene sit carefully delineated houses and commercial buildings, one of which supports a small American flag. And in the background a sun-kissed haze visually connects the tangible river and cliffs to the more ephemeral clouds and sky.[34]

Nearly ten years earlier Cropsey had urged American painters to turn their gaze upward. "Of all the gifts of the Creator," he wrote in the art journal *The Crayon*, "few are more beautiful and less heeded, than the sky."[35] Here, the Indian summer glow of the sky unites our vision of the earth's constituent parts into a seamless whole. To look up is to look down as the sky, water, and ground all share the same warm light. In such scenes, the day-to-day concerns of the small viewers in the corner (and by implication us) are visually and poetically joined with those of the villagers below. We all become imbued with the warmth. Cropsey offers us a stunning blend of sentimental and Romantic concerns: On an Indian summer day the quaintly domestic setting merges with a background at once heavenly and sublime. And meanwhile the American flag in the middle waves in the breeze.

Sentiment and Science

So far, I have been addressing the overtly literary and artistic paths by which Indian summer entered into wide circulation. We have seen how popular antebellum conceptions of the season hovered within the cultural space between Romantic and sentimental writing. But Indian summer also fig-

3. Jasper Cropsey, *Indian Summer* (1866), Founders Society Purchase, Robert H. Tannahill Foundation Fund, James and Florence Beresford Fund, Gibbs–Williams Fund, and Beatrice W. Rogers Fund; 78.38. Photograph © 2001 The Detroit Institute of Arts

ured in discussions that touched upon the overlapping concerns of sentimental literature and science. And while the participants in these discussions did not necessarily frame them as such, the Indian summer that
emerged from these conversations reveals these two discourses trying to
sort each other out.

One of the few antebellum publications that consistently strove to explain the science of Indian summer weather was Benjamin Silliman's *American Journal of Science and Arts*. A more prestigious periodical would have
been difficult to find. Edited by a Yale professor, Silliman's *Journal* (as it
was colloquially known) was the first American publication to systemize
the wide distribution of scientific knowledge. In its pages we find Indian
summer subjected to the same sort of empirical attention that Silliman
insisted his contributors pay to other natural events. Between 1825 and 1850
the journal ran several articles on the science of Indian summer weather,
each offering a slightly different explanation for the seasonal warmth.[36] And
yet science alone did not constitute the extent of the *Journal*'s seasonal
speculations, as most of these articles also included lengthy descriptions of
the season's picturesque charm and discussions concerning the origin of
the phrase. They combined anthropological theories regarding Native
American habits with detailed explanations of the weather.

One example may stand for the several articles written in this vein. In
1836 Dr. Lyman Fletcher of the United States Army devoted the first two
pages of a six-page *Journal* article to the presumed origins of the term
"Indian summer." Indians, the doctor suggested, "believe that the Great
Spirit sends this mild season in November" to assist in the annual autumnal
hunt. "If you ask an Indian in the fall when he is going to his hunting
ground, he will tell you 'when our fall summer comes.'" But for the remaining four pages Fletcher abandons his ethnographic musings to address
the science behind the season. The main cause of the warmth, we read, is
the eventual return to atmospheric equilibrium following a series of violent
storms. As September unfolds and temperatures predictably drop, heavy
rains just before and after the autumnal equinox increase the circulation of
moisture in the air. "Currents or counter currents are formed," which collide
with each other until mid-October, when "equilibrium is restored." When
that happens, a "mild bland atmosphere ensues."[37]

Modern meteorologists reject this view, but its presence in an article that
speculates so deeply into Native American ways tellingly reveals the cultural
position occupied by Indian summer. More specifically, the simultaneous
discussion of both the science and the cultural history of Indian summer

in the same journal speaks to the highly flexible state of scientific authority in the three decades prior to the Civil War. As Laura Dassow Walls has noted, antebellum scientific discourse had not yet been fully institutionalized within the academy. Authority rested in neither professional scientists such as Harvard's Louis Agassiz nor literary amateurs such as Concord's Thoreau. Each made different types of claims regarding the province of science: Agassiz strove for the objective analysis of transparent fact, while Thoreau cultivated his personal interaction with an opaque natural world. Neither spoke for the entire scientific community, yet both claimed to be scientific.[38] Such lack of clearly defined authority, however, would not have concerned early Indian summer commentators, all of whom described a season that entered vernacular discourse before the fault lines between science and literature had been cleaved. Indeed, the season emerged just before the post–Civil War division of the curriculum into highly specialized and autonomous pursuits.

All of which brings me back to the sentimental season that I discussed earlier in this chapter. No figure better exemplifies the meteorological and sentimental place that Indian summer occupied in the mid–nineteenth century than Wilson Flagg (1805–1884), a once popular but now forgotten author of natural history essays. A lifelong New Englander and astute observer of the region's seasons and birds, Flagg at first offered a scientific explanation to account for the burst of autumnal warmth. In the 1857 *Studies in the Field and Forest*, he argued that the sun's warming rays are strongest immediately after a killing frost has caused the leaves to drop. With the sudden loss of cooling evaporation that had been provided by the leaves, the newly exposed ground undergoes a sudden increase of temperature that we call Indian summer. Unfortunately, the rapid decimation of eastern forests had rendered Indian summer obsolete, or at least Flagg assumed this to be the case. In his view, there simply were no longer enough trees in the eastern states to produce such an effect. Prior to extensive settlement and clearing, Flagg claimed in 1872, the season "came without fail." But in the wake of massive forest clearings, a process that peaked during the mid–nineteenth century, there were insufficient dead leaves to produce the conditions necessary for "a true Indian Summer." "It has fled from our land before the progress of civilization; it has departed with the primitive forest."[39] In other words, Flagg reasoned, environmental facts trumped cultural legends: Indian summer no longer existed.

Flagg's scientific interests, however, did not prevent him from appending a lengthy sentimental poem titled "The Indian Summer" to his 1857 explanation of the season's warmth. In six stanzas of uneven quality he outlines scenes reminiscent of Brainard's earlier poem while highlighting the birds and flowers that return when the weather once again turns warm. During Indian summer, he writes, "The summer sun once more regains his sway" while "the brown landscape breathes a warmer day." The discussion of November in the third stanza may stand for the rest of the poem:

> Oft in this month, with bright complacent smile,
> The sun dispels the frowning clouds awhile;
> Lifts up the misty curtain that conceals
> The heavenly radiance summer's sky reveals;
> Sheds softer azure on the calm blue sea,
> And spreads a greener verdure on the leas.
> Shortly before December rules the year,
> Upon the wintry skies, new signs appear;
> A milder planet guides the hours of night,
> And fairer day-beams harbinger the light.
> Thus in an hour of sorrow, when opprest
> By anxious cares that steal away our rest,
> Will unexpected gleams of hope arise,
> And chase the clouded prospect from our eyes.[40]

The poem has some charm, but its true significance lies in what it reveals about Flagg's willingness to move from one mode of Indian summer discourse to another. In a short span of pages, he travels from a scientific explanation of seasonal warmth, to a sentimental poem of the season, to an ecologically complex debunking of cultural myth. Like Thoreau, to whom he was inevitably compared, Flagg viewed the natural world as a complex site endowed with metaphoric possibilities precisely because it was scientifically rich. But unlike his more accomplished contemporary, he could never unite his science and poetry into a seamless whole. As a result, his treatment of Indian summer—at times a scientific provable entity, at times a sentimental icon of the past—reads like the product of a man who cannot make up his mind. But perhaps such a statement is too hard on Flagg. After all, the words "science" and "sentiment" rarely appear in the same sentence. Rather than revealing an unscientific sentimentalism, his intellectual juggling act reveals a culture perfectly capable of simultaneous discussion of scientific and sentimental weather.

Flagg's divided conception of Indian summer resembles the attempts of other nineteenth-century writers to bridge the gap between measurable fact and poetic conjecture. Thoreau famously does this in *Walden*. In the course of his stay along its shores, he learns that the pond must first be described before it will reveal any philosophical or psychological insights. And in the introductory "Custom House" chapter of *The Scarlet Letter*, Hawthorne similarly remarks upon the emotional and intellectual energies required to convert the tattered woven "A" he finds in a desk drawer into the material for the romance concerning Hester Prynne that he prepares us to read. He subjects the shredded letter to rigid measurements and carefully records its size, texture, and hue. The mere physicality of the "A," however, does not satisfactorily excite Hawthorne's imagination. In fact, the exact opposite is the case. The more he stares at the "A," the more convinced he becomes that there must be "some deep meaning in it, worthy of interpretation."[41] The description, he understands, leads to the metaphor.

And so it was with antebellum Indian summer. By midcentury virtually all descriptions of the season worked in the service of the imaginary life of the country. Simultaneously caught between sentimentalism, Romanticism, and science, the early literary accounts of Indian summer offer a case study in how we might move from the thing observed to the thing imagined. As the decades progressed, cultural conditions paved the way for more and more readers and writers to find metaphoric value in this interlude of warmth. Second youth, restful death, wizened middle age—these and other sentiments found poetic expression in the season.

And yet, the movement between weather observed and weather as metaphor was never entirely innocent. For the one point that writers of Indian summer poems could not escape was that the season they celebrated carried the name of America's native peoples. As we will see in the following chapter, the conversion of Indians into a meteorological metaphor was an artistic and linguistic move fraught with complications.

3

Fighting Words: Native Americans and the Naming of Indian Summer

> When I mediate on the destiny of the prosperous branch of the Saxon family, and the unexhausted energies of this new country—I forget that what is now Concord was once Musketaquid, and that the American race has had its history— The future reader of history will associate this generation with the red man in his thoughts, and give it credit for some sympathy with that race—Our history will have some copper tints at least and be read as through an Indian Summer haze.
> —Henry David Thoreau[1]

For all its success in entering into the language of sentiment and weather, no aspect of Indian summer more thoroughly reflected the state of nineteenth-century American culture than its name. Nor does any season arrive more deeply implicated in the nation's past. Named for a people many readers and commentators believed had been safely removed to a romanticized past, Indian summer's emergence as a sentimental touchstone depended on America's collective meteorological imagination to cover up a morally uncomfortable portion of the historic record: The number of Indians in the eastern part of the country had declined dramatically. In 1820, roughly 120,000 Native Americans lived east of the Mississippi; by 1845, after a period of government-sponsored removals, fewer than 30,000 remained—a 75 percent loss that only aggravated the general decimation inaugurated nearly two centuries before.[2] By figuratively locating natives in the most beautiful and serene time of year, the violence done to them seemed less traumatic and severe. And so with each new celebration of the season's beauty, the calm autumnal warmth of the nineteenth-century present further buried the violent early spring of the colonial past. A more pronounced metaphoric reordering of the historic record would be difficult to find.

Unlike, say, El Niño weather, which takes its name from a single person (the Christ child), Indian summer is named for an entire group of people, the presence of whom represents one of the defining aspects of American life. Consequently, the "Indian" half of the phrase carries all of the metaphoric and historic baggage that America's settler culture has collectively imposed on native inhabitants. No other people on earth have been asked to bear such a heavy meteorological burden. We chuckle at the thought of a Caucasian winter or an African-American spring. Why, then, an Indian summer? Any attempt to answer this question brings us directly into the history of American racial views. More precisely, it requires us to confront how eighteenth- and nineteenth-century white Americans responded to the Indians whose land they desired. Even today, when white/Indian violence has hopefully been relegated to the past, the phrase "Indian summer" continues to rankle the American soul. Indeed, more than a few people have nervously wondered if we should in fact celebrate Native American summer in recognition of changed perceptions or continue to employ the phrase we know so well. As a recent *New Yorker* cartoon indicates, comfortable white Americans may offer ironic asides about the season's name, but they cannot escape its role in the nation's life. Drinks in hand and almost insufferably secure, the cartoon couple awaits their favorite time of year (see figure 4).

Indian languages have provided the English tongue with hundreds of words, most conspicuously in the areas of place-names, animals, and foods. "These were the sounds that issued from the wigwams of this country before Columbus was born," Thoreau somewhat patronizingly wrote in the "Chesuncook" section of the *Maine Woods*. They "have not yet died away; and with remarkably few exceptions, the language of their forefathers is still copious for them."[3] Neologisms that unite the word "Indian" with familiar English terms have also contributed to America's linguistic heritage. According to H. L. Mencken, the earliest documented use of such a phrase was "Indian hemp" (1619), a term followed by "Indian meal" (1635), "Indian harvest" (1642), and "Indian preacher" (1682). The eighteenth century gave rise to "Indian agent" (1766), "Indian file" (1758), and, of course, "Indian summer."[4] In most cases, no mystery lies behind the origin of the linguistic compound. Each describes a specific act or thing done or pos-

"I hope we have whatever it is we may or may not still be allowed to call Indian summer."

sessed by natives. Only Indian summer has inspired multiple etymological theories.

The earliest surviving speculations concerning the origin of the term "Indian summer" date to the first years of the nineteenth century, some three decades after Crevecouer but contemporary with the season's march into the weather vernacular. The practice of proposing etymological theories became a veritable cottage industry in the 1820s, and of course speculation continues today. When describing my research efforts to colleagues and friends, I am frequently asked to explain where and how Indian summer earned its name. A definitive answer, however, remains impossible to unearth. We can rule out some explanations as illogical or historically unfounded, but I suspect we will never know for sure just how and why the appellation came to be. The claims of countless commentators notwithstanding, no smoking-gun evidence regarding Indian summer's name exists.

Nevertheless, we can gainfully examine how the term was used and by whom. Ultimately, I would argue, such an examination will prove more fruitful than a rigorous antiquarian quest. We learn far more about Indian summer's place in American culture by exploring the contexts from which theories about its etymology emerged than we could ever hope to learn by selecting one of them as definitively correct. Often reflecting concerns over a troubling pattern of violence, such theories can help us uncover views that literate antebellum white Americans held about the country's native inhabitants. Unfortunately, we know comparatively little of what nineteenth-century Indians themselves thought of the subject, so I can tell only part of a much larger story. But the story is worth telling for the light it sheds on an important schism in nineteenth-century white views concerning Indians, a schism that enabled Americans to embrace the romantic appearance of their Indian brethren in the woods but to cringe in fear when those same Indians strolled down settled streets. Indeed, the etymological history of the season exemplifies the widespread wish that Indians in the American East could be folded into a seemingly natural event—the leaves fall, the frost comes, and the Indians fade away. But of course nothing that happened to American Indians followed a proscribed natural plan. As we will see, nineteenth-century Indian summer may represent the first time in human history that discourse about the weather has been asked to help clean up a nation's unpleasant past.

Good Indian/Bad Indian

The history of Indian summer etymologies reveals a season that imaginatively and meteorologically embodies the Good Indian/Bad Indian dichotomy that informed nineteenth-century literary discussions of Native Americans. As all students of American literature will recognize, the years that saw the spread of Indian summer weather also witnessed frequent treatment of natives in the nation's poetry and prose. Such treatment stemmed from the general Romantic-era desire to create a body of national writing centered on the exigencies of local material. Thus in 1815, the august Boston-based *North American Review* urged American writers to find inspiration in either the pre-Revolutionary era or "the armorial bearings and Hieroglyphic writings" of the country's Indian past.[5] Appeals of this sort reached authors across the country, particularly in the 1820s and 1830s. The best-known example remains James Fenimore Cooper's Leatherstocking novels, a series he began in 1823 and completed nearly twenty years later. But Cooper was only one of many writers who turned to native subject matter. At various times in their careers popular writers such as Catharine Maria Sedgwick, James Kirke Paulding, and John Neal all covered similar literary terrain, briefly placing Indian history and culture at the center of America's literary life.

Subtlety, however, rarely graced that center. Almost without exception, writers of the period presented fictional Indians as either malignant devils prone to unspeakable cruelty or noble savages possessed with a stoic calm. American Indians, who had been and remain decisive actors on the historical stage, thus became abstracted figures within a morality tale conceived, written, and read by whites.[6] Cooper's novels, for example, present Indians as either good or bad, a moral calculation usually based on which group best understands and accepts its eventual fate. Indians who resisted faced a violent fictional demise. Their noble counterparts, on the other hand, allowed the fruits of civilization to grow by quietly removing themselves from their native soil, a presumed nobility best exemplified by Chingachgook in *The Last of the Mohicans*. Indeed, no other nineteenth-century work more completely states the white hope that Indians would accept the dictates of history than Cooper's 1822 novel. As the story draws to a close and with his dead son lying at his feet, Chingachgook nobly urges his Indian brethren to leave: "palefaces are masters of the earth and the time of the Red Man has not yet come again."[7]

Such hopes extended far across the culture. Even Lydia Maria Child, a writer who later developed a far more trenchant critique of America's Indian policies, ended her first novel, *Hobomok* (1824), by having the title character surrender his white wife and half-English son to the wife's first lover before disappearing into the forest. As Child's biographer notes, Hobomok's departure represents the "familiar white fantasy that the Indian will somehow disappear."[8]

Two nineteenth-century explanations for the origins of the term Indian summer adopt a version of the Good Indian half of this dichotomy. The first and earliest explanation of any sort that I have seen imaginatively reconstructed Native Americans as environmental sages who happily shared their wisdom with the usurpers of their land. Indians, of course, have long been saddled with the romantic hope that they intuitively understand natural processes with acumen unavailable to whites, and occasionally Indian summer theories played on this hope by portraying Indians gladly informing colonists about the weather. First propounded in 1804 by the important early American novelist Charles Brockden Brown, this explanation claimed that the season had been "predicted by the natives to the first immigrants, who [then] took the early frosts as the signal of winter." A version of this theory, which Brown offered in a footnote within a scientific work that he translated from the French, surfaced again nearly forty years later in Zadock Thompson's 1842 *Natural History of Vermont*. An astute naturalist, Thompson reported that "it was a maxim with the aborigines of this country" that thirty smoky days must pass before winter finally arrived. "Perhaps in allusion" to this belief, Thompson suggested, early colonists applied the name "Indian summer" to honor the natives who had first informed them that such days foretell the coming cold.[9]

Though plausible, explanations of this sort assume insights into colonial-era environmental literacy that we do not have; indeed, even Thompson admitted that he could "not vouch for [the] truth" of the maxims he reported. To assess the veracity of such claims, we would need to know what colonists knew about Indian summer weather and when they knew it, even though the colonists themselves had nothing to say on the subject. The theory does, however, conform to similar white efforts to reconstruct the history of ecological knowledge when such reconstructions served desired ends. In the centuries following English settlement of Massachusetts, for example, a legend developed that the kind Indian Squanto taught colonists how to fertilize their crops with fish. But in fact, as the environmental historian William Cronon has shown, the English arrived in the New World knowing full well how to employ this technique. Squanto himself may have learned it during his European captivity just before the arrival of the Pilgrims.[10] Still, the legend of Squanto survives in part because it highlights an Indian who aided the colonial enterprise. The weather-wise natives of legend suggest that an analogous pattern followed in the case of Indian summer. Apparently, Indians freely gave their seasonal knowledge to the very people who, now blessed with such knowledge, established further dominance over the land. It's a convenient story for those who ultimately prevailed. As in the oft-repeated tales of Squanto,

Pocahontas, and Sacagawea, these friendly natives are memorialized primarily because they assisted whites.

A second explanation linked the term Indian summer to the time of year that Indians supposedly preferred to hunt. As a contributor to the *American Journal of Science* somewhat inelegantly claimed, the "appellation of Indian summer, is derived from the circumstance of this period of the year, being selected by the aborigines of the country, as their hunting season, to which it is highly conducive, not only on account of the plenty and perfection of the game, but also in consequence of the haziness or obscurity of the air." Such conditions "favor a near and unsuspected approach."[11] Others pointed to Indian summer smoke to suggest that campfires lit by native hunting parties gave rise to the season's name. Daniel Webster, for example, believed that the term derived from the confluence of flame, smoke, and fall hunting parties he first heard about as a child, parties he in turn described to later generations of children eager to hear about Indian summer. "The early settlers," he claimed, "were forced to some plain explanation, and they were satisfied with that." And because the "name was pleasant and peculiar" it quickly "grew into easy use."[12]

Webster's confidence aside, no surviving colonial records indicate that settlers viewed native behaviors in any way related to such an explanation. To be sure, fall hunting parties were essential to the native economy, but as with Brown, we have here only an undocumented recollection that earlier generations spoke of the season in the same way he did.[13] Of course, such a disparity between the historical and mythical records could prove invaluable to legend spinners. With few Indians remaining in the antebellum Northeast to challenge or rebut his story, Webster could easily construct, backdate, and impose romanticized visions of native life in the forest of the past.

At times, such stories amount to a bit of harmless fun, and we should take care to avoid dismissing efforts to tell a good yarn. But we should also remember that these Indian summer etymologies are rooted in a convenient myth in which conflicts between natives and whites give way to friendly discussions about hunting and the weather. Stories such as those told by Webster, Thompson, and Brown run the danger—all too common in discussions of native ways—of turning Indians into the subject of casual anthropological glances. What sounds plausible is inscribed within a series of legends constructed and repeated by whites. They function as meteorological palliatives that invoke the beauty of Indian summer while denying an uncomfortable past. Indeed, by relegating Indian summer to folklore or legends of the hunt, the various Good Indian etymologies helped naturalize the passing of native culture. If the past was so calm, the passing of land from Indian to white control must have been inevitable, even preordained. A contingent set of historical facts is submerged beneath a romanticized state that appears charming, natural, and benign.

Indian summer etymologies that draw upon the second half of the Good Indian/Bad Indian dichotomy stand in stark contrast to the sentimental theories we have been considering. In these cases, the tensions between Indians and settlers led fearful whites to paint Native Americans as blood-thirsty and deceitful savages who planned their most vicious attacks during the lull that the season provided.

First publicly proposed in 1824 by the Reverend Joseph Doddridge, the fear-based explanation traces the term Indian summer to the anxieties of early white colonists in western Virginia and Pennsylvania, who supposedly looked forward to winter because Indians had difficulty staging attacks through snow. Accordingly, the vigilance required during the summer and spring grew less pronounced at the end of the fall. In his 1824 *Notes on the Settlement and Indian Wars, of the Western Parts of Virginia and Pennsylvania,* Doddridge claimed "the onset of winter was therefore hailed as a jubilee by the early inhabitants of the country." Indian summer, however, provided a second chance for attack by providing a form of meteorological subterfuge. With the weather suddenly and unusually warm, Indians had "another opportunity of visiting the settlements with their destructive warfare." So dreaded was this time of year, Doddridge claimed, that a "back-woodsman seldom hears this expression [Indian summer] without feeling a chill of horror."[14]

Doddridge's theory grew out of colonial fears of the Indians' so-called "skulking way of war." As several scholars have noted, the first British colonists in the New World were perplexed and angered by the military strategies of the Indians. Rather than confronting their enemies in open battlefields, as European campaigns were fought, the Indians relied on quick mobility through the forest. For many colonists, the Indian technique of hiding behind trees and fighting without the visible support of comrades violated acceptable military practice. At first, they saw little skill in such secretive methods of war. But by striking by surprise and then rapidly re-treating into the forest, the Indians scored a number of quick, if limited, victories without incurring large losses of their own.[15] The on-again, off-again warmth of Indian summer enhanced such trickery, Doddridge assumed. The fluctuating and unpredictable weather conditions apparently provided the Indians more opportunity to skulk.

The unfortunate childhood slur "Indian giver" stems from a similar set of beliefs. Just as Doddridge's version of Indian summer inverts winter's apparent promise for peace, so to does an "Indian giver" promise one thing only to take it back. The term most likely derives from white misconception of the role of gift giving among native communities. Indian societies commonly exchanged gifts in order to cement relationships and establish status. The ability to bestow gifts on others—at marriages, at funerals, and in tribal diplomacy—secured the giver a high standing within the community. Moreover, leaders frequently exchanged gifts of unequal value in the expectation that the favor would be returned, thus cementing the relationship into the future. The failure to send additional gifts typically led to demands that the initial presents be returned. English colonists in the old Northwest Territory (where, we recall, Indian summer took early root in military camps) had difficulty understanding this system. Assuming that trade involved the equal exchange of goods, they misread the Indian insistence upon gifts as a form of bribery rather than a necessary component of social life. As one eighteenth-century almanac writer stated, to make an "Indian gift is to make a present but expect more in return than we give."[16] An "Indian giver," then, came to mean anyone who bargained unfairly or did not live up to his or her end of a deal.

With its association of skulduggery, violence, and the frontier, Doddridge's theory regarding the etymology of Indian summer proved extremely popular. Throughout the nineteenth century, publications attempted to settle once and for all where the term Indian summer originated by reprinting excerpts from Doddridge's account. In 1824, the year the theory first saw print, both the *Philadelphia Gazetteer* and the *Saturday Evening Post* published selections from his discussion, while Samuel Kercheval appended Doddridge's entire *Notes* to his popular 1833 *History of the Valley of Virginia*. And in 1849, the editors of the *New England Historical and Genealogical Register* published a version of this explanation in the pages of this venerable Brahmin publication. By midcentury, the savage Indian summer theory fully rivaled the various explanations rooted in native nobility and calm. Indeed, it remains popular today. I remember hearing this explanation as a child and encountering it again in a college assignment that drew on the work of the historian Daniel J. Boorstin.[17] I confess, too, that prior to digging too deeply into my project I repeated this explanation to my students with what I believed was certainty.

Still, though my own initial certainty may have been unfounded, Doddridge's theory conforms to the geography and timing of early Indian summer. He locates the season's origins in the same late-eighteenth-century trans-Allegheny district we considered in chapter 1. (Recall that Harmar, Denny, and Crevecouer all engaged in military action in these terrains.) As we have seen, various shifting alliances among Indian, American, English, and French interests led to an essentially permanent state of war in the region. The violence picked up considerably after 1758, when, contrary to the promises of the Treaty of Easton, Anglo-American squatters from the East began crossing the Alleghenies into Ohio, Kentucky, and the western districts of Pennsylvania and Virginia. For the remainder of the century, the region between the Ohio River and the Great Lakes witnessed one violent outbreak after another. With one group facing west and the other "facing east"—to use the title of Daniel K. Richter's native history of early America—both sides abandoned any visions of peaceful coexistence on the land.[18]

Despite the geographical plausibility, there is little evidence to suggest that Indians timed their raids on white encampments according to Doddridge's account. In fact, rather than plan their attacks to correspond with Indian summer (a move that would betray the legendary Indian aptitude for surprise), the record indicates that Indian-white conflicts erupted throughout the seasonal round. In her splendid study of Kentucky settlement, for example, Elizabeth Perkins argues it was whites, not Indians, who preferred to attack in the fall, since such late-year forays allowed for the destruction of recently harvested grain. Of the "approximately thirty major armed expeditions crossing the Ohio River between 1774–1794," she notes, "over half took place during August, September, and October."[19] Others have argued that Indians favored winter raids precisely because such forays could surprise and trap settlers who, owing to the snow and cold, had become housebound.

Doddridge, then, brings us back to the same historical conundrum that marks most Indian summer explanations. He either accurately recalled—fifty years after the fact—language of mid-eighteenth-century frontier settlements or used a contemporary term to explain a past event. Unfortunately, in the absence of further evidence we will never know. We do know, however, that he inserted a distinctly violent tone that other early discussions of Indian summer did not contain. And here lies his importance to our story. For in the end, Doddridge's legacy rests in the nature of his Indian summer explanation rather than its historical accuracy.

* * *

What, then, are we to make of these twin poles of Indian summer ety-mologies? At first glance, they seem mutually exclusive. Yet recent consid-eration of an analogous subject by the historian Jill Lepore suggests that the Good Indian/Bad Indian etymologies drew from the same imaginative well. In her study of the Wampanoag chief King Philip's place in Ameri-can culture, Lepore argues that white views concerning Indians during the 1830s and 1840s must be seen within the context of the furor over government-sponsored Indian removal policies. To make a complex story quite short, following Andrew Jackson's 1828 election to the presidency, federal policy regarding Indians in the old Northwest Territory and the southeastern United States moved from the hope of securing Indian lands through mutually agreed upon treaties toward a program of forced expul-sion to areas west of the Mississippi. White Americans would apparently no longer tolerate Indians in their midst. And yet, the very same month that Jackson sent his plan to Congress, audiences in New York wildly applauded the debut of Edwin Forrest's performance of John Augustus Stone's play, *Metamora; or, The Last of the Wampanoags*. One of the most popular productions of the nineteenth century, Stone's play ends with King Philip, the seventeenth-century leader of the most powerful Indian uprising in American history (here given the non-Wampanoag name of Metamora), issuing a dying curse to the whites who have brought his campaign to an end: "Spirits of the grave, I come! But the curse of Metamora stays with the white man!" As audiences cheered Philip's seventeenth-century defiance, nineteenth-century Indians were sent packing.[20]

As Lepore notes, "Through plays like *Metamora*, white Americans came to define themselves in relation to an imagined past. That past, however, required that there be no Indians in the present, or at least not nearby."[21] Thus audiences in the Northeast could comfortably protest the adminis-tration's plan secure in the belief that Indian populations in their region had already dramatically declined. Philip could be a hero precisely because he was dead.

The same may be said for the Good Indian/Bad Indian versions of Indian summer. New Englanders such as Daniel Webster and Zadock Thompson looked to the past through rose-colored glasses. Their Indian summer stories seemingly amount to charming and harmless fun. The vi-olent frontier of Doddridge, on the other hand, contained Indians that no one could consider fun, and in fact his widely distributed explanation could be used to justify policies of removal. In either case, Indians were dead and gone: In New England they romantically and inevitably passed on; on the frontier they were violently kicked out.

An Indian Time

So far, the explanations we have considered focus on white responses to Indian behavior. This should come as no surprise since comparatively few Indians entered the publishing marketplace in the first half of the nineteenth century. Consequently, we are left primarily with settlers' explanations for why the season carries the name it does. Few of these theories, however, take seriously the notion that Indian summer might unfold within native religious beliefs. But if we turn our attention away from the written record toward the oral narratives by which so much of native culture was transmitted, we can hear the Indian voices so strangely absent from most nineteenth-century accounts of Indian summer.

The oldest published example explicitly to link Indian beliefs to Indian summer dates from an 1812 sermon by the Reverend James Freeman of Boston's King's Chapel. A central figure in the early history of Massachusetts Unitarianism, Freeman claimed that Narraganset Indians attributed the seasonal warmth to Cautantowwit, a deity residing in the Southwest. His text that day, the last Sunday of the year, was from the First Letter of Peter: "The end of all things is at hand; therefore keep sane and sober for your prayers." Such thoughts led Freeman to describe for his parishioners a visit he had made to his father's burial site one recent Indian summer day. They also gave rise to etymological speculation. According to Freeman, "this charming season" derives its name "from the natives, who believe that it is caused by a wind, which comes immediately from the court of their great and benevolent God Cautantowwit," god of the Southwest. As he gently exhales each fall, the breeze makes audible "the spirit of the good man speaking in the wind."[22]

Unfortunately, we cannot verify the accuracy of Freeman's account. Like many nineteenth-century writers he cites no sources for his information, although this of course does not preclude the possibility that the story of Cautantowwit had been in general circulation. A deity with the power to create and destroy life, Cautantowwit certainly figured prominently in Narraganset culture. Early English accounts such as Roger Williams's 1643 *Key to the Language of America* report the native belief that corn and beans originally came from the southwestern gardens of Cautantowwit, a location that conforms to the common belief that Indian summer warmth hailed from this direction. "This is the pleasingest, warmest wind in the climate," Williams said of the southwestern breeze, one "most desired of the Indians." But Williams, whose work Freeman most likely consulted, makes no further mention of Indian summer attributes. Still, the theory gained currency among white New Englanders of the day, in part because at King's Chapel Freeman held one of the most distinguished pulpits in the region. Local historians such as William Tudor and George Ticknor, for example, placed Freeman's exact words within their descriptions of Indian summer, while the distinguished *American Journal of Science* proclaimed the story central to the "New England tradition" of the season.[23] But no one who has investigated the subject—including Albert Matthews, the greatest Indian summer source hunter of them all—has found an earlier published reference to Cautantowwit's Indian summer smoke than Freeman's.[24] For white New Englanders, at least, the New England tradition seems to start with him.

To find a more complete native New England theory regarding Indian summer, we must turn to stories recorded and written in the twentieth century. Among many other important ethnographic findings, the anthropologist Frank G. Speck collected an Indian summer explanation during his fieldwork with the Penobscot Indians of Maine. Speck first encountered and recorded Penobscot belief systems in 1909, when there still were "a score or more of aged Indians whose life span reached back to the days when European influence had not deeply affected their economic life." According to Speck's informants, the Penobscot called warm fall periods "the people's summer." One elderly man reported that as a child he heard his elders tell the story of an Indian named Zimo, who upon falling ill in the summer was left with nothing to harvest in the fall. Faced with starvation, Zimo sought assistance from "the Master."

So he went to the Master for help. He said, "I have been sick all through planting and harvesting time and now winter time is coming on and I have no provisions." And he asked him to help him. Then the Master told him, "Go ahead. Plant your things now and you will have a crop right away." Zimo went home and straight away put his seeds into the ground. The weather favored him and as soon as he had finished planting, his crops were ready to harvest. It took him seven days and at the end he had as much as other people. Then winter came in. They called that warm season "person's summer," and it comes again every year.[25]

The contemporary Abenaki storyteller Joseph Bruchac tells a similar tale that long circulated among Indians in Vermont and upstate New York. In Bruchac's words, "Long ago there was a man who was known as Notkikad," who, like the Penobscot Zimo, was left with nothing to harvest in the fall. Fearful for his family's survival, Notkikad offered tobacco to Tabaldak, "The Master of Life." That same evening Tabaldak visited Notkikad in a dream, promising him special seeds and warm weather to sow another crop. Within two days the "young plants were already waist high," and soon Notkikad and his family "harvested his crop and dried the corns and beans and squash for the winter." It is a gift returned each fall to the Abenaki.

To this day, the people say, that special time is still given to us each year, even though we have none of those magical seeds. That time, which people call Indian Summer today, was called Nibunalnoba or "a man's summer" by the Abenaki. It reminds them to always be thankful.[26]

Unlike the legends about various kindly Indians who conveniently shared their Indian summer knowledge with whites, Bruchac's story places the season entirely within the stories and life cycles of native peoples. And like Speck's elderly informants—who also leave whites out of the story altogether—he stresses the need to give thanks during Indian summer. For him, the season is more than a glorious interlude, though it certainly has its glories. Its true value lies in its promise to the Abenaki that life may be sustained when we patiently remember how to thank.

A second cluster of Indian versions of Indian summer emerged farther west than these Abenaki and Penobscot tales, perhaps most notably in the Ojibwa narratives compiled by Henry Rowe Schoolcraft. Few other nineteenth-century white Americans had as much direct contact with Indians as Schoolcraft. A professionally trained geologist and self-trained linguist, he spent fourteen years exploring the old Northwest Territory and the Mississippi Valley before becoming a federal Indian agent in Michigan in 1822, a post he held until 1841. During his long tenure, he collected and translated into English hundreds of Ojibwa oral narratives and songs, many of them supplied by his Ojibwa wife, Jane. And although they are not without their critics, his several books on the structure and history of Indian languages and tales helped launch the field of Native American ethnography. Indeed, according to one recent scholar of his work, Schoolcraft was "the first Euramerican actively and systematically to create texts from Native American oral performances."[27]

Schoolcraft traced the origin of Indian summer to the personified exhalations of a native mythological figure. Like other Algonquian peoples, the Ojibwa among whom he lived gave names to the winds, believing them to be active participants in the lives of men, animals, and plants. In a tale included in the 1839 *Algic Researches* Schoolcraft located the origin of the phrase and concept of Indian summer in the story of Shawondasee, an obese and "plethoric old man" whose father, Mudjekewis, was "the father of the winds." At Mudjekewis's behest, Shawondasee assumed control over the wind from the south. The son, however, proved lazy and grew fat because he did little but sit with his eyes locked in a gaze north. But when "he sighs in autumn," Schoolcraft writes, Shawondasee provides the northern people with a welcome interlude of warmth. At such times "we have those balmy southern airs, which communicate warmth and delight over the northern hemisphere, and make the Indian Summer."[28]

Another Ojibwa tale ascribed the warmth of Indian summer to Nanabozho, whose playful antics and extraordinary powers made him a central figure in the oral narratives of Great Lakes Indians. Nanabozho assumes multiple roles in Ojibwa tales. A giver of life and a trickster, he could take on the forms of animals and intercede, often comically, in the affairs of the world. According to narratives compiled by Homer Kidder in the late nineteenth century, he held a special place in Ojibwa affections. Nanabozho, one informant told Kidder, "was feared on account of his tremendous power but he did not know how to control his power. He could make a new earth, yet sometimes he acted like a fool, making jokes and playing tricks, though his pranks were harmless."[29]

One of those tricks, though a kindly one, may have been the annual Indian summer. According to a posthumously published description of Ojibwa religion by the Reverend Peter Jones (1802–1856), a Canadian Ojibwa and ordained Methodist minister, Nanabozho each year briefly forestalls the cold by producing warm smoke from the bowl of his pipe. Just prior to falling asleep for the winter he fills "his great pipe and smokes for several days."[30] The smoke in turn travels south to bring the people their Indian summer. Though brief, Jones's contention deserves special attention. Begun in the 1850s and brought to completion by his wife, his account contains, so far as I can tell, the only published pre–Civil War theory regarding Indian summer offered by an Indian.

With their roots in the Great Lakes culture of the Ojibwa, Schoolcraft's and Jones's tales place Indian summer within the outer limits of the contested territories that gave rise to the etymologies we considered in chapter 1. Still, as with every other theory we have considered, questions can be raised. Schoolcraft, for example, complicated any assessment of his work by adopting several conflicting approaches when gathering his materials.

On the one hand, he took native oral traditions seriously, believing them to reveal key aspects of Indian culture and history. On the other hand, he also edited his collected legends to meet the joint demands of his own strict Methodism and a reading public he correctly reasoned preferred tales in a sentimental vein. Moreover, for all his outward concern for Indian welfare, Schoolcraft ultimately believed that native folklore betrayed a congenital inability to accept the dictates of progress. Indian narratives, he argued, represented an "Oriental mentality" that naturally resisted new ideas. Only a rigorous course of education would successfully lead Indians out of the forest, and even here he was not certain a new environment would be sufficient to overcome the native genetic heritage.[31] Shawondasee and his Indian Summer smoke, then, emerge from an Indian mind that Schoolcraft assumed remained locked in its primitive ways.

Jones, on the other hand, spent his adult life trying to convert Indians to Christian ways. Some modern readers have dismissed his work for its appeal to white rather than native audiences. Yet such a charge seems harsh, especially in light of the justifiable concerns stemming from essentialist readings of race: There is no one way an author must write in order to reach specific sets of readers. As his biographer notes, Jones "lived in a period of oppression for Canada's native peoples, at a time when the Indians of present-day southern Ontario had lost their equality with whites." Certainly he made compromises with his materials, perhaps even in his tale of Nanabozho, but that does not imply that he abandoned the culture of his youth.[32]

Some empirically grounded critics might also object to using an orally transpired legend as an historic artifact, although in recent years scholars of native culture have argued (convincingly, I believe) that Indian history can be understood only if we accept the kind of evidence that exists in the nonphysical realm of oral traditions.[33] And then, of course, there is the very real possibility that Jones, Schoolcraft, and their twentieth-century successors—both Indian and white—took retrospective liberties with Indian summer, using a term from their own time to describe a phenomenon from the past (the same could be said for virtually all the etymologies we have encountered). Nevertheless, by choosing to locate the origin of Indian summer in the religious culture of Indians rather than white *responses* to Indians, Freeman, Schoolcraft, Speck, and, most explicitly, Bruchac and Jones allow the people for whom the season is named to speak. No other explanation makes Indian summer an Indian time of year.

The Vanishing Indians of Indian Summer

I want to return to a subject I raised earlier in this chapter to consider those aspects of nineteenth-century discussions of Indian summer and Indians that do not focus on the origins of the term, but instead use the season as the meteorological equivalent of the Vanishing Indian. For many writers, the season offered the ideal opportunity to present versions of this motif. Most works in this mode suggest that while the decline of Indian populations represented a cause for regret, the inevitable march of civilizing forces had virtually preordained their demise. For white Americans who recoiled at the thought of violent expulsion, the quietly disappearing native provided the perfect rhetorical antidote, an antidote that placed the retreating figure within the tragic yet romantic glow cast by the setting western sun.[34]

Sanford Gifford's elegiac 1861 painting *Indian Summer* visually captures the romantic yearnings behind this motif (figure 5). A native of Hudson, New York, Gifford was esteemed for his several Indian summer views, many of them variants of the one shown here. Indeed, according to one critic, the buying pubic took for granted "his success was possible only in this field."[35] This was decidedly not the case, but Gifford certainly understood his culture's concerns. Here three small Indians appear in the foreground while a distant canoe carries others. The surrounding leaves have reached the fullness of autumn's gold, while our vision is carried away toward some mysterious distance to where these few Indians will presumably go. With his meticulous rendering of stilled space, Gifford offers a scene that is at once noble and sad.

We see these same concerns in William Cullen Bryant's frequently anthologized "An Indian at the Burial Place of His Fathers," the work that perhaps best exemplifies the literary uses of the Vanishing Indian motif. The first stanza establishes the connection between decline, loss, and regret:

> It is the spot I came to seek –
> My father's ancient burial-place,
> Ere from these vales, ashamed and weak,
> Withdrew our wasted race.
> It is the spot – I know it well –
> Of which our old traditions tell.

In the next twelve stanzas Bryant lays out the transformation of the landscape that followed the arrival of "the pale race." Where formerly a "lithe

5. Sanford Gifford, *Indian Summer* (1861). In Private Collection.

and tall" Indian woodsman could "Walk forth, amid his reign," now the white man's "wheat is green and high," a sign that the stabilizing force of agriculture has replaced the wandering ways of the hunt. The change comes about not through violence, however, but through the unfolding of nature's plan; "like April snow / In the warm moon," the Indians "shrink away." Bryant's speaker further naturalizes the process by suggesting that the white "race may vanish hence, like mine," a possibility that renders Indian decline no more extraordinary than the various departures presumably to come.[36]

The most widely read work to link Indian summer with the Vanishing Indian motif was Longfellow's long 1855 poem, *The Song of Hiawatha*, a work that draws directly on Schoolcraft's *Algic Researches*. Although *Hiawatha* takes place along Lake Superior, its tone stems from the weather Longfellow experienced in Cambridge. As he paused in his writing in October 1854, he marveled at "the mist, the leaves, the flash of the river," of both the legendary Indian summer and the one he was experiencing at home— "all is mystical and a dream." Such a scene led him to recall the "charming tradition in the mythology of the Indians that this soft, hazy weather is made by the passionate sighs of Shawondasee."[37]

In naming his hero Hiawatha, Longfellow repeated a mistake made by Schoolcraft, who had erroneously substituted the identity of an historical Iroquoian personage for the Algonquian Nanabozho. Nevertheless, Longfellow describes a legendary being, here shorn of Nanabozho's trickster qualities, who has been sent by the gods to bring peace and plenty to the tribes of the Great Lakes. A man of peace in a land of war, Hiawatha is perhaps the definitive Good Indian of nineteenth-century American fantasy. Skilled in the ways of the forest, he is strong, courtly, and, ultimately, doomed. As Newton Arvin, Longfellow's finest biographer, has noted, the plot infuses its hero with an elegiac Indian summer glow.[38] The season itself only briefly figures in the poem, when the poet, drawing on Schoolcraft's story of Ojibwa winds, describes the lazy Shawondasee breeze of the fall:

> From his pipe the smoke ascending
> Filled the sky with haze and vapor
> Filled the air with dreamy softness,
> Gave a twinkle to the water,
> Touched the rugged hills with smoothness,
> Brought the tender Indian Summer
> To the melancholy north-land,
> In the dreary Moon of Snow-shoes.[39]

Though not explicitly stated, a sweetly melancholic feeling hovers over the descriptions of Hiawatha, a peacemaker sent to end the ancient battles that separated one Indian nation from another. In the end, he gives way to a more powerful force—French missionaries—and he sails westward in a magic canoe, a departure that assured his exploits would remain forever shrouded in legendary Indian summer mist.

Connecticut's Lydia Sigourney drew on similar sentiments in her 1849 poem "Indian Summer," although she allowed herself a bit more anger at the fate of the Indian than Longfellow ever displayed. She begins by asking, "When was the redman's summer?" a metaphoric rather than meteorological question intended to identify the prime of Indian civilization. After rejecting the other seasons of the year, she settles on the fall—and, more specifically, Indian summer—finding in that season most of the romantic conventions (fragile beauty, red leaves, approaching death) that antebellum letters draped over Indian culture. Only "When the groves / In fleeting colors wrote their own decay," she writes, did "The Indian's joyous season" begin. At such times, "the haze, / Soft and illusive as a fairy dream" envelops the "landscape in its silvery fold." But Sigourney moves beyond conventional Indian summer scenic depiction to suggest that the season's fleeting beauty resembles the tragic fate of Native Americans:

> Gorgeous was the time,
> Yet brief as gorgeous. Beautiful to thee,
> Our brother hunter, but to us replete
> With musing thoughts in melancholy train.
> Our joys, alas! Too oft were woe to thee.
> Yet ah, poor Indian! Whom we fain would drive
> Both from our hearts, and from thy father's lands,
> The perfect year doth bear thee on its crown,
> And when we would forget, repeat thy name.

Calling to mind a romanticized version of the past, Sigourney's Indian summer sanctions feelings of regret while drawing our attention to the compensatory beauties of the season. Though steeped in nostalgia, the poem invites readers to compare the season—"The perfect year doth bear thee on its crown"—with the race whose passing she laments. She rhetorically wraps both within an irretrievable past, a past that tantalizingly re-emerges once a year only to vanish once again.

Sigourney poetically linked Indians to Indian summer by appealing to the fragile state of both the season and the natives' position within American culture. Some of her contemporaries, on the other hand, made the connection by looking to the color of Native American skin. By 1830 the association of Indian complexion with autumnal colors had become a poetic commonplace, thus literally and figuratively embodying sentimental constructions of the Indian past. The simultaneous spread of Indian summer descriptions and the Vanishing Indian motif helped intensify the connection: People with red skin were once here, but now, in the Indian summer of their history in the eastern states, their presence is fading fast. Such embodiments were frequently manifested in feminine form. In his 1837 story "The Cherokee's Threat," N. P. Willis describes a perfect Indian summer day in which the "blood-red sugar maple" and "the gaudy tulip tree" evocatively suggest an Indian woman's lips. Ellery Channing similarly wrote that Native Americans' most characteristic moment occurs during "a fading week" of Indian summer weather that resembles the "cheek / Of a consumptive girl." Bright, beautiful, and departing, the red cheek of the girl matches both the color and expected life span of a nineteenth-century Indian and an autumnal leaf.[40] None will last long.

Such mawkish sentiment ran the danger of slipping into offensive caricature. Without question, the nadir of these nostalgic gestures was reached in John McCutcheon's illustration "Injun Summer," a print that appeared once every year in the *Chicago Tribune* from 1909 to as recently as 1992.

Whatever dignity was offered by the nineteenth-century sentimental version of the Vanishing Indian motif is here shred in cartoonish poor taste. The print shows a pipe-smoking old man recounting to his grandson the stories from his own youth while invoking nearly every stereotype of the now-gone Indians. The language in the captions could not be more troubling. "Yes, sonny, this is sure enough Injun summer," the old man reports. That's "when all the homesick Injuns come back to play." There "used to be heaps of Injuns around here," he continues. Not "cigar store Injuns" but the "Reg'lar sure'nuf" kind (figure 6).[41]

Nostalgia has its uses, but the faux sweetness of a grandfather recounting to his grandson the Injuns who "all went away and died," shows just how problematic white America's fascination with Indian summer could be. To be sure, the Vanishing Indian motif was based on the false premise that Indians had in fact vanished. Still, there is a vast difference between the Indian summer visions presented by Sigourney and McCutcheon. To be fondly recalled by a season's name is one thing; to be ridiculed is another.

We have to go back seventy years prior to McCutcheon's cartoon to find a poet who truly offered an alternative vision to the sentimental association of vanishing Indians with Indian summer. Though largely forgotten today, the western Massachusetts poet Josiah Canning completely rejected the conventional Vanishing Indian motif, using Indian summer imagery instead to react with anger at the fate of Native Americans. In his 1838 poem "The Indian Gone!" Canning pointedly asks, "where is he?" when pondering the whereabouts of his farm's former inhabitants. His answer does not assuage his fears that he has wrongly encroached onto native lands. While working his fields on the night of a "Hunter's moon," the speaker "heard a mournful voice deplore" the "perfidy" that "slew . . . a long-departed race." So far, this sounds like anything Bryant or Willis might have written. But later, Canning finds disturbing implications in the connection between the weather and the absent Indians:

> I wrought with ardor at the plough
>   One smoky Indian-summer day;
> The dank locks swept my heated brow,
>   I bade the panting oxen stay.
> Beneath me in the furrow lay
>   A relic of the chase, full low;
> I brushed the crumbling soil away –

INJUN SUMMER

Yep, sonny, this is sure enough Injun summer. Don't know what that is, I reckon, do you?

Well, that's when all the homesick Injuns come back to play. You know, a long time ago, long afore yer granddaddy was born even, there used to be heaps of Injuns around here—thousands—millions, I reckon, far as that's concerned. Reg'lar sure 'nough Injuns—none o' yer cigar store Injuns, not much. They wuz all around here—right here where you're standin'.

Don't be skeered—hain't none around here now, leastways no live ones. They been gone this many a year.

They all went away and died, so they ain't no more left.

But every year, 'long about now, they all come back, leastways their sperrits do. They're here now. You can see 'em off across the fields. Look real hard. See that kind o' hazy, misty look out yonder? Well, them's Injuns—Injun sperrits marchin' along an' dancin' in the sunlight. That's what makes that kind o' haze that's everywhere—it's jest the sperrits of the Injuns all come back. They're all around us now.

See off yonder; see them tepees? They kind o' look like corn shocks from here, but them's Injun tents, sure as you're a foot high. See 'em now?

Sure, I knowed you could. Smell that smoky sort o' smell in the air? That's the campfires a-burnin' and their pipes a-goin'.

Lots o' people say it's jest leaves burnin', but it ain't. It's the campfires, an' th' Injuns are hoppin' 'round 'em t' beat the old Harry.

You jest come out here tonight when the moon is hangin' over the hill off yonder an' the harvest fields is all swimmin' in the moonlight, an' you can see the Injuns and the tepees jest as plain as kin be. You can, eh? I knowed you would after a little while.

Jever notice how the leaves turn red 'bout this time o' year? That's jest another sign o' redskins. That's when an old Injun sperrit gits tired dancin' an' goes up an' squats on a leaf t'rest. Why, I kin hear 'em rustlin' an' whisperin' an' creepin' 'round among the leaves all the time; an' ever' once'n a while a leaf gives way under some fat old Injun ghost and comes floatin' down to the ground. See—here's one now. See how red it is? That's the war paint rubbed off'n an Injun ghost, sure's you're born.

Purty soon all the Injuns'll go marchin' away agin, back to the happy huntin' ground, but next year you'll see 'em troopin' back—th' sky jest hazy with 'em and their campfires smolderin' away jest like they are now.

6. John McCutcheon, *Chicago Tribune* cartoon, "Injun Summer" (first published 1909). Copyrighted Chicago Tribune Company. All rights reserved. Used with permission.

> The Indian fashioned, I know,
>   But where is he?
>
> When the pheasants drumming in the wood
>   Allured me forth my aim to try,
> Amid the forest lone I stood,
>   And the dead leaves went rustling by.
> The breeze played in the branches high;
>   Slow music filled my listening ear;
> It was a wailing funeral cry,
>   For Nature mourned her children dear.
>   It answered me![42]

Here, the smoky weather, the found relic, and the recognition that he has been plowing someone's former home cause the speaker to lose himself in an imaginary "funeral cry." Unlike Sigourney, who takes comfort in the season's annual return, or Cooper, who views the loss of native culture as necessary for civilization's progress, Canning remains unconsoled. For him, Indian summer brings neither a break from agricultural burdens nor the promise of a second youth in the fall. Rather, its very name troubles the soul.

Canning, whose haunting depictions of western Massachusetts deserve more attention, refuses to gloss the history of America's natives with either of the two standard white versions of the Indian past. He presents neither a bloodthirsty savage nor a sentimental icon. Though many regretted the apparent demise of native ways, few other writers (with the important exceptions of Dickinson and Thoreau) found the season named for natives so emotionally unnerving. Finding solace in neither Indian summer's promise of renewed youth nor the enjoyments of civilization's fruits, he instead found only a muted rage when confronting the Indian's fate.

Canning's vision, however, barely resonated in the culture, as the stoically vanishing Indian ultimately came to dominate nineteenth-century efforts to link Indian summer with the people for whom the season is named. We might even say that the season became the meteorological accompaniment to sentimental elegies to Native Americans, McCutcheon's tasteless illustration notwithstanding. Time and again, writers painted both the season and Indians with similar strokes. Vivid, strong, and soon to depart, both are remembered for the beauties they recall. Thomas De Quincey, an Englishman, captured this nineteenth-century sentimental dilemma better than any American of the time. "What the American Indian race itself at this time is, *that* the Indian Summer represents symbolically." As a meteorological symbol, he continued, the season offered perfect "revelations of grace in form and movement" while nonetheless always covering those revelations "under a *visible* fatality of decay."[43] For De Quincey and so many others, what was once beautiful remained only as a faded token of the past.

In the end, we find the perfect analogue for the vanishing place of Indians in the iconography of Indian summer in the diminishing relative thickness of seasonal smoke we considered in the previous chapter. William Faux, we recall, attributed the season's apocalyptic smoke to the wild and reckless ways of Indian burning practices, a practice lamentably continued by whites. Longfellow, on the other hand, found that the smoke induced feelings of nostalgic charm. His seasonal smoke appeared just thick enough to cast a romantic glow over the land, only to dissipate and ultimately disappear. Later in the century, when the threat of Indian violence was no longer tenable, there was little need to include native smoke in descriptions of the season; indeed Indian summer increasingly became known for its glorious warmth rather than its mysterious haze. In one notable example, an 1890 correspondent to the *American Meteorological Journal* recalled childhood tales of Indian Summer smoke and native fires by remarking that "the smell of burning grasses, so very noticeable in my youth, is no longer to be perceived by ordinary senses." And by 1913, a meteorological textbook had left Indians out of the explanation altogether. The smoke and fog, the author claimed, were produced either by "dust from roads and plowed fields" or from naturally occurring forest fires.[44] No Indians were necessary. To follow the historical progression of the smoke amounts to a crash course in the history of popular white versions of Native Americans: from violent savage, to charming relic, to dimly recalled icon, to nonexistent. Each white version of Indians came with its own form of haze.

4

Indian Summer and the Creation of New England

Those grown old, who have had the youth bled from them by the jagged edged winds of winter, know sorrowfully that Indian Summer is a sham to be met with hard-eyed cynicism. But the young wait anxiously, scanning the chill autumn skies for a sign of her coming. And sometimes the old, against all the warnings of better judgment, wait with the young and helpful, their tired, winter eyes turned heavenward to seek the first traces of a false softening.
—Grace Metalious, *Peyton Place*[1]

In chapter 2 I argued that the growth of certain cultural institutions created the conditions for Indian summer to exist. We saw how the conventions of sentimentalism and Romanticism enabled people to name and identify a form of weather they had not recognized before. Culture, I suggested, helped make the weather.

In this and subsequent chapters I alter this course to argue that Indian summer weather helped create nineteenth-century New England. Without abandoning my earlier position, here I suggest that with the new weather firmly in place (or quickly falling into place) the region's writers drew on Indian summer imagery to help define what made New England (and New Englanders) unique.

Most eighteenth- and nineteenth-century Americans assumed that regional climates contributed significantly to the formation of character. Thomas Jefferson, for example, repeated the common canard that both northern and southern sensibilities stemmed from the exigencies of the local weather. The former owed their presumed reserve to the effect of cool air, while the latter's alleged fiery nature stemmed from the heat. New England writers shared some of this deterministic view, perhaps most notably in the ethnographic writings of Francis Parkman and Louis Agassiz.[2] But whereas Jefferson correctly understood that the respective climates of the North and South existed well before the onset of human culture, antebellum New England writers who used Indian summer imagery employed a cultural/meteorological pattern that was only decades old. They turned a relatively young form of weather into an exemplar of the region's presumed beauty and charm. At the same time, they drew on Indian summer's sentimental attributes to buttress claims that New England customs were venerable and old.

The emergence of Indian summer as a fully realized literary subject paralleled efforts to mold a distinctive New England literary tradition. At the risk of oversimplifying a complex development in literary history, the years that witnessed the spread of Indian summer also saw neoclassical claims of universal subject matter give way to Romanticism's interest in local subjects. Such a move was necessary, one critic noted, if Americans were ever to "prefer indigenous rather than exotic literary productions."[3] Inspired by this advice, many writers turned their attention to natural phenomena in their own backyard. With its local vagaries and traditions, the weather (including Indian summer) offered perhaps the most geographically specific material for a writer coming of age during these decades. Such was the case with nineteenth-century accounts of Indian summer in New England. As we will see in this chapter, the writers who made the season their own helped define literary *and* meteorological traditions for the region.

Of course, writers outside New England did not ignore Indian summer. We saw in chapter 1 that the season most likely originated in the trans-Allegheny West and then moved rapidly through the Ohio Valley. Clearly people in these areas used the term to describe the local weather, as did southern writers such as John Pendleton Kennedy and Edgar Allan Poe. In his 1845 "Tale of the Ragged Mountains," for example, Poe describes a "warm misty day toward the end of November," which Americans call "the Indian Summer." Similarly, Daniel S. Curtiss's 1852 history of settlement in Wisconsin and Illinois remarks that the light and breezes of Indian summer on the prairie are "like the approach of a good man's last days" at the close of a useful and upright life."[4] Nineteenth-century southerners and midwesterners, however, never suggested that Indian summer's characteristic traits rendered their respective regions culturally distinct from others.

Typically, they described the local weather and then moved on. Only New Englanders routinely claimed the season as their own and turned to its warmth as a regionally based metaphoric sign.

The entrance of Indian summer into New England seasonal iconography reminds us how amenable to cultural change that iconography has proved to be. In his 1997 book *Snow in America*, Bernard Mergen notes that by the middle of the seventeenth century, colonial New Englanders "had made snowy winters characteristic of their identity." Having survived a series of brutally cold winters, colonists and their immediate descendants elevated the region's frigid temperatures and snow to iconic status. In the twentieth century, fall foliage replaced snow as New England's most distinctive seasonal event. As Kent Ryden notes in his recent study *Landscape with Figures: Nature and Culture in New England*, colorful foliage emerged as a regional signpost after a second clearing of the white pine forest around 1900 allowed the shade-intolerant hardwood deciduous trees to suddenly display an unimpeded view of their splendid colors. The widespread availability of cars in the twentieth century also opened previously inaccessible woodlands to day-trippers in search of leaves. To be sure, autumn colors had been praised before; but as Ryden shows, descriptions of the foliage, such as those offered by Thoreau, often bemoaned a *lack* of appreciation for its beauty. Thus, rather than assuming that everyone saw the same glorious spectacle he relished, Thoreau in his 1862 essay "Autumnal Tints" instead hoped to teach his neighbors how best to enjoy the glories of New England's fall.[5]

If New Englanders took their time to learn to love the leaves, the glorification of Indian summer experienced no such delays. On the contrary. Almost overnight the season emerged as a celebrated regional icon. As associations between the season and region crystallized, New Englanders increasingly believed themselves blessed for living where the charms of Indian summer shined most bright. The seventeenth and eighteenth centuries had their snow, and the twentieth basked in the hues of the fall. But for nineteenth century New Englanders, particularly those active between 1820 and 1880, Indian summer reigned supreme.

Of course, the phrase "New England Indian summer" conceals as much as it reveals. Despite its relatively small size, there is no one New England. The meteorological and cultural differences between northern Maine and southern Connecticut could not be more pronounced.[6] Nor can we speak of a typical New Englander or representative New England writing. Like all regions, New England contains multitudes. As we saw in the previous chapter, we know precious little about what nineteenth-century Indians—in New England and elsewhere—thought about Indian summer. The same holds true for African-Americans. For the most part, as this chapter makes abundantly clear, we know only what literate white New Englanders thought about the season, although even here the evidence is limited to whites of Anglo-Saxon descent. I freely concede these points, in part because I must, but also because my true interest in this chapter lies in the efforts by a small group of nineteenth-century writers to use Indian summer as a meteorological means by which to forge a sense of New England as a unique and special place. How and why that happened is my principal subject. As we will see, the season became a central component in the myth of New England, a myth propagated by self-proclaimed regional spokespeople who claimed Indian summer as their own.

The Connection Established

The earliest statement explicitly to link the season's charms with the region appears in the work of William Tudor, briefly the editor of the Boston-based *North American Review* and author of the underappreciated *Letters on the Eastern States*. In the 1821 *Letters* Tudor says of his home region, "one of the most agreeable peculiarities in our climate is a period in the autumn called the Indian Summer." Its beauty, he insisted, stands in the same relationship to the actual summer as a "vivid recollection of past joys [does] to the reality." A Boston-area contributor to an 1838 number of *The United States Magazine* similarly claimed that "to a resident of New England the very name of Indian Summer calls up so many essentially poetic images, that it is difficult to approach the subject without permitting the thoughts to run riot over the fairy scenes which that season presents."[7] Poets, too, made the connection, as in Frances Osgood's thirteen-stanza poem inspired by an Indian summer scene painted by Thomas Doughty, an artist active in Boston in the 1830s. For Osgood, the "wild beauty" of Indian summer belongs to "one sunny region alone." "New England, beloved New England," she writes, "the soul-waking scene is thine own!"[8]

Not coincidentally, New England's embrace of Indian summer weather occurred during the same decades that many of the region's writers consciously worked to establish a literature national in scope. Ralph Waldo Emerson, a lifelong Massachusetts resident, articulated a vision of American writing that took the vastness of the New World as its subject; rather than confining himself to the narrow and small, his ideal scholar would embrace everything that was large. Key figures in literary New England's embrace of Indian summer such as Henry Wadsworth Longfellow and Oliver Wendell Holmes also assumed that they labored to build a broadly national literature. This is a well-known story, one by which, as Stephen Nissenbaum points out, New England writers such as Emerson, Haw-thorne, and Thoreau are taught in classes on "American Literature" while their contemporary William Gilmore Simms is presented as "southern."[9] But it is a story with implications for the history of New England Indian summer, a history simultaneously told as a regional and national tale.

Nineteenth-century New England's celebration of Indian summer, then, points in two different directions, albeit for the same reason. The embrace began when local authors figuratively brought the season east. But once ensconced in the new terrain, Indian summer could in turn propel the image of New England outward to the nation at large. By the 1830s New Englanders were quite accustomed to such projections. As Joseph Conforti points out in his study of New England identity, the effort to foist regional ways onto the nation at large dates to the late-eighteenth-century geog-raphy books by Connecticut's Jedediah Morse. Issued and revised several times over the years, Morse's geographies imagined the six New England states as a definable cultural entity that served as a collective exemplar of Federalist virtue—a regional model for the nation.[10] And so it was with nineteenth-century New England Indian summer. Usurped, codified, and embraced while New England writers worked to create a nation-defining body of letters, the season became a meteorological analogue for a broader cultural and literary campaign to show New England at its best.

Although they addressed readers across the country—a rhetorical stance we might think would lead to an abstracted vocabulary—the successful celebration of the region's Indian summer required New England writers to master the use of local rather than generic materials. In other words, only by immersing Indian summer into the idiom of the region could they expect their seasonal celebrations to take hold. To make this point clear, we should recall the several New England writers discussed in chapter 2 who wrote Indian summer poems. For although poets such as John Brain-ard and William Thompson Bacon lived *in* New England, their work was not really *of* New England. That is, their strong affinity for the neoclassical formalism from which they arose prevented them from emphasizing the specific details of the local climate, even a climate they had recently adopted as their own. We see this in their poetic treatment of trees. Brainard speaks of the "mighty forest" while Bacon points out the "mellow fruit" characteristic of Indian summer. Neither poet, however, identifies trees or plants native to New England. In their case, Indian summer poetry remained closely allied with a British topographical literary tradition that favored the universal and abstract over the local and concrete.[11] By contrast, James Russell Lowell's 1848 "Indian Summer Reverie" describes a walk along the Charles River, where the speaker encounters local trees such as oak, ash, and elm. Native animals such as bobolinks and chipmunks scurry through the poem as well. Although he too could slip into delocalized abstractions, Lowell's poem (which we will consider in detail) reveals a poet far more rooted in the local environment than Brainard or Bacon ever were. In his hands Indian summer represents more than a merely beautiful time of year; rather, its beauty derives from roots buried deep in the local soil. It produces specific effects on a specific locale.

Part of Lowell's emphasis on local Indian summer details stems from a gradual transformation in writing about New England. By the time Thoreau died in 1862, a significant and distinguished body of writing featuring detailed accounts of New England's topography and natural history had been established. Thoreau's contribution to this development is well known, but Indian summer poems and stories also contributed to the rise of a sustainable literary tradition. Indeed, the season can be used as an historical measuring stick to chart the region's ability to support a full-fledged literary community capable of using local materials for artistic ends. This does not mean that all New England writing about Indian summer after Brainard's early efforts was steeped in local color. But the season did enable New England writers to construct an environmental and political history of their region in ways that deliberately (and often aggressively) set the region apart from the rest of the nation.

Early Literary Efforts

The first significant literary work to specifically link Indian summer with New England is Sarah Josepha Hale's 1827 novel *Northwood*. A more perfect beginning would be difficult to find. A farmer's daughter born in New Hampshire in 1788, Hale in the 1830s and 1840s used her editorial position at *Godey's Lady's Book* to campaign for the establishment of Thanksgiving as a national holiday. In *Northwood*, the first of several novels she would eventually write, she re-creates an idyllic Granite State farm reminiscent

of the one she enjoyed as a child. An early example of New England regional writing, the novel was also among the first significant American
literary works to address the widening gap between the North and South
over the issue of slavery. Indeed, the plot trajectory deliberately establishes
a contrast between the regions. Though born in New Hampshire, Hale's
protagonist grew up in the South after his parents, believing that their son's
prospects would be improved by such a move, consented to allow southern
relatives to raise him in a more luxurious environment. When he returns
to the family farm as a young man, he is greeted by a perfect New England
Indian summer day, a greeting that assures the hero that he has truly arrived
home. "Our autumn," the narrator claims for both New Hampshire and
New England, "has a period of peculiar and mysterious loveliness, called
the Indian summer."

This brief season, of about twelve days in the whole, though rarely following in
consecutive order, is most beautiful and most distinctly marked in New England.
The softness of atmosphere is then indescribable. The sun looks down as though
dreaming of June and its roses; while some tricksy spirit throws over the faded
earth a veil that, mirage-like, gives a charm beyond the brightness of summer noon.
This is most perfect in November.[12]

The homecoming scene that follows, replete with a lavish Thanksgiving
feast, is predictably joyous for everyone involved. At the same time, the
beautiful Indian summer day provides compensatory cover for the bittersweet emotions of the prodigal's return home. For all the advantages his
wealthy southern upbringing allowed him to accrue, the weather that marks
the hero's triumphant journey reminds him of everything he has missed.

No New England writer more consciously draped himself in Indian
summer imagery than Henry Wadsworth Longfellow. Like Hale, Longfellow developed an affinity for things New England that lasted his entire
life. Born and raised in Portland, Maine, he settled in Cambridge in the
late 1830s upon assuming a chair in languages at Harvard. Within a few
short years his house on Brattle Street became a center of Boston's literary
life.[13] Although Longfellow became an accomplished translator and critic
of European verse, his reputation rested on his poems depicting historical
events, many of them centered on New England. In catchy, cleverly rhymed
meter he elevated figures such as Miles Standish and Paul Revere to the
highest ranks of regional heroes.

New England Indian summer appealed naturally to Longfellow's sensibilities, so it was perhaps inevitable that he would turn to the season at

a moment early in his career when he felt quite cut off from the place of his birth. While in Germany in 1829, the twenty-one-year-old Longfellow proposed to a Philadelphia publishing house a series of fictional sketches on life in New England, one of which was to be called "Indian Summer." The detailed proposal called for tales on a variety of New England habits and institutions, much as Washington Irving's 1819 *Sketch Book* invoked long-standing customs of England and the Hudson River Valley. At the time, Longfellow was distressed that a promised professorship at Bowdoin College—his alma mater—had been reduced to the rank of instructor. (Bowdoin officials believed he was too young to assume a full professor's chair.) Having gone to Europe to prepare for the position, he found himself alone in Dresden, a city he did not like. Confused about his professional prospects, Longfellow began collecting materials for his proposed book of New England tales as a way to resurrect his spirits.[14]

Fortuitously for Longfellow's later career as a poet, nothing came of the book plan. Unable to convince anyone to issue his proposed collection, he opted to publish his Indian summer sketch in the 1832 edition of *The Token*, an annual gift book published in Boston.[15] The story begins with an effusive description of a New England Indian summer. He offers a picture of perfect calm before certain death:

In the melancholy month of October, when the variegated tints of the autumnal landscape begin to fade away into the pale and sickly hue of death, a few soft, delicious days, called the Indian Summer, steal in upon the close of the year, and, like a Second Spring, breathe a balm round the departing season, and light up with a smile the pallid features of the dying year. They resemble those calm and lucid intervals, which sometimes precede the last hour of slow decline.[16]

As befits such a maudlin introduction, the tale describes the accidental visit of a traveler to a deathbed scene in New England. Shortly after arriving in the unnamed village, the narrator watches the last rites of a young woman stricken by a mysterious disease. Longfellow rolls out all of the sentimental devices for this short sketch, including a final reunion between the dying young woman and her long lost brother, who had fled the idyllic village in fits of intemperance. The pause between one season and the next that Indian summer represents contributes to the sentimental scene. The unusual warmth calls to mind "those calm and lucid intervals, which sometimes precede the last hour of slow decline." The young woman, who has piously accepted her soon-to-come passing, similarly hovers between life and death.

Longfellow retained an interest in Indian summer long after his initial disappointing use of the season. We saw in chapter 3 how he infused his 1855 *Song of Hiawatha* with a romantic cloud of Indian summer smoke, a haze he initially observed while staring out the window in Cambridge. He presented a similar landscape in *Evangeline* (1847), a popular long poem that depicts a sentimental love affair that unfolds during the expulsion of the Acadians from maritime Canada at the close of the French and Indian War. Using the English term "All Saints' summer," Longfellow presents the soon to be departing Acadians within a perfectly composed and magical terrain:

> Such was the advent of autumn. Then followed
>   that beautiful season
> Called by the pious Acadians the summer
>   of All Saints!
> Filled was the air with a dreamy and magical light
>   and the landscape
> Lay as if new created in all the freshness of child-
>   hood.
> Peace seemed to reign upon earth, and the restless
>   heart of the ocean
> Was for a moment consoled. All sounds were in
>   harmony blended.
> Voices of children at play, the crowing of cocks in
>   the farm-yards,
> Whir of wings in the drowsy air, and the cooing
>   of pigeons –
> All were subdued and low as the murmurs of love;
>   and the great sun
> Looked with the eye of love through the golden
>   vapors around him;
> While arrayed in its robes of russet and scarlet and
>   yellow,
> Beneath with the sheen of the dew, each glittering
>   tree of the forest
> Flashed like the plane-tree the Persian adorned
>   with mantles and jewels.[17]

By carefully allowing the sun's soft light to illuminate the protective frame of the "russet and scarlet" trees, Longfellow conveys the picturesque still- ness of the scene. With the sounds in the landscape similarly blended into a perfect harmony, he offers the meteorological equivalent of a moment frozen in time. Moreover, our knowledge that the Acadians will soon be forced to leave such a delightful spot (a fact Longfellow counted on his readers to know) serves to underscore the melancholy tone that runs throughout the poem.

A Brahmin's Season

Longfellow's interest in Indian summer set the stage for an ongoing fascination with the season among Boston's Brahmin elite. In fact, Brahmin writers such as James Russell Lowell, Oliver Wendell Holmes, and John Greenleaf Whittier were perhaps the central figures in bringing New England and Indian summer together. Sons of New England all, their lives and work contain more than a little of the season's nostalgic glow.

Holmes first applied the term "Brahmin" to the Boston aristocracy in the opening pages of his 1860 novel *Else Venner*. "There is in New England," he writes, a caste that "by the repetition of the same influences, generation after generation" views itself as the protectors of local culture.[18] The roots of this class date to the early nineteenth century and run directly through Harvard Yard, where the sons of Boston-area merchants began the lifelong networks that sustained their commercial and philanthropic endeavors. At first, such connections served business purposes as early Brahmins founded in the 1810s and 1820s the large New England textile mills that ushered in the American industrial revolution. By midcentury, however, the children and grandchildren of the early Brahmin merchants had consolidated their control over New England's banks, factories, and transportation systems. Perched atop the region's financial houses and secure in their own livelihoods, the second- and third-generation Brahmins worked to shape the contours of local elite culture, lending their names and money to institutions such as the Massachusetts Horticultural Society and the Museum of Fine Arts. The more literary minded pursued belletristic careers, often supplemented by an academic post at Harvard.[19]

The Brahmin Indian summer poets either came from such families or married into them, thereby securing for themselves the comfortable income that allowed for a more leisurely life of letters. Lowell's grandfather, for instance, organized the Boston Manufacturing Company, the firm that financed and controlled New England's largest mills, while Longfellow married Fanny Appleton, heiress to one of the region's great fortunes. In part because they always seemed so comfortable, twentieth-century scholars downplayed the talents of the Brahmin poets, finding their work tepid, didactic, and dull. And to be sure, a certain smugness informs their work. In essays and poems as well as in their professional demeanors, they cultivated a bemused sense of detachment from the very same economic forces that had elevated their families to prominence. Nevertheless, they enjoyed wide success and occasionally produced works that possess more than mere antiquarian charm.[20]

James Russell Lowell offered the most extensive Brahmin version of the season in his 1847 poem "An Indian Summer Reverie." A Harvard graduate and heir to a local fortune, Lowell occupied a conspicuous place among Boston-area writers. Not yet thirty when he issued his Indian summer poem, he had already made a name for himself as a poet in the New England grain through the first installments of his successful series *The Bigelow Papers*, a collection of poems issued between 1846 and 1848 that presents stock Yankee characters who in colorful regional speech gently skewer politicians while voicing opposition to the Mexican War.[21]

The concerns of "An Indian Summer Reverie," however, have less to do with national politics than with Lowell's beloved Cambridge and Charles River. Running to forty stanzas of unequal quality, the poem probably goes on longer than it should. Still, Lowell shows how Indian summer weather can encourage a newfound sensitivity to the land. The poem begins with a typical depiction of the season's "visionary tints"; but whereas Longfellow merely described his scene, Lowell draws more explicitly on the tenets of Romanticism to bring the speaker into direct contact with his subject. "No more the landscape holds its wealth apart," he notes; rather, the Indian summer weather "mingles with my senses and my heart." Like the Romantic haze we considered in chapter 2, the outside weather has metaphorically seeped inside. Emboldened by such a fusion between interior and exterior states, Lowell's reverie carries him past the plants and animals that have emerged for an apparent second spring. As he travels along the riverbank, the surrounding water, land, and air teem with life; everything, his senses included, seems doubly alive. Two stanzas may stand for the rest:

> The cock's shrill trump that tells of scattered
>   corn,
> Passed breezily on by all his flapping mates,
>   Faint and more faint, from barn to barn is borne,
> Southward, perhaps to far Magellan's Straits;
>   Dimly I catch the throb of distant flails;
>   Silently overhead the hen-hawk sails,

> With watchful, measuring eye, and for his quarry
>   waits.
>
>   The sobered robin, hunger-silent now,
> Seeks cedar-berries blue, his autumn cheer;
>   The chipmunk, on the shingly shagbark's bough,
> Now saws, now lists with downward eye and ear,
>   Then drops his nut, and, cheeping, with a bound
>   Whisks to his winding fastness underground;
> The clouds like swans drift down the streaming at-
>   mosphere.[22]

Toward the end of the poem Lowell switches from detailed nature depiction to mournful recollections of scenes from the past. While he is looking toward his boyhood home in Cambridge, his seasonal reverie becomes a catalogue of loss. Because the town had grown so quickly in the ensuing years, "the fields famed in boyhood's history" now stand as little more than a "diminished green." Figures from the poet's childhood such as the painter Washington Allston and the village blacksmith—a small-town icon that Longfellow would famously develop—had died, leaving Cambridge poorer for their passing. In the final stanza, the poet likens these nostalgic images to the brief moment of perfection that an artist might recognize in his work before destroying it in anguished disgust.

> The Artist saw his statue of the soul
>   Was perfect; so, with one regretful stroke,
>   The earthen model into fragments broke,
> And without her the impoverished seasons roll.

Although the scene retains its natural beauty, the cultural changes to his native town lead the poet to conclude, "Our only sure possession is the past."[23] Lowell was not alone in this feeling. D. H. Lawrence famously remarked that Natty Bumppo, the hero of Cooper's Leatherstocking novels, grew younger as the series progressed. Natty's novelistic career, he suggested, goes "backwards from old age to golden youth" and thus reenacts the "true myth of America," a myth by which "there is a gradual sloughing of the old skin towards a new youth."[24] The same may be said for Lowell's Indian summer. For all its charm, the season awakens the poet's sense that his best days have come and gone, that to be a New Englander of the mid–nineteenth century is tantamount to being old.

Lowell's response suggests why the season proved so popular among the Brahmin class. Not yet thirty when he wrote "An Indian Summer Reverie," the poet seems already to feel old. And in some sense he was. Although they were never quite the picturesque small towns he reverentially recalls in these 1847 lines, the Cambridge and Boston of Lowell's youth had nonetheless by midcentury developed into an international center of commerce, education, and trade, a process hastened, ironically enough, by the Lowell family's lucrative textile mills. At the same time, Ireland's potato famine led thousands of immigrants to scurry toward Boston, forever altering the region's political and ethnic mix. Brahmins remained firmly in charge of the area's cultural and financial institutions, but their numerical grip on the city and region was rapidly giving way. As Lowell wrote in his 1854 essay "Cambridge Thirty Years Ago," the region previously "had a character. Railways and omnibuses had not [yet] rolled flat all the little social prominences and peculiarities." With a population "wholly without foreign mixture" the Cambridge of his youth represented the calm before a pending storm.[25]

Such unprecedented change unnerved some of Lowell's fellow Brahmin literati. The historian Francis Parkman, for instance, believed that America's educated and cultured class, among whom the Brahmins considered themselves most conspicuous, had to "assert in its histories its cultural superiority" to groups who threatened "the vigorous and good stock" of the established families.[26] Lowell was more congenial than the prickly Parkman and would not necessarily have shared such views. Still, one gets the sense from his "Indian Summer Reverie," complete with its loving attention to local detail, that even he sensed that the tide had turned. Like the new immigrants, who made him feel out of place in his hometown, Indian summer weather made him feel old before his time.

Lowell's "Reverie" notwithstanding, it was Holmes who most consistently drew the connection between Indian summer and the premature aging of the Brahmins. Age, Holmes believed, was always catching up with him. The son of a minister, he lacked the easy access to wealth enjoyed by Lowell. Still, as a leading Boston doctor and popular essayist, novelist, and poet, he eventually became a pinnacle of the Brahmin elite. Born in 1809, Holmes began writing poetry about growing old before graduating from Harvard. One of his earliest poems, significantly enough titled "The Last Leaf," employs the conventional image of a dying leaf to describe an elderly man's shuffle through the streets. After smiling at his awkward gait, the young speaker hopes that future youngsters will also smile "At the old forsaken bough / where I cling."[27] Holmes continued to write about aging throughout his long career, often by associating the process with Indian summer. When, for example, he was asked to deliver a poem at an 1856 celebration marking the twenty-seventh anniversary of his Harvard commencement, he offered lines to "Our Indian Summer," a title that no doubt caught the attention of his classmates, most of whom were still in their forties.

But the season was more than a hackneyed metaphor for advancing age. In fact, its hints of passing youth led Holmes literally to wander through the past: "This is," he wrote in 1866, "the season for old churchyards"— not the burial grounds of Boston, which have been "ruined" by that city's relentless growth, but the still quiet and unchanged plots of Cambridge and Dorchester, which remain "inviolate." Holmes was especially moved by reminders of early death he encountered during his Indian summer strolls through graveyards. Thus while in Dorchester he stood face to face with the burial stone of a child of three who had been dead for nearly two centuries. The dead child, enigmatically named Submit, had obviously wracked the heart of a "Pilgrim mother two hundred years ago and more." But in the faded epigraph, which contains a seasonal reference to the child's youth, Holmes found words to counter his own Indian summer mood:

> Submit submitted to her heavenly king
> Being a flower of that eternal spring
> Neare 3 yeares old she dyed in heaven to waite
> The yeare was sixteen hundred 48.

Unmoved for two centuries, the dead Pilgrim child still "sleeps in peace."[28]

The emphasis on age in these statements reveals Brahmin anxiety over the changing face of New England, an anxiety shared by Anglo/American writers in the region almost from the moment colonists first set foot on New England soil. By the late seventeenth century, regional writers were already claiming that New England was not what it used to be.[29] Of course, the myth that New England had a golden past is precisely that—a myth, one that the Brahmins eagerly embraced. For writers such as Lowell and Holmes, the mist of Indian summer was part of that embrace. While other young men of their generation moved away to seek fortunes farther west, they remained home to wander local burial grounds. Like Indian summer itself, which briefly brings life to the late-year landscape, they found youth while rummaging amid the old.[30]

And yet at times even a writer as conspicuously Brahmin as Holmes wondered whether the mixture of old and young during Indian summer did not have its darker sides. In his 1868 novel *The Guardian Angel*, Holmes depicts a season that may encourage the violation of one generation by another. Set in an unnamed New England town, the novel concerns Myrtle Hazard, a beautiful fifteen-year-old girl who becomes the subject of erotic fantasies for the town minister, the doctor, and virtually all of its young men. One Indian summer afternoon, the married minister and Myrtle wander through the countryside as the older man imagines himself with the girl. As the sun warmed their faces he "was getting bewitched and driven beside himself by the intoxication of his relations with her." Eventually, he tries to coax her to the ground, but the girl successfully resists. Without absolving the minister of blame, the narrator nevertheless attributes at least part of the girl's near assault to the Indian summer weather: "To those who know the Indian summer of our Northern States, it is needless to describe the influence it exerts on the senses and the soul." Precisely because the landscape seems so still, "all natures"—including the minister's lecherous ways—"seem to find themselves more truly" during Indian summer. Indeed, it was just at the moment when "the strange light of the leaves irradiated the youthful figure" of the girl that he tried to convince her to join him on the ground.[31] Fortunately, Myrtle is wise enough to refuse the plea to sit in the grass, but the minister's intentions leave us wondering just how much Indian summer contact the generations should have.

The Aging of Indian Summer

Though frightening in his inability to accept either the limitations or the niceties of age, Holmes's minister was the exception. In the second half of the nineteenth century increased age became the major rhetorical strand around which New Englanders wove their Indian summer tales. In part, this reflects a growing interest in the subject of old age in the years after the Civil War. As the historian David Hackett Fischer notes in his study *Growing Old in America*, publishers found a ready market for anthologies containing poetic tributes to people who still enjoyed life in their advanced years.[32] In collections such as Lydia Maria Child's *Looking Toward Sunset* (1865) and Kate Sanborn's *Indian Summer Calendar* (1904) readers encountered uplifting essays and poems showing the consolations of peaceful retirement within a country otherwise obsessed with the accomplishments of the young. Sanborn, in particular, focused on New England, where she found "a brilliant galaxy of authors" of "more than three score." Their experiences led her to conclude that "there does exist an Indian summer of the soul and mind and heart, ay, and the body too, if rightly cared for."[33]

No post–Civil War author with ties to New England did more to solidify the link between Indian summer and advancing age than the novelist William Dean Howells, author of the unjustifiably obscure 1886 *Indian Summer*. Howells was not a New Englander by birth. He first came to Boston at the age of twenty-three in 1860 by way of Ohio; an aspiring writer, he was thrilled to be welcomed to town by such luminaries as Hawthorne, Lowell, and Holmes. After spending the Civil War years as the American consul in Venice—a reward for having written a campaign biography of Abraham Lincoln—Howells settled in Cambridge in 1871 to take over the editor's position at the *Atlantic Monthly*, a post he held until he moved to New York in 1890.[34]

The phrase "Indian summer" does not appear in the novel named for the season, but everything in the story suggests that Howells believed his title carried sufficient metaphoric weight to stand unambiguously for wizened middle age. The novel concerns the forty-one-year old Theodore Colville, an Indiana newspaper editor visiting Florence, a city he last visited in his early twenties. While walking through the streets he runs into a female friend he knew during his previous visit; now in her late thirties, the friend, a widow named Lina Bowen, is chaperoning a twenty-year-old American girl named Imogene Graham. (The girl's parents remain in Buffalo.) Colville, a lifelong bachelor, is taken aback by the girl's beauty and vitality. At the same time, he finds her youth a cause of regret: "the spectacle of that young unjaded capacity for pleasure touched him with a profound sense of loss." After a few meetings the two become engaged, although Colville tries to warn her that the twenty years that separate them might someday prove difficult. At first, Imogene dismisses his caution, wanting instead for Colville to know that "I am your youth—the youth you were robbed of—given back to you." Eventually, however, she realizes that such a marriage could not work. Colville, who has suspected as much all along, instead quite happily weds the far more appropriately aged Lina Bowen, a woman who throughout the novel displays a maturity and common sense commensurate with her years. In the end, he claims, "I have married a young person," a belatedly gracious statement that Lina nonetheless finds "irresistible."[35]

John Updike recently remarked of *Indian Summer*, "A midlife crisis has rarely been sketched in fiction with better humor, with gentler comedy, and more gracious acceptance of life's irrevocability."[36] There is, indeed, an exquisite delicacy to the language that we don't always find in Howells, although I confess that the forty-one-year-old Colville does not strike this particular author as especially old. But the hero's eventual recognition that his age calls for a form of serenity not required of his youth certainly hits home. Early in the novel Colville is reminded of just this point by an expatriated Unitarian minister from Massachusetts, the nineteenth-century home of Indian summer. "At forty," the minister claims,

one still has a great part of youth before him – perhaps the richest and sweetest part. By that time the turmoil of ideas and sensations is over; we see clearly and feel consciously. We are in a sort of quiet in which we peacefully enjoy. We have enlarged our perspective sufficiently to perceive things in their true proportion and relation; we are no longer tormented with the lurking fear of death, which darkens and embitters our earlier years; we have got into the habit of life; we have often been ailing and we have not died. Then we have time enough behind us to supply us with the materials of reverie and reminiscence; the terrible solitude of experience is broken; we have learned to smile at many things besides the fear of death. We ought also to have learned pity and patience.

Forty, the minister concludes, "is a beautiful age."[37]

But as the nineteenth century drew to a close, neither Howells nor his Brahmin predecessors could ignore that for all its implied serenity, Indian summer also implied a loss of vitality. To some observers, New England letters seemed especially drained of such vitality. The twentieth-century critic Van Wyck Brooks argued in *The Flowering of New England* (1936) that Emerson, Hawthorne, and the other figures of the American Renaissance created New England's finest literature between 1840 and 1860. This is not the place to challenge such an overly broad statement. It is, however, noteworthy that when Brooks next turned his attention to the years between 1865 and 1914, he titled his study *New England: Indian Summer*. To be sure, he found occasional moments of brilliance during these later years, particularly in Henry James and Henry Adams. But overall he noted a general drop in literary vigor. (Adams himself remarked in his *Education* that "the summer of the of the Spanish War (1898) began the Indian summer of life to one who had reached sixty years of age.") Wherever Brooks turned, he found the region stuck in a cultural torpor: "Society had lost its vital interests, and the Boston mind was indolent and flaccid, as if the struggle for existence had passed it by." Such complaints were not exactly new. Nor were they entirely accurate, as Brooks confined himself to the writing of Anglo-descended whites as if they alone constituted New England literature. Nevertheless, when Brooks surveyed the post–Civil War

New England literary landscape, he noted that "a mood of reminiscence possessed the people, for whom the present offered few excitements." In cities and towns, the men (he says nothing of the women) seemed "torpid and listless"; their "ambitions seemed be to atrophied except on the practical plane." By the 1880s the signs were clear: "A haze of Indian summer hung over New England."[38]

Which brings me back to the Brahmin depictions of Indian summer, most of which were written in the years *before* the Civil War, when literary New England was supposedly at its peak. Their statements reveal a prescience for which the Brahmins are not often credited. Powerless to stop the transformation of their region, a transformation that saw New England lose its central place in American cultural and political life, they welcomed the arrival of Indian summer's haze. Nowhere near as talented as Emerson or Hawthorne, the Brahmins may nonetheless have been ahead of their illustrious contemporaries on at least one front: They described the Indian summer of New England while the literary flowering (to use Brooks's terms) remained in full bloom.

Creating New England's Weather Past

I want to turn now to the common assumption that Indian summer weather had been enjoyed by the earliest English settlers in New England. Assertions of this sort continue to be accepted as self-evidently correct, even though no evidence suggests such a history. Indeed, without question, this has been the most consistent misperception about the season. An 1855 article in the art journal *Crayon* claimed, for example, that "accounts of the New World sent home by the earliest Pilgrims dwelt with especial wonder at delight upon Indian Summer."[39] And although he admitted that "we look in vain for any recognition of it in pages not more than half a century old," the naturalist Bela Hubbard in 1887 likewise reported that "early New England writers speak of this serene portion of autumn as peculiar to America, hence the name they gave it."[40] In fact, the warm and sunny glow of the invented Indian summer past conceals what we know about the meteorological record. Rather than praising the weather, the earliest English colonists were generally stunned by how frigid their new homeland could be. Assuming that its lower latitude would produce warmer temperatures than the more northerly England, colonists such as William Bradford and John Winthrop tried to explain why Massachusetts was so cold.[41]

Never did they pause to consider why it might suddenly become warm in the fall.

The assumption that colonial New England enjoyed Indian summer has roots in the same feelings of loss we have been considering in this chapter. As several nineteenth-century writers discovered, one way to ameliorate the Brahmin fear that New England had fallen from grace was to backdate the contemporary weather. For many, the glorious nineteenth-century Indian summer represented a natural link to the climates of the past. As a result, celebrations of a brief period of meteorological bliss often amounted to a rewriting of history. Continuities were established where none existed.

But why either wish for or assume that a newly discovered season had a distinguished meteorological pedigree? Once again, Eric Hobsbawm's notion of invented traditions sheds light on the matter. As we saw in chapter 2, such traditions "attempt to establish continuity with a suitable historic past."[42] Mid-nineteenth-century New England—roughly 1830–1870—was particularly susceptible to such inventions, as increased urbanism, industry, and immigration had produced the most modern region in the country. Indian summer's presumed history helped relieve those New Englanders who felt threatened by these transformations. It allowed them to believe that so long as Indian summer weather continued to arrive, the region still possessed a natural connection to days gone by. By concealing the central factors of New England life—no region had more advanced factories and railroad networks, for example—Indian summer writings rearranged the present along with the past. While perhaps not doing so intentionally, those who referred to New England's Indian summer glories, almost all of whom stressed rural outdoor pursuits, ignored the region's most characteristic physical qualities, even as they strove to define what made New England unique. Though produced, distributed, and read by urban New Englanders, nineteenth-century Indian summer idylls did their very best to deny from whence they came.

Claims that New England and Indian summer perfectly suited each other contributed to or paralleled a series of historical reconstructions by which the region reconceived its past to serve present ends. Historians have generally looked to the last decades of the nineteenth century to identify the origins of elite New England's interest in such filiopietistic endeavors as historic house preservation or genealogical research. But as Michael Kammen has noted, New England writers, clerics, and political figures from the antebellum era laid the groundwork for what would become the later systematic embrace of local history.[43] Poets such as Longfellow and politicians such as Daniel Webster mined New England's colonial and Revolutionary past for both political and moral reasons, linking the issues of the day with the struggles of years gone by.

The hagiography surrounding the Pilgrims makes this point clear. In the late eighteenth and early nineteenth centuries, the Pilgrims were newly venerated as the prescient fathers of New England religious and political liberty, a process that only accelerated as the 1820 bicentennial of Plymouth's founding loomed. The *Mayflower* Compact (a phrase unused by the small Separatist community) and Plymouth Rock (on which there is no evidence that the Pilgrims ever set foot) became regional icons to which nineteenth-century New Englanders could point as physical and emotional reminders of the region's first inhabitants. But as Joseph Conforti points out, the later version of the Pilgrim was almost wholly an invention, one that subsumed the much larger and historically more significant Puritan communities to the north into a mythic story of national origins that began at the tip of Cape Cod. Everyone in seventeenth-century New England became a Pilgrim.[44] Indian summer provided the meteorological cover for this filiopietistic embrace. As the Pilgrims grew in stature, the season's champions backdated their own period's most glorious weather to allow New England's first white settlers to bask in its glow.

We find examples of such a process in several different genres. An 1851 history of Litchfield, Connecticut, for example, asks readers to imagine the landscape that greeted "the first hardy explorers to these pleasant valleys, two hundred years ago." The native inhabitants of this landscape, we are told, looked forward each year to the "golden days of Indian summer," a period when native inhabitants "mused of the Great Spirit, the giver of corn, beans, and tobacco." In his 1857 poem "Mabel Martin," John Greenleaf Whittier likewise suggests that during the height of the 1692 Salem witch trials Indian summer paid a visit. Consciously seeking to "call the old times back," Whittier describes the plight of the title character, who had been convicted and executed for witchcraft. Her daughter, obviously distressed at the disaster that struck the family, was so overcome with grief that "she scarcely felt the soft caress" of "Indian summer's airs."[45]

In some sense, these gestures resemble the desire to preserve the Vanishing Indian within Indian summer that I discussed in chapter 3. As the above-quoted contributor to the *Crayon* conceded, we "love to associate it [Indian summer] with the fading memories of that race whose history, alas! is like the vague shadowing of an autumn distance."[46] In other words, the hoped-for Pilgrim Indian summer allowed seventeenth-century New Englanders to somehow survive into the nineteenth century. Like Native Americans, Pilgrim settlers and their immediate descendants briefly halted their fade into the distance when Indian summer reigned. The irony, of course, is that Indians and Pilgrims ended up on opposite sides of the historical fence. Nevertheless, the language of Indian summer proved pliable enough to embrace anyone in need of embracing. Both the natives for whom the season is named and the people whose arrival ultimately doomed those same natives could be simultaneously memorialized and preserved.

Once the Pilgrims and Puritans had been covered with Indian summer mist it was only a matter of time before late-eighteenth-century New Englanders came in for similar treatment. Thus, in her 1868 novel *Oldtown Folks*, Harriet Beecher Stowe employs the nineteenth-century season to describe an autumnal ritual of a much earlier time.[47] A Connecticut native whose family bulked large in nineteenth century New England literary and religious life, Stowe depicts an eighteenth-century New England Indian summer that lends bucolic charm to a fictional village in the years just after the American Revolution. It is a town not unlike the one she lived in as a girl. Whenever the "warm, late days of Indian summer came in," she writes, "the Deacon began to say to the minister, of a Sunday, 'I suppose it's about time for the Thanksgiving proclamation.'" At such times, there "came over the community a sort of genial repose of spirit," as if the weather helped facilitate cohesion. And cohesion was precisely the point she wished to make. As in her several post–Civil War historical novels, Stowe in *Oldtown Folks* drew on her deep knowledge of local history and customs to present idealized glimpses into New England's past. In the preface, the narrator remarks that the work "endeavors to show you New England in its seed bed, before the hot suns of modern progress had developed its sprouting germs into the great trees of today." Accordingly, when Indian summer arrives just before Thanksgiving, the fictionalized premodern New England shines as only New England during Indian summer can. The community is united, the weather is glorious, and together the town relishes the "sense of something accomplished."[48]

The rereading of the meteorological past outlined by Stowe, Whittier, and so many others was part of a broader cultural program that sought to reimagine the history of environmental interactions in New England. I mentioned in chapter 3 the continuing myth that Squanto showed Pilgrims how to fertilize their fields with fish. In another example, the geographer Martyn Bowden has shown that the popular notion that an impenetrable primeval forest greeted the initial settlers took shape *after* the first colonists had passed away. In fact, the earliest descriptions record surprise at the amount of open space, most of it produced through Indian fire practices. Wanting to believe that they and their ancestors had created a garden in the wilderness, Americans of subsequent generations conceived a colonial-era forest that was larger, thicker, and more intimidating than either the written or botanical record suggests.[49]

In the nineteenth century, much of this rereading focused on the appearance of earlier towns. Though Stowe describes an era nearly fifty years prior to New England's wholesale embrace of the season, the arrival of Indian summer in her mythic village nonetheless suggests that the annual glowing warmth could help transform the region's small towns into icons of stability.[50] Lowell, we recall, similarly turned to Indian summer when recollecting the Cambridge of his youth. His "Indian Summer Reverie" led him to recall the apparently cohesive Cambridge of his youth in which a few houses stood clustered around a common. As with Stowe, it was the ideal weather for the ideal town. "There gleams my native village," he writes in a late stanza:

> There, in red brick, which softening time defies
> Stand square and stiff the Muses' factories; –
> How with my life knit up is every well-known scene![51]

But as several recent studies have shown, the dignified town center of Lowell's youth did not possess the venerable history he assumed. What we imagine as the traditional New England village—a community centered around a common, a steepled church, and a few substantial houses—represented a clear and distinct break from colonial-era settlement patterns, which tended to be far more dispersed across the land. While celebrants of the communal ideal (recall Stowe's invocation of Indian summer cohesion) pointed to small nucleated New England villages as embodiments of virtue, such spaces first sprang into existence in the early nineteenth century—after a burst of post-Revolutionary town building and economic consolidation created the densely organized commercial nodes that we today celebrate as picturesque reminders of the past. Nevertheless, the center village emerged in the antebellum decades as a key ideological motif linking the region with its colonial past.[52]

Historically ideal townscapes and weatherscapes, then, served the same function: The nucleated village had apparently always been there, while the annual turn of the seasons had apparently always produced a moment of beauty and calm. Both linked New England to a romanticized and dehistoricized past. A series of conflations, then, defined nineteenth-century New England Indian summer. For just as the urban landscape was imaginatively collapsed into its premodern form, so too did the extremes of New England weather collapse into a celebration of serenity and calm. Summer's heat and winter's chill figuratively vanish when Indian summer is held up as the region's most distinctive meteorological event.

To even speak of New England Indian summer requires us to imagine the region as a cohesive whole. Yet if we look at the arrival of killing frosts, which most people would say is the most reliable predictor of an Indian summer, we find great variety across the six states. According to statistics compiled by New Hampshire state climatologist Barry Keim, nearly two months separate the average date for the first killing frosts in different New England locales. Farmington, Maine, can expect one by September 28, while Block Island will not see one, on average, until November 26. Similarly, Concord, New Hampshire, has its first killing frost on or about October 2, while Hartford, Connecticut, must wait until October 24.[53] Clearly, no one part of New England has a monopoly on the arrival of Indian summer, and yet we continue to speak as if the entire region could be condensed into one definable and containable weather event. What is experienced in quite different ways in quite different places at quite different times becomes a uniform New England Indian summer.

The historical and geographical trajectory of these celebrations also collapses the large into the small. It is no coincidence that the first New England poems about Indian summer were written in Connecticut in the 1820s, which, as Stephen Nissenbaum points out, was perhaps the last decade the state could be identified as the seat of New England culture. By the 1840s and 1850s, Massachusetts writers were speaking of New England Indian summer, and indeed the Bay State had by then come into its own as a literary and cultural hub. It made perfect sense, then, for Holmes, a resident of the region's largest city, to speak quite broadly about the season in the region. And sure enough, in the twentieth century, when many people found the heart of New England to lie in the farm towns of Vermont and Maine, the locus of Indian summer works moved farther north. As the "true" New England fades north, it brings its Indian summer along for the ride. (figure 7).[54] As the history of New England Indian summer shows: First we conflate, then we celebrate.

All of which brings me back to nineteenth-century New England and Indian summer. For better or worse, the idea of New England as both a natural and cultural whole has persevered over the years. To think of New

7. Willard Leroy Metcalf, *Indian Summer, Vermont* (1922). Dallas Museum of Art. Gift of the Jonsson Foundation.

England inevitably requires us to collapse distinctions, a process that enables us to think of the region as a place with its own customs, its own habits, its own weather. As Kent Ryden notes, "For many Americans both within and outside the region, New England is popularly defined not by a certain set of geographical boundaries but rather by a cluster of images, icons, historic episodes, character types: the white village, the steepled church, the Revolution, Puritan times, the Yankee."[55] To this list I would add Indian summer, a season that came into its own as an emblem of faded glory just as elite New Englanders were beginning to find their own glories in the past. Old and wise but with enough rekindled youth in its belly, the season's momentary gift of beauty suggested that New England might just survive its Indian summer days. It held out the hope of any parent (and New Englanders certainly thought of themselves as national parents) that the beautiful child in one's arms would not lose the sparkle in its eyes.

5

With Faith as in Spring: Thoreau's Indian Summer

I do not know what constitutes the peculiarity and charm of this weather.
—Henry David Thoreau (IX:91)[1]

Indian summer resonated deeply in the imagination of Henry David Thoreau, more so than anyone we have yet considered. A New Englander through and through, he loved everything about the season—its warmth, its strange atmospheric light, the flowers and shrubs that rebounded to life. Such beauty, he remarked during a ten-day Indian summer spell in October 1857, "is enough to make the reputation of any climate" (X:92). Like many of his contemporaries, Thoreau found ample opportunity to express hope during Indian summer. And like others before him, he rejoiced in the season's gift of newfound energies, taking comfort in its warmth much as a late-year bloom thrives in its glow. More than a merely glorious spell, Thoreau's Indian summer provided the meteorological backdrop for an annual spiritual and physical reinvigoration. "May my life not be destitute of its Indian Summer," he wrote in 1851, so that "I may once more lie on the ground with faith as in Spring" (4:62).

Yet Thoreau also recognized that while hope may spring eternal, even the most resilient spirits must come to their end. Indian summer weather prepared him for this eventuality. A too confident "faith in immortality" can only disappoint, he wrote in "Autumnal Tints," an essay first published in October 1862, five months after Thoreau himself had died at age forty-four. A modest "Indian Summer serenity," on the other hand, allows for graceful passage from one world into the next. Braced with such serenity, the dead can calmly "shed their bodies, as they do their hair and nails."[2]

The bulk of Thoreau's Indian summer reflections occur in his post-1850 *Journal*, pages that also contain the increasingly learned accounts of the zoological and botanical history of the Concord region upon which his reputation as a naturalist rests. The two developments are closely related. Scholars have long recognized that the passing of the seasons figured prominently in Thoreau's work, but he seemed particularly drawn to this one.[3] Even a casual reading of the *Journal* turns up phrases such as "the most perfect day of the year" (3:123); "these are the finest days" (IX:108); and "another Indian Summer day, as fair as we've had" (XII:447). Time and again he drew upon the same picturesque, regional, and sentimental associations that others had constructed around the season. In each case, however, he moved beyond his contemporaries to forge a new form of transcendental weather, one that pushed the season's symbol-making potential to its limit.

To be sure, there is an autumnal quality in much of Thoreau's late work. "October answers to that period in the life of man when he is no longer dependent on transient moods," he wrote on November 14, 1853. Every "root, branch, leaf of him grows with maturity. What he has been and done in his spring and summer appears. He bears his fruit" (V:502). As several scholars have noted, Thoreau's *Journal* entries for the fall months reveal his fascination with the changing leaves and ripened fields. Yet his embrace of autumnal imagery and the season's obvious beauty produced descriptions that were no mere aesthetic paeans; almost always, they remained grounded in scientific fact. As the literary historian William Howarth notes, "the season aroused in Thoreau a joyous, sensuous mysticism, but underneath his entries ran the firm current of empirical knowledge."[4] Thus in "Autumnal Tints," his late essay tracing the unfolding changes in New England foliage from August to November, he fuses exquisite painterly descriptions with a thorough understanding of the processes of autumnal change. But like all seasons, autumn has its nooks and crannies, its moments of odd variability. "If you penetrate to some warm recess under a cliff," Thoreau wrote on "the first really cold day" of November 1850, "you will be astonished by the amount of summer life that still flourishes there" (3:146, 145). As we will see, such late-year recollections of warmer days show up again and again in Thoreau's Indian summer musings.

Thoreau's eagerness to explore seasonal variations led him to construct a remarkably fluid sense of when Indian summer occurred. He reports its appearance on dates ranging from mid-September to mid-December, both before and after the telltale frost that Wilson Flagg believed essential for the season. Part of this seasonal elasticity accorded with Thoreau's sense that the natural world operated at several different temporal levels. Yet the movement of seasons also provided perhaps the best test of the Emersonian doctrine of correspondence, a belief that man and nature mirrored each other in both symbolic and actual ways. At times, this interest led him to follow the standard course of plotting his own life against the seasonal round. But rather than conform to the conventional poetic tendency to link spring with youth and autumn with middle age, Thoreau looked for signs that both natural and historic times follow multidirectional paths. Sometimes he subsumed the seasons within himself, figuring that he *and* their changes functioned in tandem, that they were "simply and plainly phenomena or phases of *my* life" (X:127, emphasis added). At others, he found himself and the seasons operating according to different temporal sequences: "I am differently timed," he claimed in July 1851; "my seasons revolve more slowly than those of nature, for which I am contented" (3: 313). In either case, he looked to seasons such as Indian summer to explore the workings of natural and psychic phenomena both through and in time.[5]

We can follow the development of a typical Thoreauvian Indian summer through the pages of his *Journal* of 1853. September begins with temperatures still at summer's peak. On the seventh, he reports "some hours of very warm weather, as oppressive as any in the year, one's thermometer at 93" (V:421). But by the eleventh "signs of frost" loom (V:423). On October 2, just days after returning from his second excursion to Maine, he notes the "frost-bitten" appearance of local gentians, a fall flower that was the frequent subject of Emily Dickinson's muse. The witch hazel, however, "is raised above the frost," its yellow blooms announcing that the year still has more life to give (V:435). On the fifteenth, a killing frost leaves the ground "white long after sunrise" (V:439). Despite the midmonth chill, the next several days prove unseasonably mild, leading to "A week or more of fairest Indian-summer" that seemingly end when it rains on the twenty-second (V:442). The idyll resumes, however, on the very next day as Thoreau finds that "many phenomena remind me that now is to some extent a second spring" (V: 448). Sadly, another severe frost on the morning of the thirtieth at last "settled the accounts of many plants which lingered still" (V:460).

As November dawns, however, Thoreau finds signs of Indian summer life in the plants still in bloom. "I might put by themselves the November flowers which survive severe frosts and the fall of the leaf," he wrote on the second (V:475). Snapdragons, yarrows, autumnal dandelions, and tansies attract his attention until the year's first snow on the tenth brings his search to an apparent end. But then on the twenty-third, a date well after the frosts and snow, Thoreau awakes to "a pleasant, calm, and springlike morning" that leads him to conclude that the "Indian-summer itself" amounts to "the reminiscence or rather the return, of spring—the year renewing its youth" (V:517). It is a time, he proudly proclaims, "said to be more remarkable in this country than anywhere" (V:518). And through it all, he watches the leaves, noting their final dates on the trees and their appearance on the ground.

More than any writer we have considered, Thoreau understood that Indian summer occupies a strange temporal position. It can arrive for a brief visit early in October or settle in for a longer stay in mid-November. He relished the season's paradoxical challenge to our everyday sense that time moves in one direction. On the one hand, he depicted a season that gestures backward toward warmer months, an interlude that interrupts the standard movement of temperatures that carry us from spring into summer and on into fall. As he came to discover, the warm, lazy quality of Indian summer days encourages the notion that the present can extend indefinitely. Like the summer months described in *Walden*, which take up nearly two-thirds of a book theoretically devoted to a year, Thoreau's sense of time on such days stretched every which way.[6]

On the other hand, Thoreau also used the odd unfolding *of* Indian summer time to sharpen his awareness of how natural entities such as trees, animals, and shrubs change *through* time. Throughout the 1850s he grew ever more fascinated by and kept detailed records of minute changes in the landscape, noting the date, sometimes even the hour, of when an animal departed for the winter or a particular flower bloomed. Indian summer weather helped him understand processes of change precisely because it so dramatically alters meteorological conditions. On one day the land appears prepped for winter, on the next trees bloom as in spring. Such dramatic and delightful change sent Thoreau running outdoors to measure and record whatever he saw. So while the weather might have encouraged a timeless lazy stroll through the woods, it also drew Thoreau's attention to the day by day, even hour by hour, alterations on the land. And thus the paradox of a Thoreauvian Indian summer: It is the season of temporal deviance that reveals him as the most temporally aware American writer of his day.

A Different Sort of Season

We can begin to trace Thoreau's departure from conventional Indian summer concerns by briefly considering two common aspects of the season for which he displayed little apparent interest. First, unlike Brahmin writers such as Longfellow and Holmes, Thoreau rarely felt the pull of nostalgia on Indian summer days. Though he was a student of New England history, his conception of the past did not come shrouded in Indian summer mist. Indeed, he once suggested, "a tradition of these days might be handed down to posterity," a statement implying that such a tradition had not yet been established (X:92). When he did look back one "very warm Indian Summer day" in 1856, he recounted a conversation that focused on the specific facts of his own past rather than the mythic history of the region. Noting that "Father told me about his father the other night," he describes his grandfather's actions during the Revolutionary War and early efforts as a Boston merchant. The recollection, however, comes unadorned with the patina of charm so frequently employed by the Brahmins. We learn that the grandfather "was a short man, a little taller than my father, stout and very strong for his size (IX:129, 132). But nowhere in the passage does Thoreau suggest, as his Brahmin contemporaries so often did, that an Indian summer haze enveloped earlier generations. The elder Thoreau stands as a man sure of himself with no need for a romantic glow.

Almost without exception, Thoreau's references to Indian summer in the *Journal* are either written in the present tense or recall events just a day or two old. In October 1852, for example, he writes, "I *sit* on Poplar Hill. It *is* a warm Indian Summerish afternoon. The sun *comes* out of clouds and *lights* up and *warms* the whole scene" (3:366; emphasis added). Later that month he reports, "this may be called Indian Summer. It is quite hazy" (3:381) And again in November 1859 he finds that "the musquash *is* active. Swimming about in the further pond today, – this Indian Summer day." As if to underscore the present-mindedness of the day, elsewhere in this last quoted passage Thoreau employs the past tense to note, "I have been so absorbed of late in Captain [John] Brown's fate as to be surprised whenever I detected the old routine running still"—a sentence that moves from the present perfect tense to the infinitive to the past (XII:448). But when he describes the current Indian summer weather, he returns to an unambiguous use of the simple present. Neither a before nor an after time, Thoreau's Indian summer simply is.

The refusal to inject layers of nostalgia into Indian summer seems in keeping with what we know of Thoreau's character. But his second major departure from Indian summer convention comes as a surprise. For unlike virtually every writer we have considered, Thoreau rarely speculated on the origin of the term. He came closest in an undated early 1840s *Journal* passage that jointly addresses discussions of Indians and the weather. The entry reads like a Cooperesque assumption that Indians had gently faded from the scene. Future Americans, Thoreau predicts in rather conventional Romantic language, "will associate this generation with the red man in his thoughts"; like the Indians themselves, "our history will have some copper tints at least and be read through an Indian Summer haze" (2:38). Otherwise, he refrained from linking the season to the lives and history of American Indians.

Such silence seems surprising given Thoreau's deep interest in Indian history. As a young man, he shared the predominant Romantic view that Indians were a noble but vanishing race, a belief implied in the above assumption that they had been enveloped by the season's haze. "The Indian does well to remain Indian," he wrote in the "Sunday" section of *A Week*, a statement typical of the abstracted quality the young Thoreau assigned to native people.[7] Eventually, however, he came to a more complex understanding of the continent's original inhabitants. Between 1845 and 1860 he filled eleven notebooks on Indian subject matter, drawn primarily from his extensive reading of the available ethnographic and historic literature. By the mid-1850s, by which point his journeys to Maine had brought him into contact with actual rather than abstracted Indians, Thoreau arguably possessed as much knowledge concerning Native Americans as publicly renowned experts such as Schoolcraft.[8] But rarely did he use this expertise to speculate on the origin of the term "Indian summer."

Though perhaps surprising at first glance, Thoreau's lack of curiosity regarding the origin of the phrase "Indian summer" makes sense. As he well understood, to identify a natural process amounts to bringing it into human culture. "With the knowledge of the name comes a distincter recognition and knowledge of the thing," he recorded in the *Journal* on August 29, 1858. A natural object becomes "more describable, and poetic even" when attached to a vernacular phrase (XI:137). Indeed, he typically relished the opportunity to coin a term for those parts of the natural world that did not possess a common name. In June 1851, for instance, he suggested that the year's full moons should all enjoy folk names as popular as September's harvest moon, proposing the planter's moon for May and either the traveler's or the whippoorwill's for June (3:267). Well read in the new historical and cultural geography of Alexander von Humboldt, he yearned for geographic knowledge that moved beyond simple accounts of physical forms on the land to stress the interactions of man and nature.[9] Whenever possible he employed popular names such as the harvest moon precisely because they shed light on how people use and experience the natural world. But Indian summer had already been named by the time Thoreau started to write, leaving him little reason to explore historic sources. So rather than embarking on yet another dubious etymological explanation, he simply employed what had become an accepted and useful meteorological term.

A Journal Maker's Season

When Thoreau began referring to Indian summer with regularity in the early 1850s, he occupied an extremely precarious position in American letters. His 1849 *A Week on the Concord and Merrimack Rivers*, upon which he had staked his literary reputation, had been a resounding commercial failure and only lukewarm critical success. Having himself covered the printing costs, Thoreau, who turned thirty in 1847, was left carrying a considerable debt.[10] Still, he had not given up hope that important work lay ahead; on the contrary, he used these same years to prepare himself intellectually for the burst of creative activity that led to the 1854 publication of *Walden*. As his most famous book took shape through several drafts, Thoreau also read widely in natural sciences such as geography, botany, and zoology. And perhaps most important for his eventual Indian summer musings, he also began regularly to embark on the extended walks that emerged as the principal subject of his *Journal*.

The *Journal* itself took on a new form in these years. Begun at age twenty in 1837, it eventually became a central document in the Thoreauvian corpus. For most of the 1840s, Thoreau recorded sporadically, using the *Journal* to discuss literary and philosophical ideas, many of them in response to his reading, and to draft material for public presentation in essays and lectures. But toward the end of 1850, after the hoped-for success of *A Week* was clearly not going to come, the *Journal* became less preparatory for literary material and more an independent project devoted to accounts of the natural world. Rather than occasional or aphoristic entries, Thoreau now wrote virtually daily, using his long walks to gather detailed information on the flora and fauna of the Concord region. Whereas it once served as a rather conventional account of his readings and reflections, which many of his Concord neighbors kept, the post-1850 *Journal* reveals Thoreau working toward a new literary genre that combined transcendental yearnings with the collection of scientific facts. No mere recording tablet simply to document the moments of a day, the post-1851 *Journal* became, in H. Daniel Peck's words, "a place to tally those moments against the present as a way of measuring change."[11] With this new practice, the *Journal*, which had always been important, became central to Thoreau's life as a writer.

As a literary form, the *Journal* offered Thoreau the opportunity to explore Indian summer's most salient points in ways that his other chosen genre, the essay, did not. As Joan Burbick shows, the *Journal* of the early 1850s reveals Thoreau returning again and again to similar scenes to record the progress of seasonal change. "In the *Journal*," she writes, "an individual natural event is visited, observed, and described repeatedly, yielding the 'truth' of the event over time."[12] Indian summer weather is ideal for just such a project. Indeed, with its sharp interruption of one meteorological pattern for another, it may be the perfect season for the diarist of natural change, a time of year when we can't help but notice that something feels different. The *Journal* proved especially valuable when charting the arrival of fall's first frosts. As Thoreau noted on the bitterly cold morning of October 11, 1859, early frost could serve as "a season ripener, [an] opener of the burs that inclose Indian summer," a claim he certainly understood was best measured if he had accurate records of when the frosts arrived (XII: 375). The *Journal* provided just such a record.

Thanks to the recent Princeton University Press editions of Thoreau's *Journal*, we can locate the start of the new journalizing format to a few days of Indian summer weather in 1850. Beginning in April of that year entries had become longer, richer, and more carefully dated; moreover, whereas he formerly routinely removed pages when composing an essay, the number of leaves torn out substantially diminished. Sometime after September 19, Thoreau opened a new notebook and seemed to commit himself to the larger conception of the *Journal* as a literary project separate from his published works. Except for the forty-two manuscript pages that he transferred to an essay about his trip to Canada, the new notebook contains a hitherto unseen structural integrity.[13] For our purposes, the key date is October 31, the day Thoreau wrote his first extended description of Indian summer. "Our Indian Summer I am tempted to say is the finest season in the year," he proudly proclaims near the middle of his first fully realized *Journal* notebook. Indeed, "Here has been such a day as I think Italy never sees" (3:123, 124).

The entry is startling for its lack of Indian summer sentiment, for though he believes "this has been the most perfect afternoon in the year," the weather leaves Thoreau conflicted. On the one hand, he hopes to avail himself of the opportunity to "study the dead & withered plants" so that they will "live not in memory only, but to the fancy & imagination" as well. But the very same "perfectly still & dry & clear" weather also causes Thoreau to confront his fear of growing old, although he is just thirty-three. "After the era of youth is passed," he writes, "the knowledge of ourselves is an alloy that spoils our satisfactions." Worse still, the day leaves him feeling isolated. As he looks through a nearby stand of pine, he is reminded "of houses we never inhabit. That commonly I am not at home in the world." Like a penitent, he reproaches himself for unspecified sins, believing himself unworthy for such grace. "The thought of what I am – of my pitiful conduct – deters me from receiving what joy I might from the glorious days that visit me" (3:123, 124). As Emily Dickinson would also discover roughly ten years later, Thoreau here identifies Indian summer as a season of emotional complexity—not of the sweetly melancholic sort preferred by the Brahmins, but a more probing time when the light and quiet can find us strangely alone.

Despite the bleak statements of October 1850, such days typically appealed to Thoreau because they encouraged a walking and journalizing pace that was simultaneously deliberate and relaxed. With its pleasantly warm temperatures and soft atmospheric light, Indian summer stretches the afternoon's hours—and hence the available walking time—to create the pastoral illusion that time has been slowed. An inveterate saunterer—to use his own odd term—Thoreau believed that the talent for engaged walking "comes only by the grace of God."[14] He could turn churlish when others could not match his enthusiasm. During a remarkable ten-day Indian summer spell in October 1857, for instance, Thoreau privately raged against those who refused the opportunity for strolling that the weather provided. "I do not know how to entertain one who can't take long walks," he wrote on the seventh. "In the midst of the most glorious Indian-summer afternoon, there they sit, breaking your chairs and wearing out the house, with their backs to the light, taking no note of the lapse of time" (X:74). On

the fourteenth, "the tenth of these memorable days," he declared his in-
dependence from the casual Indian summer walker:

I am a reaper; I am not a gleaner. I go reaping, cutting as broad a swath as I can,
and bundling and stacking up and carrying it off from field to field, and no man
knows or cares. My crop is not sorghum nor Davis seedlings. There are other crops
than these, whose seed is not distributed by the Patent Office. I go abroad over
the land each day to get the best I can find, and that is never carted off even to
the last day of November, and I do not go as a gleaner. (X:94)

An early example of Thoreau's Indian summer walking occurs in a November 1851 *Journal* entry recounting an excursion he took to Dudley Pond,
just east of the Wayland-Sudbury border. A year before, he reported, "Our
Indian summer I am tempted to say is the finest season in the year," and
his entry for this day confirms why (3:124). It was a morning seemingly
designed to brighten a New Englander's soul. Although they were not
looking for anything in particular, Thoreau and his walking companion,
the poet Ellery Channing, remained alert to discrepancies between current
meteorological conditions and the weather otherwise expected for the first
week of November. They found several. As the afternoon drew to a close,
Thoreau noticed that an inch of ice had formed under the north side of a
nearby wood, a sure sign of winter's pending onset. Channing, on the other
hand, reported that he had found ripe strawberries in the Berkshires just
the week before, evidence that springlike weather had extended well into
the fall. While indicative of the general unpredictability of New England
weather, such discoveries also propelled Thoreau toward a deeper understanding of his native region. While lying on the sand along the pond, he
fused speculations regarding the autumnal warmth and his passing youth
(he was thirty-four) into an image of Indian summer that characterized
much of his later writing on the season:

When I saw the bare sand at Cochituate I felt my relation to the soil. – these are
my sands not yet run out. Not yet will the fates turn the glass. This air have I title
to taint–with my decay. In this clean sand my bones will gladly lie. Like viola
pedata I shall be ready to bloom again here in my Indian summer days. Here ever
springing–never dying with perennial root I stand. – for the winter of the land is
warm to me–while the flowers bloom again as in spring – shall I pine? When I see
her sands exposed thrown up from beneath the surface–it touches me inwardly–it
reminds me of my origin–for I am such a plant–so native to N.E. methinks as
springs from the sands cast from below. (4:168–69)

The passage contains four elements central to Thoreau's conception of Indian summer. First, as the enthusiastic final sentences make clear, he roots himself firmly in New England soil. Thoreau of course rarely strayed from the Concord area for extended periods, so it seems only fitting that he would lay claim to a permanent resting place in his beloved New England ground. At Dudley Pond, then, he draws on the region's most glorious season to announce that in this "clean sand my bones will gladly lie." Second, the excursion provides evidence for his growing conviction that metaphoric and actual second springs can reveal signs of life in even the most dormant landscapes. Identifying himself with the *Viola pedata*, a local violet that blooms a second time in the fall, he hopes he too will be nurtured by the respite provided by the autumnal warmth. Third, and closely connected to the desire for new beginnings, Thoreau insists that he still has important work to do: "not yet will the fates turn the glass," he declares. And finally, the passage reflects his sense that Indian summer is, above all, a season that forces us to confront the complexities of time. On one level, the unusual warmth experienced at Dudley Pond reminds him that discrepancies between seasonal and calendrical time render problematic any attempt to draw direct correlations between them. But more significantly, the Indian summer scene offers the ideal opportunity to explore the paradoxical nature of time itself.

As he observes the pond and its environs, taking note of which flowers are still in bloom, the sand on the beach pushes his thoughts toward sand in an hour clock. Although he insists "my sands are not yet run out," the clock image reveals a fear that time relentlessly slips away in linear fashion: Time passes, and the sand pile grows. At the same time (that word again!) the Indian summer weather confirms the circular nature of temporality by creating the conditions for the return of the violets. Like the flipping of an hourglass, which sends the sands dripping back to the other side, seasons return in predictable ways, albeit without necessarily conforming to what the calendar says. Indian summer, then, stands poised between Thoreau's awareness of cyclical processes (which he so elegantly mapped in *Walden*) and a competing notion that history proceeds in but one direction. Its backward gesture toward the warm summer months momentarily halts the stately march that carries autumn's cool toward winter's cold. Balanced between two irreconcilable forces—one shooting forward, the other rounding back—Thoreau's version of Indian summer carves out and defines a season that others had only hinted at before.

The momentary temporal pause of Indian summer offered Thoreau protection against charges that he wasted precious time with his outdoor pursuits. He sorely needed such protection during the professionally trying Indian summer of 1851. That fall he earned a living as a surveyor, an occupation for which he had considerable talent but which also took him away from his preferred methods of spending his time.[15] Although outdoor work, and hence preferable to the family pencil-making business, surveying put such demands on his writing and natural history projects that it became a source of frustration. At one point he complained that he had been "surveying for 20 or 30 days – living coarsely – even as respects my diet." His mood changed, however, following an hour of Indian summer weather on December 13th. Reenergized by the warmth, he reconsidered the value of time spent engaged in remunerative work.

We had one hour of Indian summer weather in the middle of the day. I felt the influence of the Sun– It melted my stoniness a little. The pines looked like old friends again. Cutting a path through a swamp where was much brittle dogwood &c &c I wanted to know the name of every shrub. This varied employment to which my necessities compel me serves instead of foreign travel & the lapse of time– If it makes me forget somethings which I ought to remember, it no doubt enables me to forget many things which it is well to forget. By stepping aside from my chosen path so often I see myself better and am enabled to criticize myself. Of this nature is the only true lapse of time. It seems an age since I took walks & wrote in my journal– And when shall I revisit the glimpses of the moon? To be able to see ourselves–not merely as others see us–but as we are–that service a *variety* of absorbing employments does us. (4:203–4)

With his surveying chain in hand, Thoreau welcoms the Indian summer weather for its capacity to transform the work he is doing. The brief burst of sunlight and warmth in the middle of his workday necessities helps him temporarily to ignore the lost opportunities for the unfettered writing and walking time he so greatly prefers. Precisely because surveying forces him to "step aside" from his chosen path, he finds temporary solace in the notion that paid work occasionally allows him to "see myself better." Like Indian summer itself, surveying highlights Thoreau's writing because it interrupts and redirects what has been the normal use of his time. As the Indian summer hour defines the larger day, so too does the foray into surveying force Thoreau to come to terms with his literary work. Both are aberrant times that clarify normal time.

Still, Thoreau yearns to return to his preferred work before too much more time passes him by. Paraphrasing Hamlet, another young man deemed silly or ineffectual by those who thought he dabbled morosely, he asks, "And when shall I revisit the glimpses of the moon"?[16] Thoreau sounds defensive here, as he certainly could be, but the Hamlet reference in the midst of an Indian summer reverie reveals a young man not yet sure of his place in the world. Like Shakespeare's hero, Thoreau was blessed and burdened by a father figure who believed he frivolously wasted his time. The ghost of Hamlet senior could not understand why his moody son took so long to get his revenge, while Thoreau had to contend with Emerson's barely concealed belief that the younger man lacked professional drive. The two had been friends since 1837, when the thirty-four-year-old Emerson took the twenty-year-old Thoreau under his wing, but now their contrasting temperaments and interests highlighted their differences. "Thoreau wants a little ambition in his mixture," Emerson famously wrote in his journal. "Instead of being head of American engineers he is captain of a huckleberry party."[17] Although the two men remained cordial and in some ways quite close, Thoreau felt the sting of this charge and occasionally responded like a son defending himself against a father's wrath in the wake of disappointing results at school. On an Indian summer day earlier that same fall, for instance, a day when Thoreau found "many things to indicate the renewing of spring," the younger man could not commit himself to renewing the once intimate friendship: "We do not believe in the same God," he confided in his *Journal*. "I am not thou– Thou are not I" (4:137).[18]

But during the hour of Indian summer on a December afternoon Thoreau finds that his time is not wasted. In fact, his "varied employment," so different from his preferred form of work, leads him to cryptically conclude "nature is the only true lapse of time" (4:204). Whereas most of his contemporaries would have simply enjoyed the unexpected break from the cold, Thoreau embraces the hour's respite to turn the tables (albeit within the privacy of his *Journal*) on those who question his life's work. With the progress of time seemingly halted by the weather, the differences between literary and remunerative labors become less apparent. On an Indian summer afternoon, even work has literary potential.

A Luminist Season

Thoreau's sense of Indian summer time is closely allied with the momentary temporal freeze depicted in some Luminist paintings. As several critics have noted, his descriptive vocabulary shares, and in some cases predicts, the work of painters such as Sanford Gifford, Martin Johnson Heade, and other similar artists who removed the signs of brush strokes from their canvases to create the illusion of an immediate yet timeless present. A form of landscape painting with roots in the Hudson River school, Luminism emerged in the 1840s and '50s. But whereas its older cousin stressed hugely sublime scenes, the newer version presented quieter and more contemplative terrains. According to John Conron, who has done more than anyone to establish the connections linking Thoreau to nineteenth-century painting, Luminist works rely upon "a rigorously conceptualized sense of composition."[19] They divide space into a series of receding horizontal planes that articulate a clearly defined foreground, middle ground, and background. Typically, the scenes are illuminated by the mode's characteristic light, a sharply focused and spiritual glow that draws attention to the outlines of both natural and man-made forms. As the art historian Barbara Novak puts it, "luminist light tends to be cool, not hot, hard not soft, palpable rather than fluid, planar rather than atmospherically diffuse."[20] It contains a purity that gleams.

Sanford Gifford's 1861 *Indian Summer* (figure 5), a painting I considered in chapter 3, offers a classic luminist construction of the season by bringing together the mode's horizontal and atmospheric attributes. From the smooth foreground of water the scene recedes plane by plane. The mountains of the middle ground, which themselves recede toward a distant horizon, are enveloped by a sky infused with light. Elana Weiss, Gifford's twentieth-century biographer, calls the style on display in this painting "aerial-luminism," in which the light hovers in air "as a semiobscuring veil, lending the mystery of marginal visibility" to the terrain.[21] Indeed, a haunting quiet pervades the scene. If, as Novak asserts, "the visual corollary of silence is stillness," then this exceptionally still scene produces not a sound.[22] The result is a deeply poetic vision of controlled calm.

The quiet atmospheric light of Luminist sunsets has much in common with the visual and psychological effects produced by an Indian summer day, particularly during late afternoons. Such interludes compress Indian summer's extended calm into a matter of hours, offering the diurnal round the same momentary pause that my subject affords its seasonal counterpart. Walk outside late in the day during Indian summer, and you will understand this point. There is a quiet in the air at such a time, one that grows quieter still as sunset looms. Even the promise of the setting sun's glowing warmth is enough to make the day. As Thoreau remarked one "remarkably

warm" Indian summer day in 1858, "there is an advantage to walking east-
ward these afternoons," since upon returning home you are sure to "have
the western sky before you" (XI:228, 230).

Thoreau's mastery of painterly terminology increased dramatically after
reading the works of the British landscape theorist William Gilpin in the
early 1850s. As Robert Richardson points out, Thoreau had been working
to add richness to his landscape descriptions for several years before he
encountered Gilpin. But after reading his eighteenth-century English predecessor he was better equipped to apply the language of light and color
to his landscape depictions.[23] We can trace this development by looking to
a series of Indian summer landscapes presented in his *Journal*. The first
describes a scene amid the haze of a warm October afternoon in 1849,
before he read Gilpin. "Some afternoons," he recorded in his *Journal*, "when
the lower strata of the atmosphere is filled with a haze like mist[,] the hills
in the horizon seen from an eminence are visibly divided into distinct
ranges." On one level, this could be an exemplary verbal construction of
Luminist geometry. The terrain presents as one plane receding from the
next until the final hills rise "above the mists which fill the vallies" (3:38).
Still, the effect of color and light remains largely obscure.

We can see Gilpin's picturesque influence more clearly in a *Journal* entry
made one "beautiful, warm and calm Indian-summer afternoon" in October
1853. Thoreau begins by remarking on the panoramic views that opened to
his eyes while plying the Concord River in the company of his sister. Seen
from the boat, the river's shore appears "like the ornamented frame of a
mirror." The water's smooth surface captures the reflection of the sky and
buttonballs that line the edge, while the actual flowers (that is, the unre-
flected ones) "are seen against the russet meadow" that the two drift by (V:
463). Two years earlier, Thoreau remarked that he was "always struck by
the centrality of the observer's position," that he "always stands fronting
the middle of the arch" (3:298). Such awareness informs the visions that
unfold before his eyes on this Indian summer day, as one perfectly constructed scene after another reveals itself to the Thoreau siblings' eyes.

A still more successful and more rapturous entry from the Indian summer of 1859 takes full advantage of the available light and color, placing
them within clearly defined frames of view. It is a passage remarkable for
its attention to painterly detail. While sitting atop Pine Hill Rock over-
looking Walden, Thoreau first notes the "thick haze" that envelops the
scene:

What strikes me in the scenery here now is the contrast of the unusually blue water with brilliant-tinted woods around it. The tints generally may be about at their height. The earth appears like a great inverted shield painted yellow and red, or with the imbricated scales of that color, and a blue navel in the middle where the pond lies, and a distant circumference of whitish haze. The nearer woods, where chestnuts grow, are a mass of warm, glowing yellow (though the larger chestnuts have lost the greater part of their leaves and generally you wade through rustling chestnut leaves in the woods), but on the other sides the red and yellow are intermixed. The red, probably of scarlet oaks on the south of Fair Haven Hill, is very fair. (XII:378–79)

Thoreau apparently rarely saw paintings by his contemporaries, but he senses on this Indian summer day that the season's warmth and light easily lend themselves to the verbal sketch.[24] With the haze providing a mysterious background and the leaves forming a shield of yellow and red, he creates with words the same visual dynamic that Gifford does with paint. Rarely has the language and imagery of Indian summer been so seamlessly one.

The Natural History of Thoreau's Indian Summer

Earlier in this chapter I mentioned Thoreau's lifelong interest in seasonal change, an interest he displayed in his oldest surviving school-age essay titled, appropriately enough, "The Seasons."[25] The ongoing curiosity stemmed from his initial adherence to the Emersonian doctrine of correspondence, the transcendental position that led him to link the external evidence of the seasons to his internal psychic states. But as Thoreau became more expert in the sciences, his seasonal meditations increasingly substituted (without entirely abandoning) his youthful moral and biographical considerations with detailed analyses of natural change. Armed with an ever increasing knowledge of botany, forestry, and zoology, he recorded seasonal markers such as the arrival and departure of birds and the dates that particular flowers bloomed, charting each against his own precise measurements of when fall or spring, for example, ended or began. Nearly always, he found room for a more complex understanding of the progress of seasons than the conventional cyclical movement, so beloved by sentimental poets, would allow. "The year has many seasons more than are represented in the Almanace," he remarked in 1850 (3:74). Seasonal change, he came to see, was an ongoing process: "If you are not out at the right instant the summer [or any season] may go by & you not see it" (3:379). Whether the calendar says winter or fall, "each season is drawn out and lingers in certain localities," the movement of the sun and stars notwithstanding (3:146).

Thoreau's fascination with the machinations of seasonal change led to him to construct a natural history of Indian summer that explored specific changes to flora and fauna against the backdrop of the season's conventional promise of second youth. But first he had to learn what natural changes to expect, a process he found easier in some disciplines than others. His struggles to identify local birds, for example, reveal just how difficult it could be to place his scientific acumen in the service of seasonal lore. Birds flitter throughout the pages of Thoreau's Indian summer *Journal* entries, as they do throughout New England in the fall—some just passing through from regions farther north, others taking tuneful advantage of the newfound warmth. Paddling on the Concord River one eighty-degree Indian summer day in October 1856, for instance, Thoreau recorded "quite a flock of wild ducks" along the shore. Resplendently filled with life, the ducks, like the "very Indian Summer itself," signaled the "renewal of the year" (IX:108). Despite such enthusiasms, Thoreau's reputation for ornithological expertise does not match the esteem he eventually earned in forestry. His interests in birds ran deep, but his knowledge was slow to come. As a young man he helped his brother and sister compile a journal of sightings in and around Concord, but several twentieth-century naturalists and scholars have questioned the identity of many of those birds. Indeed, the nature writer Joseph Wood Krutch, typically a sympathetic reader of his predecessor's work, found the nature-loving Thoreau's lack of bird knowledge "almost disconcerting."[26]

Overcoming this deficiency emerged as one of Thoreau's primary scientific quests of the 1850s, one for which the suddenly warm skies of Indian summer proved ideal. During an Indian summer spell in 1853 he admits that the identity of specific birds eludes him. Upon spotting birds at the edge of a meadow he half asks/half states, "They must be either sandpipers, tell-tales (not the greater or lesser), or plovers(?). Or may they be the turn-stone?" We get the sense here of Thoreau the would-be birder working to match the songs he hears with the birds he sees. With each passing year, however, the descriptions grow richer and more accurate. Three years later, for example, an Indian summer day finds him confident enough to identify birds without seeing them, relying instead on the reports of his ears: "In the woods I hear the note of the jay, a metallic, *clanging* sound, sometimes a mew. Refer any strange note to him" (IX:110).

By October 1859, an "Indian-Summer-like" day inspires a rapturous catalogue of the birds, as Thoreau confidently relies on his eyes and ears to differentiate among the species, pushing himself to learn more. "Birds are now seen more numerously than before," he writes. "I see and hear probably flocks of grackles with their split and shuffling note, but no red-wings for a long time." As he continues along, he detects the "*sveet, sveet, sveet*" of shore larks while still spying robins and "probably purple finches." In the background, "the sweet *phe-be* of the chickadee" enlivens the "half-strains" sung by sparrows and bluebirds" (XII:372–73). These last quoted sentences from 1859 show Thoreau at both his most eager and his most sure; he knows his birds and especially relishes the joy they take "in the warm, hazy light" of the season. With the breathtaking sight of the birds at last the subject of his ornithological mastery, he awaits the arrival of a full-blown Indian summer: "Now the year itself begins to be ripe, ripened by the frost, like a persimmon" (XII:373).

If bird knowledge represented a struggle, Thoreau displayed no such difficulty when it came to the flowering trees and shrubs of Indian summer. Surviving and often thriving after a late-year frost, Indian summer blooms fused his knowledge of the physical world with the hope that the season just might offer a second lease on life. To be sure, Thoreau did not have to look far to find contemporaries turning to fall flowers as botanical ex-emplars of spring's reprise, of renewed youth. The transcendental poet Jones Very, for instance, noted, "Within our hearts we find them a place / As for the flowers, which early Spring-time grace." Thoreau, too, found solace in the asters and goldenrods he described in the autumnal "Friday" section of *A Week*, likening their yellow blooms to "Brahminical devotees, turning steadily with their luminary from morning till night."[27] But Indian summer flowers carried especial meaning for Thoreau beyond what others typically ascribed to ordinary fall blooms such as the aster. Briefly glorious signs of life, they became emblems of his own desire to remain creative and alert.

Two flowers, the witch hazel and the *Viola pedata*, particularly stand out in Thoreau's botanical Indian summer. Of those, poets most typically as-sociated the season with the witch hazel, whose yellow autumnal blooms brighten this common eastern shrub. Thoreau no doubt understood the alleged magical properties historically ascribed to the plant. There is "something witch-like in the appearance of the witch-hazel, which blossoms late in October and in November," he wrote in *A Week*.[28] But whereas earlier New Englanders used its branches as divining rods and its bark for medicinal tea, he found its true value in its promise of life. "I love to be reminded of that universal and eternal spring when the minute crimson-starred female flowers of the hazel are peeping forth on the hillsides," he wrote on October 27, 1853—"when Nature revives in all her pores" (V:457).[29]

Thoreau's most elaborate statement about the witch hazel may be the richest nineteenth-century account of any late-blooming flower. Though the passage does not mention Indian summer specifically, his *Journal* entry of October 9, 1851, basks in the warmth of an autumn afternoon, a time when the witch hazel's color and aroma offer incontrovertible sensory evidence that "all the year is a spring."

The witch-hazel here is in full blossom—on this magical hill-side—while its broad yellow leaves are falling—some bushes are completely bare of leaves, and leather-colored they strew the ground. It is an extremely interesting plant—October & November's child—and yet reminds me of the earliest spring. Its blossoms smell like the spring – like the willow catkins—and by their color as well as fragrance they belong to the saffron dawn of the year. – Suggesting amid all these signs of Autumn – falling leaves & frost—that the life of nature—by which she eternally flourishes, is untouched. It stands here in the shadow on the side of the hill while the sun-light from over the top of the hill lights up its topmost sprays & yellow blossoms. Its spray so jointed and angular is not to be mistaken for any other. I lie on my back with joy under its boughs. While its leaves fall – its blossoms spring. The autumn then is indeed a spring. All the year is a spring. I see two blackbirds over head going south, but I am going north in my thought with these hazel blossoms. (4: 135–36)

The miraculous sight of flowers after the frost leads Thoreau to marvel at their centrality to late-year cycles of life, particularly for bees. Although he initially assumes that the yellow blooms arrive too late to benefit the nearby bee colony's honey works, he soon discovers by their buzzing sound that the bees will continue to thrive so long as enticing flowers remain. "How important then to the bees this late blossoming plant," he notes (4:136). With its gentle colors delighting the eye and the aural evidence of nature's subtle work buzzing in the air, a more Thoreauvian moment than this chance encounter with the witch hazel may be difficult to find. A flower he had always found beautiful and suggestive had assumed a central part in his catalogue of life.

The only rival to the witch hazel for Thoreau's Indian summer affection was the *Viola pedata*, otherwise known as the bird's-foot violet. A delicate purplish flower that blooms each fall throughout eastern Massachusetts, its importance grew as the 1850s progressed. In the decade's first year, he lumped its arrival with other seasonal blooms, noting that "there seems to be in the fall a sort of attempt at a spring—a rejuvenescence as if the winter were not expected by a part of Nature—violets—dandelions—and some other flowers blossom again" (3:142). Twelve months later—to repeat a phrase I mentioned earlier in this chapter—Thoreau hoped that "like viola pedata I shall be ready to bloom again in my Indian summer days" (4:168). And as the decade drew to a close in the fall of 1859 he used the flower to introduce a several-page discussion on the virtues of John Brown. "No flower by its second blooming," he said of the *Viola pedata* then in its glory, "more perfectly brings back the spring to us" (XII:418).

Thoreau's Indian summer botanical reveries remind us how reluctant he was to shed the Emersonian transcendentalism of his youth. As a young man he had been captivated by Emerson's notion that natural facts correspond to moral laws. But neither Emerson nor the youthful Thoreau were particularly good naturalists; they loved nature in the abstract without truly knowing the birds and plants that their respective 1840s journals celebrate. Yet much to Emerson's bemusement, Thoreau eventually devoted himself to the hours upon hours of close observation and reading necessary to master nature's ways. Ultimately, this extended crash course convinced him that natural processes were too complicated and subtle to stand for simple moral laws. His scientific and literary projects of the 1850s were thus rooted in the relations between living things, *not* the presumed moral correspondence that connected values to facts.[30] But now the Indian summer flowers, so redolent of symbolic power, seemed to bring Thoreau back to the Emersonian view of nature as a repository of human values. Wanting so much a second spring for himself, he looked everywhere for one on the land, hoping that through their undeniable natural beauties Indian summer flowers could propel him to new heights of creative renewal.

Still, to fault Thoreau for intellectual backpedaling is to miss the larger implications of his 1850s Indian summer flowers. In many ways he remained an Emersonian throughout his adult life, as his frequently quoted 1853 explanation for why he turned down membership in the Association for the Advancement of Science reveals: "I am a mystic, a transcendentalist, and a natural philosopher to boot" (V:4). So even as he became a master of science and could draw upon layers of factual knowledge of the natural world, he remained alert to the symbolic potential unleashed during his walks in the woods. A clump of bird's-foot violets on a hill or witch hazel in a copse became the raw data for his scientific understanding of what blooms when. But they were also moral and aesthetic keepsakes, reminders that Indian summer days could still usher in periods of newfound joy. We might even call them transcendental icons—scientific and symbolic at the same time.

The Gossamer Days

No natural process more tellingly suggested the transcendental possibility that Indian summer weather could reveal nature as a vibrant and living whole than the mysterious gossamer webs spun by tiny spiders on warm autumnal days. Typically bunched together in shimmering cottony patterns, the webs are best seen in fields of grass as dawn's early dew begins to rise. Though Thoreau never determined how they came to be, the origin of gossamer webs displays nature's remarkable ingenuity. When competition for food forces them to disperse, some spiders use their silk as a form of parachute to carry them elsewhere. Such spidery flights typically occur on warm still days and can be accomplished only by the lightest species. As the warm breezes begin to lift the early dew, the webs get carried along for the ride, propelling the spiders by a mode of travel entomologists call ballooning. If meteorological conditions are right (that is, if the winds are sufficient enough to allow flight but not too strong to destroy the webs), spiders can transport themselves across surprisingly large distances. On Indian summer mornings the process can be startling to watch, especially when as many as a thousand spiders decide to disperse at the same time, each of them producing several strands of silk prior to attaining flight.[31]

Thoreau was hardly the first natural history writer to marvel at the strange appearance of gossamer. In his famous 1723 Spider Letter, for instance, the American divine Jonathan Edwards noted that on "a very calm day" he often discovered "multitudes of little shining webs and glistening strings, brightly reflecting the sunbeams." Gilbert White likewise remarked in his *Natural History of Selborne*, a work Thoreau first read in March 1853, that "every day in fine weather, in autumn chiefly, do I see these spiders shooting out their webs and mounting aloft."[32] No one, however, marveled at their appearance with the same intensity as Thoreau.

He returned to them again and again in his 1850s *Journal*, though never with the wide-eyed wonder he displayed on October 31 and November 1,

1853, days remarkable for their Indian summer warmth. The passage begins with a description of a lazy trip along the Sudbury River that Thoreau took with his sister Sophia. As they row, the siblings become mesmerized by the smooth meadow along the river's shore and the tiny gossamer filaments that join the blades of grass into a pattern of complex beauty. "I slowly begin to discover that it is a gossamer day," he writes. The sheer number of strands, some of them extending to lengths of eight feet, suggests they "have been suddenly produced in the atmosphere" by some mysterious quality in the air. "I find that they are everywhere and on everything." But when he approaches for closer inspection he loses sight of what had just moments before seemed so open to the eye. The webs move in and out of view, like reflections on a clear but choppy pond—now you see them, now you don't. The key determinant is the sun, whose warm rays have beckoned the spiders to their tasks. As they pass some nearby black willows that stand "between us and the sun," Thoreau and his sister note that their branches are "completely covered with these fine cobwebs." But when they float just a few feet back into the shadows, "not a thread can be seen on it" (V:465–66).

The very next day Thoreau returned for another view, only to find that the wind was too strong for the webs to remain in place. "So it would seem," he concludes, that it must be "a perfectly fair Indian-summer day," ideally during those "peculiarly clear and resonant" hours that follow a cool morning in November, if one hopes to glimpse "this wonderful display." For Thoreau, such a brief existence is nothing short of "remarkable" (V: 470–71). The webs disappear almost as they are spun.

The mysterious appearance of gossamer was compounded by Thoreau's inability to fathom a reason why minuscule spiders would spin such intricate designs. "I am at a loss to say what purpose they serve," he confesses. Unlike common household spiderwebs, they seem to catch no prey, nor do they lead in any discernible direction, even as they sometimes reach spans of several feet. But since "no industry is vain," Thoreau concludes, "this must have a reason," although he admits he can find none beyond the sheer delight of their beauty. Perhaps the spiders have embarked on "a mere frolic spending and wasting of themselves" now that the year is nearly done (V: 469–67). If so, they have awaited the most glorious days to weave the announcement of their demise.

Today, we most commonly use the term "gossamer" to describe intricate laced patterns such as we might find on a delicate shawl, but the word's etymological history suggests it was first used to designate a time of year.

Only later was it applied to the silky substance that Thoreau observed. According to the *Oxford English Dictionary*, the word derives from the Middle English phrase "goose summer," which in turn earned its name from the traditional killing and eating of geese in the fall. An obvious contraction of "goose summer," the term most likely first denoted a summerlike period akin to the American Indian summer. Thoreau was aware of a similar conflation of season and substance from German folklore. In a phrase he copied directly into his *Journal* from his sourcebook on insects, Kirby and Spence's *Introduction to Entomology*, he notes, "in Germany these flights of gossamer appear so constantly in autumn that they are there metaphorically called 'Der fliegender Sommer' (the flying or departed summer)."[33] (A similar German phrase, *altwiebersommer*—the old woman's summer—also refers to both the webs and a summerlike period in late autumn.) So when Thoreau likened the Indian summer of October and November 1853 to the gossamer days, he drew upon meteorological folklore with roots on both sides of the Atlantic that extended through centuries of time. It was a connection that few, if any, of his contemporaries would have been prepared to make.

For several reasons, the term "gossamer days" has never carried the same suggestive power in American culture that Indian summer has enjoyed. Thoreau himself recognized as much; other than his one extended treatment of the subject, he generally preferred the newer term for the weather he so admired. A student of local custom and lore, he would have betrayed his proclivities had he abandoned the native term for the exotic. Nevertheless, his encounter with and description of the gossamer webs enabled him to plumb the depths of his scientific, cultural, and local knowledge to bring the full panoply of Indian summer imagery to the pages of his *Journal*. In so doing, he uncovered an Indian summer landscape of startling beauty. More than anything else, his discovery of gossamer led him directly toward a meditation on patterns and webs—webs of nature, webs of language, webs of beauty. What had begun innocently enough on a "beautiful, warm and calm Indian Summer afternoon" led him to conclude that no other time of year better revealed nature's intricate ways.

Thoreau's Indian Summer

As I mentioned at the very start of this chapter, Thoreau cautioned himself against a facile hope in eternal life, his affection for the witch hazel notwithstanding. His model for maturity was the dying leaf. "How beautifully they go to their graves," he wrote in "Autumnal Tints." With little or no fuss "they troop to their last resting place, light and frisky." Leaves, Thoreau believed, "teach us how to die." Indeed, he wondered "if the time will ever come when men, with their boasted faith in immortality, will lie down as gracefully and as ripe" as the leaves, and with the same "Indian-summer serenity" shed their bodies, as they do their hair and nails."[34]

Thoreau's fascination with autumn took on new urgency in the late 1850s. He turned forty in July 1857, at which point *Walden* had been in print for three years, his mature *Journal* was in its seventh year, and his masterful essay on tree succession lay three years ahead. That fall, he began in earnest his study of changing leaves, a project that culminated in the posthumously published essay "Autumnal Tints." His *Journal* for October patiently records the sequence of change. He continued his research the following fall, going into ever greater detail without once losing sight of the display's beauty. "No annual training or muster of soldiery," he wrote on October 18, 1858, "could import into the town a hundredth part of the annual splendor of our October. We have only to set the trees, or let them stand, and Nature will find the colored drapery,–flags of all her nations, some of whose private signals hardly the botanist can read" (XI:220). Finding a way to read those signals, from both a botanical and a transcendental perspective, became central to Thoreau's late-in-life work.

But as Thoreau grew more expert on the sequence and method of foliage change, his discussions of Indian summer lost much of the early emphasis on late-year second springs. By the fall of 1860, the last full year he recorded in his *Journal*, his discussions of the season are purely descriptive, carrying almost no metaphoric weight. This is not to say that Indian summer had lost its attraction for Thoreau. In fact, as his *Journal* entries for the falls of 1859 and 1860 make clear, Indian summer was very much present as he began his final, though sadly short-lived, creative burst. What changed was the narrative implied in the metaphor. As Thoreau in 1859 and 1860 moved toward the study of tree succession and seed dispersal, the areas where he made his greatest scientific contributions, images of autumnal renewal figuratively gave way to his knowledge of regeneration, the processes by which nature constantly unfolds in ever shifting patterns across the land.[35] Succession rather than renewal became his preferred trope.

We can begin to detect this switch during the fall of 1859, a period when Thoreau was preoccupied with the arrest, trial, and execution of Captain John Brown. October began quite cool, "the frost of September 15 and 16" having "put an end to the summer" (XII:368). Thoreau spent the early weeks inspecting the leaves, entering into his *Journal* much that would he include in "Autumnal Tints." In the month's first two weeks he was out daily inspecting the leaves. Never had he been surer of their history. But then on the thirteenth, he recorded his last extended commentary on Indian summer's promise of renewed life. It is worth quoting at length:

The swamp amelanchier is leafing again, as usual. What a pleasing phenomenon, perhaps an Indian-summer growth, an anticipation of the spring, like the notes of birds and frogs, etc., an evidence of warmth and genialness. Its buds are annually awakened by the October sun as if it were spring. The shad-bush is leafing again by the sunny swamp-side. It is like a youthful or poetic thought in old age. Several times I have been cheered by this sight when surveying in former years. The chickadee seems to lisp a sweeter note at the sight of it. *I* would not fear the winter more than the shadbush, which puts forth fresh and tender leaves on its approach. In the fall I will take this for my coat of arms. It seems to detain the sun that expands it. (XII:376–77)

Never again would he allow himself such Indian summer exuberance.

Although his involvement does not directly explain the switch, the big change came as Thoreau grew deeply immersed in the affair of Captain Brown. On October 16, Brown, along with his sons and a small band of loyal followers, attacked and briefly held the federal armory at Harper's Valley, Virginia, where they hoped to ignite an armed revolt against the institution of slavery. Thoreau, who had met the captain during his occasional visits to Concord, threw himself into the turmoil surrounding Brown's subsequent trial with gusto. His *Journal* of October 19 includes the first of many lengthy defenses of Brown and his aims. He certainly understood that he was bucking conventional wisdom, as most commentators denounced the assault as a violent deranged act. Even the antislavery press was cautious not to support the Virginia raid, to say nothing of Brown's murderous activities in Kansas. Still, Thoreau rushed to his defense, finding in Brown the ideal of uncompromising principle. He delivered "A Plea for Captain John Brown" at the Concord Town Hall on October 30, and again in Worcester and Boston in the following days. As Brown's execution loomed in late November, he took the lead in organizing an appropriate service in Concord. On the day of the execution—an unusually warm December 2—Thoreau read from Sir Walter Raleigh and Tacitus at a ceremony he helped arrange.[36]

Yet for all the national and personal trauma, November was a glorious month, one of the finest Indian summer spells in Thoreau's adult life. But nowhere in his *Journal* does that glory receive more than passing mention. Indeed, his November entries never once reach beyond the purely descriptive realm. Thus on the fifth, a day he had traveled to Boston, he records, "the first Indian-summer day, after an unusually cold October." Indeed, it was so warm he "sat at the end of Long Wharf for coolness." On the ninth he writes, "A fine Indian-summer day. Have had pleasant weather about a week." Likewise, the fifteenth is "A very pleasant Indian-summer day"; and while he is able to enjoy the day's gossamer, his remarks about the weather are otherwise subdued. On the seventeenth, "as fair" an Indian summer day that he has ever experienced, Thoreau concedes, "I have been so absorbed of late in Captain Brown's fate as to be surprised whenever I detected the old routine running still" (XII:441–47). And finally, on the thirtieth, just two days before Brown is to die, he offers himself only a mild dose of his old Indian summer hope:

This has been a very pleasant month, with quite a number of Indian-summer days, – a pleasanter month than October was. It is quite warm to-day, and as I go home at dusk on the railroad causeway, I hear a hylodes peeping. (XII:458)

Thoreau was far from idle during these months and the ensuing year, however; in fact, he embarked on a series of projects that ultimately became his greatest scientific legacy. Sometime in 1859 Thoreau began compiling indexes and lists for what seems to have been a natural history calendar of the Concord region. His exact intentions remain unclear, as only a few months of his manuscript calendar have survived. He evidently had in mind a history that would draw upon his own extensive *Journal* entries to chart the sequence of natural phenomena through the years. Between 1860 and 1862 he made hundreds of lists that included the dates and descriptions of such things as bird arrivals, insect migrations, flower blooms, and frosts. He then transferred these lists to a series of grids with the years proceeding along one axis and each of the various phenomena down the other. It was a monumental and ultimately unfinished project that seemed designed to map patterns, to make clear how natural processes work in one place through time.[37]

A related study of sequences absorbed his intellectual energies in 1860. For several years, Thoreau had been fascinated by the succession of forest trees, wanting to know, in his biographer's words, "why and how trees and plants seemed to spring up when there seemed to be no obvious source for their seed."[38] He had been steadily working toward an explanation since the mid-1850s, but his understanding of the process began to clarify after reading Darwin's *Origin of Species* in February 1860, just weeks after it had been published in London. With Darwin's aid, he became more sure than ever that the mechanism for natural change was nature itself and that the apparent anomaly of, say, an oak stand quickly replacing a series of felled pines could be explained by looking to such seed dispersal mechanisms as animals, birds, or wind. A cleared pine lot, he discovered, will reveal healthy oak seedlings ready to take advantage of their day in the sun. On September 20 he delivered the fruits of his tree succession research in a lecture titled, appropriately enough, "The Succession of Forest Trees."

Thoreau's remarks that day were part of a much larger project titled "The Dispersion of Seeds," a project unfortunately left unfinished but recently published for the first time thanks to the Herculean efforts of Bradley P. Dean. Thoreau's research convinced him that nothing in nature generated spontaneously, but always came from a "root, cutting, or seed" that had been carried to an appropriate spot on the ground.[39] With Darwin as his theoretical perch and his *Journal* entries providing the necessary data, Thoreau was now prepared to view the natural world as an ever changing, life-creating force—a dynamic place characterized by complex interactions of succession and alteration rather than simple moments of renewal.

It is thus no coincidence that Indian summer virtually disappears from Thoreau's *Journal* in 1860, since these discoveries were bound to affect his seasonal muse. Indeed, Thoreau's *Journal* for the fall months bristles with excitement over the development theory while remaining largely silent about Indian summer. On October 19, for example, he notes "Indian summer and gossamer" but nothing else specific to the season. The day before, on the other hand, he could not contain his glee at his newfound understanding of how succession works. "See how an acorn is planted by a squirrel," he writes, "just under a loose covering of moist leaves," where it will lie "ready to send down its radicle next year." Elsewhere in the same entry he notes that a woodlot of white pine, which he estimates to be forty years old, has sprung up on a site still covered with oak stumps of at least that same age. Meanwhile, new oaks of approximately five years have reached six inches high in the same stand of pine. Just west of this site, he notes that a pasture where small pitch pines had been removed two years earlier is "now even more generally green with pines" than before. Everywhere he looks he finds one species of tree working (or waiting) to replace another, each according to a logic he is beginning to understand. The "development theory," he concludes, "implies a greater vital force in nature, because it is more flexible and accommodating, an equivalent to a sort of constant *new creation*" (XIV:143–48). As the last statement implies, we live in a world of constant creation, not of periodical or seasonal renewals.

And yet, it just may be that rather than replacing his early earlier enthusiasm for Indian summer renewals Thoreau incorporated this enthusiasm into his new understanding of succession. To see how, we can turn briefly to a late discussion of the witch hazel, the bewitchingly beautiful yellow fall bloom that provided so much to Thoreau's enjoyment of the season. Among the more intriguing qualities of the plant are its seed capsules, which ripen as nuts while the flowers bloom. In September 1859 Thoreau gathered several such nuts and brought them home. One evening he heard a "snapping sound and the fall of some body on the floor from time to time" only to discover that "it was produced by the witch hazel nuts on my desk springing open and casting their seeds across the chamber, hard and stony as these nuts are." When Thoreau began drafting his final work on seeds, he included a detailed analysis of this process, drawing directly from his *Journal* of September 1859. Apparently, the nuts had been "shooting their shining black seeds about the room for several days," both aurally and visually telling of the next generation. Thus projected, an individual witch hazel plant can "spread itself by leaps of ten or fifteen feet at a time."[40] And so Thoreau's favorite Indian summer flower, a plant that in 1853 showed him "when Nature revives in all her pores," had near the end of his life become a sign that nature needs no revival.[41] The seeds are always spreading.

To some observers Thoreau's concerns here might seem merely pragmatic, a way to explain how the witch hazel blooms. But if we keep in mind his altered metaphor whereby the notion of succession incorporates that of renewal, the magic from the moment is hardly lost. In fact, the magic increases. For as the witch hazel nuts and blooms demonstrate, change, dispersal, and renewal come together in this botanical exemplar of Indian summer beauty. If you listen carefully and know how to look, Thoreau found, next year's bushes can be seen and heard popping into existence while this fall's flowers first show their face.

This discovery came in the nick of time, for Thoreau had little energy left as 1860 drew to a close. In December he caught a cold that only worsened as the month progressed. He spent most of 1861 trying to revive himself, but his illness developed into the tuberculosis that eventually killed him. Thoreau kept writing, but the strain made sustained effort difficult. In the early months of 1862 he completed drafts of the essays "Autumnal

Tints," "Walking," and "Wild Apples," all of which appeared posthumously in the *Atlantic Monthly*. But his health never returned, and on May 6, 1862, he died two months shy of forty-five.[42] Legend holds that while on his deathbed Thoreau was questioned about his preparation for the afterlife, to which he replied, "One world at a time." If true, he passed on with the perfect Indian summer serenity he always hoped he would possess.

6

Emily Dickinson and Indian Summer: Beneath the Second Sun

In many ways, we have reached the Indian summer of Indian summer. Like the calendar that has run through most of its pages when the season suddenly arrives, our story is almost done. For by the time Henry David Thoreau died in 1862, writers and artists had placed Indian summer weather in the service of virtually all the imaginative constructions to which the season could be appropriately applied. It had already been, to repeat a phrase I used in the introduction, a "sentimental touchstone and a transcendental icon." This is not to say that nineteenth-century Americans no longer usefully spoke of Indian summer, for they did. But anyone reviewing the cultural significance of the season beyond, say, 1875 will encounter figures and images that had become deeply familiar to those who created and consumed the works we have already considered. The same may be said for New England's embrace of Indian summer, as those residing inside and outside the region continued (and continue) to identify the season as central to its iconography. By midcentury no account of the New England climate was complete without a nod toward Indian summer light and warmth.

The story, however, is only *almost* over, for we have not yet considered Emily Dickinson, Thoreau's sole rival for Indian summer daring. In her own allusive way, she stands as the season's final bloom, the last artist of any kind to add significantly to my subject's metaphoric package.

It should come as no surprise that Dickinson's Indian summer poems attain a higher aesthetic quality than those of her contemporaries. She simply wrote better verses than the season's other celebrators. But Dickinson distinguished herself thematically as well, largely by refusing to surrender herself to the season's enticements. By the time she turned to the

season in 1859, Indian summer poetry had settled into a comfortable sentimental pattern, a pattern that continued in the decades to come. For the
most part, poets followed one of two paths. Either they offered generic
praises of fall flowers in bloom or shrugged their shoulders in gestures of
sentimental regret. Dickinson's Indian summer poems, however, remain
sharply unsentimental. Any rejuvenation brought about by the sudden
warm weather fails to compensate for the equally sudden demise she knew
would come. As Ernest Sandeen noted a generation ago, her poems about
the season demand an "ascetic state of reflective awareness."[1] To be sure,
Dickinson understood the season's sentimental possibilities. Like Whittier,
she could marvel at the flowers once again springing to life. "Like a
Dream," she wrote in one poem, the season's flowers "Elate us – till we
Almost weep" (F 408). And like Longfellow, whom she read with interest,
she could trace the melancholy outlines of a landscape bathed in light.[2] But
whereas Longfellow and Whittier remained rooted in fireside gentility,
Dickinson flipped Indian summer's apparent gentleness on its head. Even
as she draws on the season's conventional images, she directs us toward its
capacity to catch us off guard, toward its strange disruptive quiet. "These
Indian Summer Days with all their peculiar peace," she wrote to her cousin
in 1869, "remind me of those still things that no one can disturb."[3] They
freeze us in moments of time.

Indian summer represented an ongoing concern throughout Dickinson's
poetic career. While not as numerous as, say, her many poems about death,
her lines to the season nonetheless represent a significant segment of her
work.[4] Her consideration of the season began with two works of 1859:
"These are the days when Birds come back" (F 122) and "Besides the Autumn poets sing" (F 123).[5] The prolific Civil War years, during which she
wrote the bulk of her poetry, gave rise to "Like some Old fashioned Miracle" (F 408), "God made a little Gentian" (F 520), "There is a June when
Corn is cut" (F 811), and the frequently anthologized "Further in Summer
than the Birds" (F 895). She returned to Indian summer in the 1870s in
such poems as "Summer has two Beginnings" (F 1457), "How know it from
a Summer's Day" (F 1412), and "A Field of Stubble, lying sere" (F 1419).
All told, she wrote approximately fifteen poems to the season. They are,
without question, the most consistently complex statements ever uttered
about Indian summer.

Dickinson also represents, if I may be forgiven the personal digression,
the writer whose work first led me to believe that one could write a book
about Indian summer. She has been with me throughout. I want, therefore,

to begin with the poem that inaugurated the journey. Several years ago while I was preparing to teach a unit on Dickinson, I read widely in her work looking for poems my students might enjoy that were not included in the standard anthologies. Somewhere in that process (I wish I could recall the date) I stumbled upon the 1877 "A Field of Stubble, lying sere." Not one of her better-known works, the poem nonetheless struck my interest for its stark depiction of a late-year scene. The second line particularly grabbed my attention, as it named a physical and emotional space for those, like myself, who had become smitten with New England's Indian summer weather. I knew I had discovered the title of the book I hoped to write in the second line of the poem.

> A – Field of Stubble, lying sere
> Beneath the second Sun –
> It's Toils to Brindled people thrust –
> It's Triumphs – to the Bin –
> Accosted by a timid Bird
> Irresolute of Alms –
> Is often seen – but seldom felt,
> On our New England Farms –
>
> (F 1419)

At first glance we have a typical New England postharvest poem, a work that like Longfellow's "Aftermath" presents an agricultural scene after the reaping of fall grains. More specifically, the poem shows the stubbled and sere conditions that remain in the wake of the second crop of hay that has been mowed from the once grain-laden fields.[6] Despite the clear signs that winter's cold approaches, such scenes evoke the fullness of the year. With the farmers' triumphs safely placed in the bin, the autumnal bounty eliminates the need for alms. Just as Indian summer itself recalls the year's earlier glory, the shorter second harvest echoes the intensity of the first. When we stand "Beneath the second Sun," we come back outside to feel the rays touch our skin, to once again embed ourselves in the palpable experience of warmth. We bathe ourselves with Indian summer aromas, colors, and glow. For most of us, the physical joy we derive from the experience matches whatever psychic pleasures we also attain. Both body and soul are revived.

In the final two lines, however, Dickinson claims that the true power of such scenes has escaped the notice of her neighbors. New Englanders may *see* the days of the second sun, but they have not *felt* them, at least not in any meaningful way. I am reminded here of Thoreau's lament that his neighbors missed the true glory of autumn's leaves. "We cannot see anything," he wrote in "Autumnal Tints," "until we are possessed with the idea of it, take it into our heads, – and then we can hardly see anything else."[7] Dickinson makes analogous accusations concerning New Englanders and the beauty of the "second sun." They stare at that beauty (which is easy enough to do), but they ignore Indian summer's darker possibilities—the isolated moments in time, the sharp angularity of the seasonal divide, the portents of death. In short, they avoid the psychological complexity of the season.

Despite her inventiveness, one fact becomes immediately clear to anyone who considers Dickinson an Indian summer poet: Nowhere in her nearly 1,800 poems does she specifically identify the season. (The phrase does appear in her letters.) She alludes to the same collection of images that her less cagey contemporaries employed without naming the season that ushers them forth. At times, we see her struggling to find just the right words to label the time of year.

> It cant be "Summer"!
> That – got through!
> It's early – yet – for "Spring"!
> There's that long town of White – to cross –
> Before the Blackbirds sing!
> It cant be "Dying"!
> It's too Rouge –
> The Dead shall go in white –
> So Sunset shuts my question down
> With Cuffs of Chrysolite!
>
> (F 265)

The struggle to name the season was compounded by the difficulty of distinguishing the initial summer of June and July from the Indian summer that came later in the year. They seemed so similar, at least to the eye.

> How knows it from a Summer's Day?
> It's Fervers are as firm –
> And nothing in the Countenance
> But scintillates the same –
> Yet Birds examine it and flee –
> And Vans without a name
> Inspect the Admonition
> And sunder as they came –
>
> (F 1412)

We can attribute part of this silence to the triumph of Indian summer imagery, which by Dickinson's time had become so pervasive that one did not need to use the phrase to convey the meaning. (Recall that Howells does not use the term Indian summer in the text of his novel carrying the season's name.) We can also point, as many critics have done, to the poet's characteristic evasiveness, to the linguistic gymnastics that made the construction of evocative metaphors one of the hallmarks of her verse.[8] But I do not think we should consider her Indian summer silence as yet another typical Dickinson dodge. Rather, her refusal to name the season goes straight to the heart of what she, more than any poet of her time, understood to be Indian summer's own characteristic allusiveness—its unstated place in the calendar, its uncertain duration, its mysterious give and take of life. During Indian summer, the weather is warm and winter awaits, but just what this weather should be called the speaker of her poems seems unable or unwilling to decide. For a season whose name itself remains such an historical puzzle, such silence seems strangely fitting. By refusing to identify her subject, Dickinson allows its enigmatic qualities to shine.

A Season Transformed—The Poems of 1859

The story of Dickinson's Indian summer begins in the Connecticut River Valley town of Amherst, Massachusetts, where she lived from her birth in 1830 until her death from kidney failure in 1886. Such a setting placed her in the geographical and chronological center of nineteenth-century New England's embrace of the season. More specifically, the story begins in the Indian summer of 1859, the year of her first significant poems to the season. As Thoreau noted of the same year in Concord, it was one of the most splendid on record, the highlight of a remarkable eight-year stretch that from 1856 to 1864 brought stunning Indian summers to the Amherst region.[9]

We can follow the season unfold in the pages of the *Hampshire and Franklin Express* and the *Springfield Republican*, two local newspapers to which the Dickinson family subscribed. Frost came early that year; by September 1 nighttime temperatures had dipped below the freezing point. Despite the early chill, temperatures fluctuated in October, leading the *Express* to claim that the weather "has been as fickle as a woman," a conceit that echoes the alleged native trickery memorialized in the phrase "Indian summer." November, however, proved uncommonly warm. By the eleventh the region had been enjoying "beautiful weather" for nearly two weeks; it seemed only fitting "that young men and maidens take advantage" of their good luck. As late as the nineteenth, "soft, clear Indian summer days" still prevailed. Finally on the twenty-fifth, after nearly three weeks of glorious warmth, the idyll ended and winter's cold could be felt. "Our beautiful Indian summer," the *Express* sadly noted, "has now disappeared."[10]

Sometime that fall—the exact dates remain obscure—Dickinson sent two poems about Indian summer to her sister-in-law Susan, who lived next door in the house she shared with the poet's brother, Austin. At the time, Susan was the poet's most intimate friend and had been receiving poems enclosed within letters for nearly a year, a sisterly correspondence that eventually led to over two hundred poetic exchanges. The two Indian summer poems—"These are the days when Birds come back" and "Besides the Autumn poets sing"—emerged at a crucial turning point in the poet's career. For the past year, the twenty-eight-year-old Dickinson (she turned twenty-nine in December) had been gathering her scattered poems into the hand-sewn fascicles found shortly after her death, an indication that he had begun to think of her poetry in a new, perhaps more permanent, light. Other poems written during this crucial year include such well-known works as "Success is counted sweetest" (F 112) and "Safe in their Alabaster Chambers" (F 124). She was still two or three years away from the great burst of creativity of the Civil War years, during which she wrote nearly 1,000 poems. But her future vocation as a poet was apparent in the 82 poems she wrote that year, a total that nearly doubled the output of 1858.

I want to look at these two 1859 Indian summer poems in detail, paying particular attention to the ways Dickinson drew upon the rhetorical figures of deception and sacrament. After all, for many white readers and writers of the time, the phrase "Indian summer" owed its name to fears of deception. Sacrament, on the on the other hand, invoked the Christian promise of second life—perhaps not here on earth, but in the peace of heaven. As we will see, the deceptive promise became a hallmark of the poet's Indian summer.

Of the two, "Besides the Autumn poets sing" makes Dickinson's transformation of conventional seasonal imagery most transparently clear. Written in the hymn meter and exact rhyme typical of her early career, the poem cleaves a space that separates Indian summer's "Haze" from the chilling "snow" to come.[11] It is, she notes, a place where poets must occasionally turn to prose, the first of several contradictions that propel the poem.

Besides the Autumn poets sing
A few prosaic days
A little this side of the snow
And that side of the Haze –

A few incisive mornings –
A few Ascetic eves –
Gone – Mr Bryant's "Golden Rod" –
And Mr Thomson's "sheaves."

Still, is the bustle in the Brook –
Sealed are the spicy valves –
Mesmeric fingers softly touch
The yes of many Elves –

Perhaps a squirrel may remain –
My sentiments to share –
Grant me, oh Lord, a sunny mind –
Thy windy will to bear!

(F 123)

Although there is much that is familiar here, the poem presents a sharp poetic terrain new to nineteenth-century Indian summer verse. The speaker begins by identifying a precarious yet enlightening period that briefly keeps other seasons at bay. By placing herself "A little this side of the snow / And that side of the Haze," she carefully delineates the in-between realm to which the entire poem refers. She does not straddle the two realms so much as she stands caught between them. Equally ascetic and incisive, such sharp moments lay beyond the reach of the oft-repeated images of Thomson and Bryant, to whom the speaker somewhat derisively refers. Their lines about seasonal change (especially Thomson's) may have once resonated with life, but by Dickinson's time had run their course. While perhaps lamenting the departing year, the speaker seems eager to replace a tired poetic habit with language that can more directly accommodate the season: "Gone – Mr Bryant's Golden Rod," a farewell bid to both Bryant's seasonal imagery and the late-year flower that was its source.

Having rejected Bryant's shopworn image, Dickinson in the final two stanzas suggests that the incisive moments of Indian summer days result from a paradoxical fraud. The first line of the third stanza—"Still, is the bustle in the Brook"—demands to be read in contradictory ways. The speaker describes either something that *still* moves or movement that has been *stilled*. Meanwhile, mesmerists, those trance-inducing healers who attracted large audiences in mid-nineteenth-century America, gently go to work. Mesmerism succeeds, of course, only when patients accept its attendant somnambulant state as evidence of improved health. For those willing to suspend belief, as many were inclined to do, mesmerists could invoke a suspended calm that allegedly eased psychic and physical ills. But as most patients soon learned, and as Dickinson surely knew, to be mesmerized was to be duped. Calm trances produced no cures. Like the false spring of Indian summer, their benefits were fleeting at best. Having begun so promisingly, the season now seems a contradiction and a trick. No wonder, then, that the speaker needs "a sunny mind" to help her "bear" the beautiful ruse.

"These are the days when Birds come back"—the other Indian summer poem of 1859—similarly reveals Dickinson reworking conventional imagery to present a season whose primary quality rests in deceit.

> These are the days when Birds come back –
> A very few – a Bird or two,
> To take a final look –
>
> These are the days when skies resume
> The old – old sophistries of June –
> A blue and gold mistake.
>
> Oh fraud that cannot cheat the Bee,
> Almost thy plausibility
> Induces my belief,
>
> Till ranks of seeds their witness bear,
> And swiftly thro' the altered air
> Hurries a timid leaf –
>
> Oh Sacrament of summer days!
> Oh last Communion in the Haze –
> Permit a Child to join –
>
> Thy sacred emblems to partake

typically do not engage in reverse migration during the fall, so the speaker is most likely observing species such as the white-throated sparrow or dark-eyed junco, two Canadian birds that travel south through the Connecticut Valley in November.[12] But whatever their ultimate destination, the effect of the poem does not really depend on their direction. What matters is that the birds have been caught off guard by the warmth, and indeed the speaker soon realizes that mistakes and frauds characterize the scene. The skies in the second stanza, for example, resume the "old sophistries of June," suggesting that the "blue and gold" beauty of the fall mistakenly repeats a trick attempted earlier in the year. The second summer, we learn, is as deceptive as the first. Of course, we do not expect a coquettish June, a month of supposedly naive pleasures when the landscape bursts with life. Instead, we innocently believe the sun's promise to warmly light the world for us to see. Everything, it seems, stands open to the eye. But for the speaker of this poem, who does not reveal the nature of June's original trick, the present Indian summer scene amounts to an unwelcome simulacrum, an imitation of an imitation. Only "the Bee" remains wise to the weather.

By the third stanza, the speaker recognizes her susceptibility to fraud and steps out of the mirrorlike trick-within-a-trick. To be sure, the "plausibility" of the scene had "Almost" induced her "belief." She nearly played the fool, but caught herself just in time. By the fourth stanza she dismisses the false promises offered by returning birds and June-like skies and instead recognizes the "ranks of seeds" that blow in with the leaf to mark the entrance of winter's chill.[13] A hard-earned realism has replaced a sentimental and duplicitous mirage.

But before we can become too comfortable with such a reading, Dickinson once again shifts gears as the speaker in the final two stanzas now seeks communion with the very forces that deceive. If the first part of the poem denies the life-affirming nature of Indian summer, the final section anticipates a communion ceremony (the paradigmatic symbol of a promised afterlife) amid the "Haze," one of the season's most persistent images. The faith in Indian summer's life-returning powers that had been rejected in the first part of the poem is here restored through the essential "emblems" of the "last Communion"—"the consecrated bread" and the "immortal wine." June's original trick, which the speaker would not reveal, now becomes an original sin to overcome. The communion rite, of course, figures prominently in Christian belief, but here Dickinson, who herself never received the sacrament, invokes its promise within a pantheistic hope that the natural world can meet both physical and spiritual needs. A supplicant at the table, she asks that she be permitted "to join" the other communicants for a final meal. Such a quest, however, ultimately remains unfulfilled. A request to join the ceremony has been made, but the poem ends before an answer is granted. The poem, then, offers no salvation, only desire, and a strained one at that.[14]

Certainly the most theologically challenging Indian summer poem we have yet encountered, "These are the days when Birds come back" brings us directly to the heart of Dickinson's struggle with Amherst's orthodox God. Raised within the doctrinally conservative Connecticut Valley version of Congregationalism, Dickinson knew the language of the communion sacrament as well as any poet of her day. As Jane Donahue Eberwein points out, communion, along with baptism, were the two principal sacraments recognized by the family's church.[15] One of the last New England congregations to restrict participation in the ceremony to the community of elected saints, the Amherst parish could not induce Dickinson to undergo the conversion experience necessary to share the consecrated bread. Having stopped attending services sometime in the late 1850s, she turned her back on the enticements offered by the rite. She did not, however, outright reject a belief in God. Indeed, according to Cynthia Griffin Wolff, "she retained a deeply rooted conviction in the *existence* of God until the day she died."[16] It was the conventional notion that God promised life in the Hereafter to those who submit to His will that she could not abide. Such a creed required believers to ignore the world's obvious signs of pain and death, a form of denial that no amount of Indian summer warmth could convince her to indulge.

The poem can be (and has been) read in any number of ways. We might focus on the two forms of language, the sentimental and the theological, which characterize the separate segments of the work.[17] Dickinson certainly knew these discourses well. Here, they stand at a face-off, each unable to penetrate the other. They arrive at this juncture as the poem arrived at Susan's door, sent, as it were, without warning. Like the Indian summer interlude, whose arrival suddenly and unpredictably severs the fall, they simply show up to stare each other down. The poem also suggests the paradoxical nature of faith by locating acts of restoration *after* the testimony of the senses has proved faith wrong. Unlike the Apostle Thomas, who upon seeing believes, the speaker's announced desire for salvation begins when she rejects what she sees. Still another possibility lies in the mystery of sacrifice, the act behind the communion language the poem employs.

The meaning of Christ's sacrifice, the unconverted Dickinson understood, remained too complex to comprehend through the sentimental language she gently skewers in stanzas one through four.

A Season of Sacrifice

Whether Dickinson was aware of it or not, the poem's sacrificial language complimented the imagery others employed during the glorious Indian summer of 1859. Indeed, that year's prolonged Indian summer proved a particularly apt moment to ponder the meaning and implications of sacrifice. As we saw in the previous chapter, the arrest, trial, and execution of Captain John Brown aroused passions across New England. Though opinion of course varied, Brown's December 2 execution was seen by at least some commentators as a modern-day analogue of the Crucifixion.[18] Although the raid had virtually no chance of success, and indeed was loudly condemned for its violence, Brown's Jeremiac belief that slaveholding represented America's great sin led many to view his actions in a sacrificial light. "You who pretend to care for Christ crucified," Thoreau wrote, should "consider what you are about to do to him who offered himself to be the saviour of four millions of men" (XII:424). Even Emerson departed from his customary political caution to declare Brown a "new saint" who would "make the gallows glorious like the cross."[19]

Although he was quick to denounce the violence of Brown's raid, one commentator who urged against his execution was Samuel Bowles, the influential editor of the *Springfield Republican*. A close friend and possibly the object of the poet's romantic affections, Bowles looms large in Dickinson's biography. He entered the family circle sometime in 1858 and soon became a regular visitor at the home of Austin and Susan, who lived just next door to the house Dickinson shared with her parents and sister. Along with the other members of the family she read the *Republican* daily and relied on Bowles's knowledge for insights into the political and military events connected to the Civil War.[20] At first, Bowles celebrated Brown the man but condemned his raid, lest its rashness become associated with his paper's antislavery position. But in the weeks leading up to the execution—weeks of splendid Indian summer weather—the captain's pending fate led Bowles to praise the virtues of the man who had sacrificed himself to the abolitionist cause. "Whatever we may say of the folly and utter desperation

of Brown's enterprise," Bowles wrote on November 4, "no man can contemplate the personal qualities he has exhibited during his trial without
hearty respect and admiration." On the twelfth, he urged against Brown's
execution, claiming, "we can conceive of no event that could so deepen the
moral hostility of the free states to slavery."[21]

Finally, on the morning that Brown stood on the gallows, Bowles's paper
listed Brown's death as central to the meaning to the recent glorious Indian
summer of 1859. The "November which has just left us," Bowles wrote in
the first sentence of his page-one editorial, has been a remarkable month,
on account alike of its weather and events." The remainder of the paragraph
is worth quoting at length:

> [November] has completely forfeited its traditional reputation as the most dismal
> month of the twelve, and has given us an almost unbroken Indian summer. Several
> efforts at wintry weather have been made, but they were short lived, and the light
> sifting snow soon melted away in warm rain and sunshine. Whether the unnatural
> heat prevalent in Virginia has effected the temperature, as it has the temper of the
> whole country, we shall know better [at a later date]. . . . Certain it is, that in
> terrestrial and human heat the late November offers an unprecedented record. And
> winter came in with a warm, spring like rain, doing escort to days bright and sunny
> enough to relax the conscience of a dyspeptic, or to start early peas if they were
> only in the ground. The trees, in some sections, deceived by appearances, are really
> entertaining spring hopes, and blossoming fruit buds and opening leaves are among
> the marvels of the inauguration of the winter of 1859. But we shall "catch it" before
> long.

And "catch it" they did; for unfortunately the beautiful weather could
prevent neither Brown's death nor the coming cold. The very next paragraph opens with a sentence that concedes as much: "By the time this
paragraph will be read John Brown will have been hung by a South Carolina
rope on Virginia gallows." Nevertheless, the stunning juxtaposition of the
beautiful weather and the Captain's death, whose actions the editor insisted
had stemmed from "the highest motives to which human nature is capable,"
helped propel Brown into martyrdom's ranks.[22]

Although Dickinson did not comment directly on the Brown affair, she
may have come to view "These are the days when Birds come back" as a
memorial to those who in the Civil War that followed sacrificed their lives
to the same cause that had inspired his raid. More than four years after she
sent the poem to Susan, it appeared in the March 11, 1864, edition of the
Drum Beat, a short-lived Brooklyn newspaper that through its connection

to the United States Sanitary Commission raised funds to care for wounded Union soldiers. (Two other early works—"Blazing in Gold and Quenching in Purple" and "Flowers – well – if anybody"—appeared in previous editions of the same publication.) Precisely how "These are the days," issued anonymously under the title "October," came to the paper remains unclear. Its editor, the Reverend Richard Salter Storrs, had graduated from Amherst College in 1839 and was often the guest of Austin and Susan Dickinson during the annual commencement week ceremonies. Karen Dandurand, whose detective work led to the discovery of the *Drum Beat* publications, suggests that Storrs may have persuaded Dickinson to offer submissions during one such visit.[23] Or, as Martha Nell Smith suggests, Susan Dickinson may have quietly brought it to the attention of the editor, since she had similarly sent other poems in her possession to Samuel Bowles.[24] At any rate, as Dandurand points out, Dickinson apparently did not object to its publication, as she did when other poems were published against her will.[25]

By no means do I want to suggest that Dickinson wrote "These are the days when Birds come back" in direct response to the Brown affair. Nor would I claim (in the absence of definitive evidence) that she specifically chose this poem for inclusion in a publication intended to aid the Civil War wounded. I would argue, however, that the sacrificial language the poem invokes was in perfect keeping with the popular mood and was hence utterly appropriate for the *Drum Beat*'s aims. Perhaps no other moment in American history so poignantly pointed to the collective need to sanctify and atone. As Christopher Kent Wilson notes in his study of harvest imagery during and after the Civil War, northern clergymen such as Horace Bushnell and political figures such as Abraham Lincoln often spoke of the need to make sacred the efforts of the wounded and the dead. "As the war continued," Wilson writes, "the harvest of death became a recurring theme in the popular press."[26] An anonymous poem published in *Harper's* in October 1863, for example, compared a recently reaped New England farm with the harvesting of souls that would be required on the war's great battlefields:

> In the still New England autumn
>   The work of the year was done,
> But afar were fields unsickled
>   Under the southern sun—
> Fields to be reaped in battle—
>   Harvests by victory won.[27]

Indian summer lends itself to such concerns. Itself a harvest time, it sends us out to reap the fullness of the year, to take in what can be gathered and to remember what has been left behind.

It is thus no coincidence that the Civil War years represent the apex of Indian summer's popularity in nineteenth-century works of poetry and art. Among the painters who turned to the season during and immediately after the war years were such well-known figures as Sanford Gifford and Jasper Cropsey as well as lesser talents such as Jervis McEntee and William Sanford Mason. Poets, too, could not resist the connection between the season and the bloody sacrifice unleashed by the war. As Henry Howard Brownell's popular 1866 poem suggests, the season's haze offered the perfect natural backdrop for the memorialized dead:

> The haze of Indian summer seemed
>   Borne from far fields of sulphry breath –
>   A subtile atmosphere of death
> Was ever round us as we dreamed.
>
> . . . .
>
> To us the glory or the gray
>   Had still a stranger, stormier dye,
>   Remembering how we watched the sky
> Of many a waning battle day,
>
> O'er many a field of loss or fame:
>   How Shiloh's eve to ashes turned,
>   And how Manassas' sunset burned
> Incarnadine of blood and flame.[28]

Five years later, the poet Mary Clemmer Ames found that the "miracle" of Indian summer helped her overcome the initial shock she experienced upon encountering Antietam's tragic fields. An occasional contributor of sentimental verse to the *Springfield Republican*, Ames was standing over the fields of carnage when she detected an Indian summer breeze that "pervades you like a presence before you behold a visible token of its assent." At first words eluded her, but ultimately, the second summer, "serener [and] softer than the first," convinced her that the men [or at least the northern men] "died not in vain."[29]

Which brings me back to the appearance of "These are the days when Birds come back" in the *Drum Beat*. The poem's sacramental language and Indian Summer scenes take on new meaning when read in the context of the Civil War.[30] No longer simply a pantheistic wish to commune with the haze or an acknowledgment of the season's deceit, the poem—at least as it appears in the magazine—now memorializes the wounded and the dead. The same may be said for the speaker of "These are the days when Birds come back." Having initially sought her own consecration, she enacts through the pages of the *Drum Beat* a consecrating act of her own.

Reading Dickinson's Amherst

Before we take up additional Dickinson poems, I want to pause to consider how her lifelong residence in Amherst contributed to her Indian summer sensibilities. As Dickinson came of age in the 1840s and '50s, her hometown straddled two worlds. On the one hand, the community had historic and ongoing ties to the evangelical strains of American religious life. Indeed, pre–Civil War Amherst, one biographer notes, "remained one of the last outposts of America's Puritan past."[31] Much of that theological energy emanated from Amherst College, an institution primarily concerned with preparing young men for service in orthodox Trinitarian ministries and which the poet's father and brother served as treasurer. As late as 1860, the college proved fertile territory for the intermittent revivals that periodically swept through the town, including one in 1850 that brought Dickinson's father and sister to conversion. Although the college curriculum underwent rapid secularization after the Civil War, during Dickinson's formative years it retained the doctrinally conservative spirit that had led to its founding in the 1820s.[32]

At the same time, the presence of Amherst College also assured the presence of a sophisticated and well-read population with ties to the region's commercial and literary elite. Known for its distinguished science faculty, Amherst College brought to town scholars well versed in such fields as botany, geology, and paleontology. And although she herself did not attend the all-male college, Dickinson was well aware of its curriculum. The nearby Amherst Academy, where the future poet studied from 1840 to 1847, employed many of the same instructors as the college, thus assuring that she received as up-to-date a scientific education as was available anywhere in New England.[33]

The persistence of Puritan orthodoxy in the Amherst of Dickinson's youth partly explains why her Indian summer visions lacked the sentimental touches of the Brahmin poets we considered in chapter 4. Like Lowell's Cambridge, Amherst embodied a New England hurtling toward its modern form. With each passing decade new industries and railroads brought increased urban densities to a region only recently blanketed with farms, changes that Dickinson's father, a lawyer and longtime fixture in Massachusetts politics, helped bring about. Lowell and other similarly inclined poets, on the other hand, operated within a community that as early as 1800 had forsaken Puritan orthodoxy for the gentler religious strains of Unitarianism. They experienced the same modernizing forces that Dickinson witnessed, but they came to such experiences from a completely different cultural and theological perspective. As a result, they could cover the past of their region with a melancholy Indian summer haze without fearing the retribution of a God ill disposed to syrupy sentiment. The past of Dickinson's Amherst, on the other hand, was still very much present. She may have turned her back on the strenuous conversions experienced by her family, but Dickinson's poetry attests to her lifelong wrestling match with her forefathers' God. Lowell covered up the disjuncture between past and present by appealing to the mist—nostalgia always won out. For Dickinson, the same disjuncture could not be concealed precisely because she lived it every day.

And yet, Dickinson's voracious reading habits assured that she would also assimilate the sentimental Indian summer enjoyed by her contemporaries. In an oft-quoted 1862 letter in which she lists her preferred reading, she cagily identifies a short but impressive list: "For Poets—I have Keats—and Mr and Mrs Browning. For Prose—Mr Ruskin—Sir Thomas Browne—and the Revelations." But as Jack L. Capps has shown in his study of the poet's reading, such a list barely hints at the breadth and depth of Dickinson's knowledge of both canonical and popular literature. For our purposes, her knowledge of the popular press is what matters, for this is where she encountered the bulk of whatever Indian summer verse she read. Capps identifies several publications that regularly entered the family home, among them many that frequently printed Indian summer stories and poems. In addition to the aforementioned *Hampshire and Franklin Express* and *Springfield Republican*, the two local papers, the list also includes nationally distributed periodicals such as *Harper's New Monthly Magazine*, *Scribner's Magazine*, and the *Atlantic Monthly*. All were eagerly read by the reading-mad Dickinsons. In Capps's words, books may have been "the principal means by which Emily extended her horizons," but "most of her knowledge of the detail and action in a world thus discovered came through her habitual reading of periodicals."[34]

Two publications especially stand out for the Indian summer imagery they brought into the Dickinson parlor. First is the Boston-based *Atlantic Monthly*, a magazine to which the Dickinsons subscribed from its inception in November 1857. Closely associated with Thomas Wentworth Higginson, with whom Dickinson famously corresponded, the *Atlantic* in its early years aspired to both a literal and figurative Indian summer haze. As Barton Levi St. Armand notes in his study of Dickinson's cultural influences, the "heyday of American nature writing belonged not to the seed time of the Transcendental revolt, but rather to its harvest, to the ripe and mellow numbers of the *Atlantic Monthly* of the late 1850s and early 1860s."[35] In these issues, the features that soon became characteristic of the American nature essay, from the thoroughness of observation to the deliberately poetic style of prose, began to take shape. At the same time, the *Atlantic* promoted itself as the voice of New England maturity by drawing on the wizened Indian summer perspective of writers such as Lowell and Holmes. In issue after issue, the magazine articulated what one scholar has called Yankee humanism.[36] With the important exception of its Thoreau essays (and even these were autumnal in tone) its articles, poems, and stories lacked the verve of early transcendentalism. Instead, they presented a vision of an enlightened New England intellectual aristocracy, comfortable in its cultural authority but perhaps just nervous enough to feel that authority slipping.

The fall numbers of 1862 reveal the kind of Indian summer imagery Dickinson encountered in her monthly perusal of the *Atlantic*. September included Higginson's "Life of Birds," a gentle and learned piece of amateur ornithology. In twelve tightly written pages, Higginson, who would eventually become Dickinson's most important contact with the broader literary world, lovingly describes the movements and habits of birds, including those that "linger in the autumn." October and November featured Thoreau's posthumously published essays "Autumnal Tints" and "Wild Apples," two works that as I mentioned in the previous chapter show the Concord naturalist especially alive to the nuances of fall. The December issue, in turn, begins with "The Procession of Flowers," still another of Higginson's closely observed nature essays. Following an outline similar to Thoreau's "Autumnal Tints," which traces the changing colors as they unfold through the fall, Higginson describes the blooming sequence of local flowers from one season to the next. The paradoxical orderliness and mystery of the process leaves him struggling for words. "We strive to picture heaven," he notes near the close, "when we are barely at the threshold of the inconceivable beauty of the earth."[37]

Although she read the *Atlantic* without fail, Dickinson would have most consistently encountered works about Indian summer in the *Springfield Republican*, the paper edited by her close friend Samuel Bowles. One of the poet's early biographers claimed that the *Republican* was "next in importance to the Bible in determining the mental climate of [Dickinson's] formative years."[38] Unlike most nineteenth-century papers, which tended to bury the season in layers of sentiment, the *Republican* presented an Indian summer that would have appealed to Dickinson's more complex emotional response to the warmth. At times it offered nostalgic visions, but just as often the paper included darker seasonal thoughts. A series of Indian summer musings during the fall of 1860 reveals the various components of this complexity at work. Bowles begins by predicting an ominous entrance for the season. As the weather first grows cold in September, "there is death in the air," a feeling intensified by the "Indian Summer breezes" blown in from the southwest. In October, however, he finds only sentimental joy when such weather has actually arrived. "What employment can be more poetical," the editor asks, "than cutting up corn in the midst of so glowing a scene, with a heap of pumpkins in the center of the field?" With their freedom to romp the fields, children—those beloved figures of sentimental literature—become "the objects of our especial envy." Who can blame them, he adds, if they run "away from school" for an afternoon of games? But before the nostalgia runs too deep, Bowles in November suggests that far from recalling more innocent times, Indian summer days instead force us to confront what we might hope to avoid. They "steal into the soul like the memory of forgiven sins and conquered struggles." Rather than gentle tugs at the heart, such weather operates like a moral canker, constantly reminding us of all we have done wrong.[39]

A similar combination of sentimentalism and darker visions informs the *Republican*'s better Indian summer poems. An anonymous November 1860 poem simply titled "Indian Summer" does this most obviously. The five-stanza work begins innocently enough, with the speaker sitting and watching through an open window "The gorgeous clouds that are passing by." The southwest air carries "Perfumes as sweet as in June" so that "Even the bees are humming today." So far, this reads like virtually every other sentimental poem to the season, but as the poem progresses the scene becomes increasingly tense. The second stanza, for example, presents "reapers binding their golden sheaves," a perhaps common but nonetheless foreboding image of the final harvest of souls. The warm air and sighing leaves, the speaker notes, are "like the prelude to grief." Death looms. By the fifth and final stanza, the speaker, who at first so innocently enjoyed what she saw, recognizes that the beautiful weather will leave her hanging in a theological lurch, caught somewhere between heaven and earth:

> At the open window I still remain
> And my soul is vainly trying to see
> Over the losses – on to the gain,
> Knowing how much that gain would be;
> Teach me, Oh teach me, how to wait
> For the summer so endless – Heaven so great.[40]

I do not want to belabor the point that the *Republican* printed Indian summer poems. We would expect nothing less from a nineteenth-century newspaper. For our purposes, the key point is the extent to which Dickinson transformed the standard seasonal imagery she gleaned from her habitual reading of the contemporary press. What David Reynolds said generally of canonical nineteenth-century American literature can be here applied to the specifics of Emily Dickinson. Classic literature during the American Renaissance, Reynolds argues, "resulted not from a rejection of socio-literary content but rather from a full assimilation and transformation of key images and devices from this context."[41] Consciously or not, Dickinson followed such a path. In her 1862 poem "Like Some old Fashioned Miracle," for example, she draws on the same admixture of Indian summer fun, imagery, and regret found in Bowles's paper, albeit to much greater effect.

> Like Some Old fashioned Miracle –
> When Summertime is done –
> Seems Summer's Recollection –
> And the affairs of June –
>
> As infinite Traditions –
> As Cinderella's Bays –
> Or Little John – of Lincoln Green
> Or Blue Beard's Galleries
>
> Her Bees – have an illusive Hum –
> Her Blossoms – like a Dream
> Elate us – till we almost weep –
> So plausible they seem –
>
> (F408)

Like the poems I discussed at the beginning of this chapter, Dickinson here looks backward on an Indian summer day to recall "the affairs of June." She recounts traditions involving Cinderella and Blue Beard, stories that seem as infinite and ongoing as the weather is miraculous.⁴² And yet, Dickinson carefully avoids falling into nostalgic naiveté. In the end, Indian summer's blossoming flowers and buzzing bees prove illusive, like a dream, but one "so plausible" that we "almost weep."

Two years later, Dickinson achieved a more complex (and more successful) reworking of conventional imagery in "There is a June when Corn is cut" (F 811). As with "These are the days when Birds come back," we must contend with a tricky June intent on repeating itself in the fall:

> There is a June when Corn is cut
> And Roses in the Seed –
> A Summer briefer than the first
> But tenderer indeed
>
> As should a Face supposed the Grave's
> Emerge a single Noon
> In the Vermillion that it wore
> Affect us, and return –
>
> Two seasons, it is said, exist –
> The Summer of the Just,
> And this our's, diversified
> With Prospect – and with Frost –
>
> May not our Second with it's First
> So infinite compare
> That We but recollect the one
> The other to prefer?

The poem begins simply enough, with the speaker announcing a second and more tender June that returns when autumn's corn is cut. It is a classic Indian summer motif. But in the second stanza the bucolic scene suddenly becomes horrific. Indeed, it reminds us of the old truism that we should be careful of what we ask for. For rather than seeing the return of warmth as a promise for resurrected life, the speaker compares the season to the terrifying sight of a fleshy corpse rising from the grave. With the return of the warmth we are left with two seasons to contemplate—one for "the Just," the other "diversified" with frost. One brings with it a heavenly beauty, while the other seems to promise a far less ennobling reward. The final stanza, which Timothy Morris rightly remarks "is as baffling as any-thing Dickinson ever wrote," ask us to compare the second June with the first.[43] The problem is, we do not know which one is "the other" to which the speaker refers in the final two lines. In preferring one summer over the other, should we cast our lot with the frightful ruse, with the unsought resurrection of a "Face supposed the Grave's," or with the one whose pass-ing made the resurrection possible in the first place? The speaker refuses to say, though neither choice seems all that comforting. Life that comes back in the fall, she suggests, that briefly thrives when corn is cut, will ultimately "Affect us, and return" to from whence it came. We are left wondering whether life that has returned in the fall promises more or less than the original life that departed so many months ago.

A similar collection of motifs and concerns drives "Summer has two Beginnings," an 1877 poem whose speaker also finds troubling implications in the return visit paid by summerlike warmth.

> Summer has two Beginnings –
> Beginning once in June –
> Beginning in October
> Affectingly again –
>
> Without, perhaps, the Riot
> But graphicer for Grace –
> As finer is a going
> Than a remaining Face –
> Departing then – forever –
> Forever – until May –
> Forever is deciduous –
> Except to those who die –
>
> (F 1457)

A more subdued version of the original summer, the second one nonethe-less leaves the speaker unsure of just where she stands. Though both are equally fine, we cannot tell which warm face is going and which one re-mains. Nor do we know what will survive once October's summer at last departs, since the promise held out by deciduous trees seems impossible to keep. The season's fallen leaves will certainly be replaced in spring, but the ongoing deciduous cycle is of no use to those who die. Lucy Larcom, we recall from chapter 2, thought Indian summer's beauty and charm would provide the perfect setting to begin a march toward heaven. The speaker of this poem, though appreciative of the season's "Grace," seems far less sure of who will survive the coming cold.

The Gentian Poems

Perhaps nothing Dickinson wrote better shows her transformation of conventional Indian summer imagery than the several works devoted to the fringed gentian, one of New England's most beloved late-year flowers. Typically seen along roadsides and in low-lying meadows, gentians bloom from late August to mid-October and often survive the fall's first frosts. Not surprisingly, they have frequently served as the ideal botanical correlative for writers seeking signs of life in the autumnal landscape. The delicate blue flower—Thoreau once said gentians were "bluer than the blue sky"— owes its special place in nineteenth-century American culture to William Cullen Bryant, a poet Dickinson knew well. His often republished 1829 "To the Fringed Gentian," which appeared in an 1861 issue of the *Springfield Republican*, established the flower as a beacon for the late-year hope that the joys of the season would continue in heaven when death finally came.[44] The final two stanzas are indicative of the life-sustaining qualities many ascribed to its autumnal bloom:

> Then doth thy sweet and quiet eye
> Look through its fringes to the sky,
> Blue – blue – as if that sky let fall
> A flower from its cerulean wall.
>
> I would that thus, when I shall see
> That hour of death draw near to me,
> Hope, blossoming within my heart
> May look to heaven as I depart.[45]

A final shot of beauty to grace the departing year, Bryant's gentian exudes autumn's central promise: that life will continue in the spring.

Like many women of her generation and class, Dickinson understood both the botany and symbolism of flowers, so she was well prepared for the poetic embrace of the gentian.[46] But as always, she reached her own conclusions. As Elizabeth Petrino notes, the poet shared the Victorian tendency to see flowers as "emblems of fragile innocence" imbued with "religious and cultural significance." But she also used flower imagery to reject or "revise many of the romantic positions women assumed in nineteenth-century verse."[47] Though appreciative of their charms she remained skeptical of the promise held out by the unexpected return of blooms:

> When they come back – if Blossoms do –
> I always feel a doubt
> If blossoms can be born again
> When once the Art is out –
>
> (F 1042)

For Dickinson, the abrupt eruption of the gentian's bloom amounted to an audacious claim on her attention. It is "a greedy flower," she wrote in 1859, one that "overtakes us all" when we are not prepared.[48] A four-line poem from the year before succinctly suggests what lies beneath its troubling bloom.

> The Gentian weaves her fringes –
> The Maple's loom is red –
> My departing blossoms
>   Obviate parade.
>
> (F 21)

As the fringes reach toward the sky, the flower unceremoniously departs, a departure emblazoned against the Indian summer red woven upon the maple's loom. She returned to the flower in the 1863 "God made a little Gentian," one of 295 poems that flowed from her pen that year. Having failed to bloom in the summer, as it must, the flower now ravishes the Indian summer countryside "just before the Snows" bring the scene to an end.

> God made a little Gentian –
> It tried – to be a Rose –
> And failed – and all the Summer laughed –
> But just before the Snows –
>
> There rose a Purple Creature –
> That ravished all the Hill –
> And Summer hid her Forehead –
> And Mockery was still –
>
> The Frosts were her condition –
> The Tyrian would not come
> Until the North – invoke it –
> Creator – Shall I – bloom?
>
> (F 520)

The imagery recalls Bryant's lines, but Dickinson draws far different implications than her famous counterpart. Whereas Bryant values the gentian for its heavenly promise, Dickinson's speaker finds a distressing void cleaved by winter's pending chill. Her flower seems reluctant to surrender its ground. Noting its preference for a frosted landscape, the speaker reports that the Tyrian (named for a purple dye with properties similar to indigo) would not lie down until the cold wind of the north invoked its final demand. The gentian's stubbornness of course ultimately proves fruitless, leaving the speaker, herself a personified flower, to wonder if she should even bloom in the first place. To spring to life in the face of such anticipated desolation seems an act of folly rather than hope. Death in the midst of beauty seems the only fate.

"The Gentian has a parched Corolla," Dickinson's final poem to the late-year flower, once and for all places the autumnal blue bloom into the category of Indian summer tricks. The last poem she wrote in 1877, it shows the forty-seven-year-old poet no longer even tempted by the promised second spring of "These are the days when Birds come back." She begins by describing a purposeless return of life to an already dried-out stem:

> The Gentian has a parched Corolla –
> Like Azure dried
> 'Tis Nature's buoyant juices
> Beatified –
> Without a vaunt or sheen
> As casual as Rain
> And as benign –

While the "Fringed career" of the gentian may briefly come to "aid an aged Year," the aid proves to be too little too late. The "parched Corolla" has been "Beatified" with no particular significance. Ultimately, no second spring results, only a hard-earned acceptance that truthfulness trumps the seasonal ruse:

> It's lot – were it forgot –
> This truth endear –
> Fidelity is gain
> Creation o'er –
>
> (F 1458)

It is perhaps tempting to read the gentian poems within the context of Dickinson's religious struggles. For the unconverted poet the "Fidelity" of death no doubt seemed, at least on the surface, a more gainful stance than the hope of returned life, either here on earth or above in heaven. But we might also usefully read these poems and the flowers they describe as botanical analogues for the idea of deception, an idea that runs deep in the nineteenth-century conception of Indian summer. By finally dying at the end of the season, the fringed gentian takes back its initial gift of late-year life, a gift that Dickinson understood could in no way withstand the onslaught of the cold. What had been an emblem of eternal life for the publicly renowned Bryant became a warning for the far more private Dickinson—not so much a warning of pending death, but a reminder of the necessity to keep one's hopes in check.

The Crickets Depart: The Sounds of Indian Summer

We have one final natural and poetic feature of Dickinson's Indian summer to consider. Earlier in this chapter I mentioned the poet's dismay that New Englanders felt neither the psychological nor the physical complexity of standing "Beneath the second Sun." We have considered the psychological aspects at length, but we need briefly to examine the season's varied sensual textures. In a much quoted line, Dickinson in 1861 claimed to "see New Englandly," a phrase by which the poet hoped to root herself in the particularities of the regional landscape. But as I suggested in my discussion of "A field of Stubble, lying sere," Dickinson assumes that sight alone will never suffice, at least not in the case of Indian summer. Other senses are required. Like the farmers in "A field of Stubble," we must replace mere sight, the least palpable of our senses, with the full panoply of physical and psychical tools at our disposal. For Dickinson, no sensory organ recorded richer Indian summer data than her poetically sensitive ears. Nor did any sound more evocatively suggest the season than the songs of crickets eerily broadcasting their presence in fields and trees. As her several cricket poems make clear, the silencing of their song at the end of Indian summer aurally and psychologically brings the season to a close.

Cricket behavior lends itself to Indian summer verse. As the sounds of summer fade, the high-pitched chirps of males seeking mates briefly dominate the sonic stage. When the cool nights of autumn settle in, so too do northern field crickets and snowy tree crickets settle down for their late-year calls of love, calls that must succeed if next spring's eggs are to be laid before a killing frost wipes out all the adults. As the temperatures rise during Indian summer, the frequency of the chirps increases, making them all the more prominent. Frequently heard but rarely seen, crickets are also masterful tricksters. As Vincent Delthier notes in the beautifully written *Crickets and Katydids, Concerts and Solos*, the songs are "clearly ventriloquial, but the cricket [is] not a ventriloquist." Rather, the sound is "reflected, refracted, and absorbed by different stems, leaves, and clumps of vegetation."[49] We may hear them in one place, but they are nearly always in another. Anyone who tries to find one should expect to be fooled.

Above all, the cricket song seems imbued with Indian summer melancholy. Its sounds, Nathaniel Hawthorne suggested, amount to "audible stillness." Walk outside on any Indian summer evening and you will understand Hawthorne's point. The silence between each individual chirp divides the night into segments of stilled time. For Dickinson, such sounds assumed an especially elegiac tone, as they were sung by creatures about to die.[50]

> September's Baccalaureate
> A combination is
> Of Crickets—Crows—and Retrospects
> And a dissembling Breeze
>
> That hints without assuming
> An Innuendo sear
> That makes the Heart put up it's Fun—
> And turn Philosopher
>
> (F 1313)

Still chirping during the ninth month's "dissembling Breeze," the crickets foretell the coming cold. Their song, a duet performed with crows, "hints" that a new season nears, a time for the heart's fun to be recast in philosophical stone.

For these reasons and more, crickets have been heard in dozens of English and American poems. Their songs, however, assume a special poignancy in Dickinson's Indian summer verse. In " 'Twas later when the summer went," for instance, they hum like a "gentle Clock," producing a sound that disturbs the poet's soul. For no sooner after the cricket "went away for the year" did winter's cold come in. The "pathetic Pendulum" of this entomological timepiece, she concludes, "Keeps Esoteric Time" (F 1312). A more haunting sound informs "The murmuring of Bees, has ceased" (F

1142), a poem in which the song of the cricket (which here goes unnamed) replaces the buzzing of the bees, who have completed their year's work:

> The murmuring of Bees, has ceased
> But murmuring of some
> Posterior, prophetic
> Has simultaneous come.
> The lower metres of the Year
> When Nature's laugh is done
> The Revelations of the Book
> Whose Genesis was June.
> Appropriate Creatures to her change
> The Typic Mother sends
> As Accent fades to interval
> With separating Friends
> Till what we speculate, has been
> And thoughts we will not show
> More intimate with us become
> Than Persons, that we know.

Written at the very end of 1867, the poem starkly recalls the promises of earlier seasons. When the bees have stopped murmuring, we know we have entered the "lower metres of the Year"—an allusive phrase for the later months. But now some other murmuring can be heard, a "Posterior" sound that is "prophetic" of the days to come. At such times, the speaker suggests, Nature can only laugh at our folly. The joyful Genesis that commenced in June has been replaced by an inversion of the Book of Revelations.[51] Rather than the promised glories of heaven, the gentle sounds presage an encroaching silence that will leave us far more intimate with our thoughts and speculations than with persons "that we know."

By any measure, Dickinson's most memorable crickets appear in "Further in Summer than the Birds" (F 895), a poem she first wrote in 1865 and continued to revise throughout her career. We might quibble that the poem describes late August or early September rather than Indian summer. But its depiction of a mysterious late-year change of weather nonetheless resembles the psychological effects of the season. The poem begins as the birds depart:

> Further in Summer than the Birds –
> Pathetic from the Grass –
> A minor Nation celebrates
> It's unobtrusive Mass.

No Ordinance be seen –
So gradual from Grace
A gentle Custom it becomes –
Enlarging Loneliness –

Antiquest felt at Noon –
When August burning low
Arise this spectral Canticle
Repose to typify –

Remit as yet no Grace –
No furrow on the Glow,
But a Druidic Difference
Enhances Nature now –

Though the changes at first seem imperceptible, the altered soundscape calls the poet's attention to new sonic textures. She cannot see what has transpired, as the sun displays "No furrow on the Glow," but the insect songsters allow her to hear the change of the year. Once the departing birds announce the arrival of fall, the unseen crickets, the "minor Nation" in the grass, celebrate their "unobtrusive Mass"—an echo of the sacramental language of "These are the days when Birds come back." They do not sing a song of joy, but instead offer a "spectral Canticle" of repose. The speaker, however, finds little comfort in the song's promise; rather, the "gentle Custom" of the grassy chirp only enlarges her sense that she is now terribly alone.

Several scholars have noted that the poem moves backward in time. The early stanzas invoke the Christian mass, which in turn leads to a solemn rendition of the Canticles, a song form, which, as Cynthia Griffin Wolff points out, had been perfected in the otherwise joyous Song of Solomon.[52] By the close of the poem the speaker attains a "Druidic Difference," a state of mind named for an ancient and mysterious set of beliefs, which carries her quietly and unobtrusively beyond the conventional language of her culture.[53] The poem thus leaves the speaker in an eerie and lonely natural world, a place enhanced, paradoxically enough, by sounds produced just this side of the grave. And meanwhile, the crickets still chirp—but for how long, we do not know.

Dickinson clearly wanted people to read this poem. Between 1865 and 1883, she sent at least five versions in letters to various correspondents, including one to Thomas Niles, a Boston-based editor with whom she might have been considering publishing some of her work. And although she does not name the insect in the poem, she at least twice asked its recipients to think specifically of crickets; once in her 1883 letter to Niles, in which she referred to the work as "My Cricket," and again in a letter sent that same year to Mabel Todd, her brother's mistress. Todd, who subsequently became the poet's posthumous editor, received her copy along with a dead cricket wrapped in paper.[54] The critical attention paid to the poem corresponds with Dickinson's obvious interest in its fate. It remains one of the most frequently anthologized and analyzed poems in all of nineteenth-century American verse. And with its "unobtrusive" crickets singing an "Antiquest" song, it also brings the season to a close.

Near the end of 1884, the last year she wrote a significant number of poems, Dickinson again turned to the cricket to announce the year's demise, and with that announcement she also signaled the end of Indian summer's poetically vibrant days. It is a simple poem but revealing nonetheless, for with the silencing of the cricket everything else comes to a close.

> The Jay his Castanet has struck
> Put on your muff for Winter
> The Tippet that ignores his voice
> Is impudent to nature
> Of Swarthy Days he is the close
> His Lotus is a chestnut
> The Cricket drops a sable line
> No more from your's at present
>   (F 1670)

The poem's path from sound to silence begins with the jay's castanet, a percussive signal that winter now looms, that the "Swarthy Days" of Indian summer have come and gone. To ignore the jay now would be impudent. Meanwhile the cricket, whose chirps we expect to hear during warm days in the fall, drops a mysterious dark line: "No more from your's at present." The season has ended. The songs are done. We do not know what will happen next year. And so with the death of the crickets, Dickinson brings us to the far side of the frost. Whether conceived as "a minor Nation" in the grass or as the senders of poetic lines, their songs mark the beginning of the end.

Thoreau once remarked that November's crickets "sing the requiem of the year" (4:169). With their song gone for the winter, Indian summer landscapes quickly go quiet. Their passing marks the end of an era. We can say the same for Dickinson's passing and Indian summer. Like Thoreau's crickets, her poems were the final requiem for nineteenth-century Indian summer. Her death in May 1886—less than two years after her final poetic cricket announced "No more from your's at present"—brought the season to a fitting poetic end. Others would continue to write Indian summer poems, but never again would the full complexity of the season be so starkly and so concisely put into words.

7

Coda: Indian Summer in the Twentieth Century

With Dickinson's death in 1886 our story essentially comes to a close. By the time she died that May, some seven months short of fifty-six and still four years away from the first published collection of her poems, the season had lost its last vital connection to nineteenth-century American culture. Though it continued (and continues) to breathe life into late-year landscapes, it had, for the most part, run its artistic course. To be sure, in the century that followed, authors and artists routinely recycled Indian summer images, but their efforts were usually just that—tepid imitations that amounted to little more than cliché. As the year 1900 loomed, there seemed little more to say about a season so indelibly linked to the closing century's literature and art, as neither the sentimental nor transcendental version of the season could be expanded upon in any meaningful way. Even the Vanishing Indian, which had been a central Indian summer motif, lost its place in popular American culture, first to the Indians of late-nineteenth-century Wild West shows and then to the horseback-riding and cowboy-slaying Indians of Hollywood.

Dickinson's death, which occurred the same year that Howells fictionally solidified Indian summer's connection to wizened middle age, thus offers a compelling bookend for the history I have presented. If we identify Crevecoeur's 1778 reference as a rough approximation of the season's birth and Dickinson's passing in 1886 as an equally rough approximation for its death, we are left with a period of just over one hundred years. We might call this period the century of Indian summer.

Of course, Indian summer poetry did not follow Dickinson to the grave. Far from it. In the years just before and after the turn of the century the season remained a popular topic for versifiers, particularly those who published in genteel general-interest periodicals such as *Scribner's* and *Century Magazine*. An 1897 Indian summer poem by Martha Gilbert Dickinson, Emily's niece, offers a case in point. Published in the October issue of the *New England Magazine*, Martha Dickinson's "Indian Summer" draws on the same aftermath imagery that Emily employed in poems such as "A Field of stubble, lying sere," albeit without the masterful touch. The first two stanzas invoke a postharvest scene.

> The sun slants warm through empty fields
>   Whose crops are harvested serene,
> Where memory her echo yields
>   Of spring's quick pulse and tender green.
>
> The spurned bough reveals the path
>   Her bird has flown; as unaware
> A gentle sense of aftermath, –
>   Renunciation fills the air.

Although it is unfair to compare Martha Dickinson with her famous relative, her "Indian summer" clearly lacks her aunt's verve. It contains nothing new, as even the speaker seems to admit in the final lines.

> With chastened hopes to sober joys full grown,
>   How of like her the aged sit apart,
> Within a mellow season of their own, –
>   Sweet Indian Summer of the heart![1]

In Martha Dickinson's hands, Indian summer is a time for the tired and old.

A turn-of-the-century poem written by Dr. S. Weir Mitchell further suggests the moribund state of Indian summer verse in the years after Dickinson's death. In a 1905 poem written for the *Century Magazine*, Mitchell, the same literary-minded physician who infamously prescribed months of enforced bed rest as a cure for postpartum depression, attempted to rekindle the sentimental qualities that earlier poets had ascribed to the season. The effort, however, seems forced.

> The stillness that doth wait on change is here,
>   Some pause of expectation own the hour;
> And faint and far I hear the sea complain
>   Where gray and answerless the headlands tower.

> Slow falls the evening of the dying year,
>   Misty and dim the patient forests lie,
> Chill ocean winds the wasted woodland grieve,
>   And earthward loitering the leaves go by.[2]

Though not utterly without charm, Mitchell's poem exemplifies the overall low state of American verse at the dawn of the twentieth century, a period after the deaths of Dickinson and Whitman but before the World War One–era modernist experiments of Eliot, Pound, and Frost. Still, his poem seems unusually derivative, even for its time. Shorn from nineteenth-century sentimentalism's initial driving force, he offers lines that read like store-bought greeting cards rather than heartfelt expressions of longing or loss.

Fortunately, a few twentieth-century highlights prevented the season from fully slipping into the hackneyed realm occupied by Mitchell. The most enduring has proved to be Al Dubin and Victor Herbert's 1939 "Indian Summer," a song that became a staple of the jazz repertoire. Unlike most hit songs, on which the composer and lyricist work closely together, "Indian Summer" was over two decades in the making. Herbert's tune came from his 1919 piano piece "Indian Summer: An American Idyll." Twenty years later, Dubin, a onetime Tin Pan Alley lyricist best known for the urbane songbook he wrote for the 1934 film *Forty-Second Street*, added words to Herbert's score. The lyrics recall many of the season's conventional motifs while presenting the bittersweet aftermath of a love affair gone awry:

> Summer, you old Indian Summer
> You're the dream that comes after June time's laughter
> You see so many dreams that don't come true
> Dreams we fashioned when summertime was new
> You are here to watch over
> Some heart that is broken
> By a word that some left unspoken
> You're the ghost of a romance in June
> Going astray, fading too soon
> That's why I say
> "Farewell to you, Indian Summer!"[3]

As several singers soon discovered, Dubin's words roll off the tongue with an ease any tunesmith would admire. And after Tommy Dorsey scored a number one hit with the song in December 1939—with Jack Leonard on vocals—the tune itself became a much recorded instrumental standard.

Over the next thirty years musicians as diverse as Count Basie, Sidney Bechet, Coleman Hawkins, and Stan Getz improvised to Herbert's gently swinging tune, a tune made easy to remember by Dubin's lyrics.

Without question, Frank Sinatra and Duke Ellington recorded the most compelling version of the song during their December 1967 collaboration, the only occasion the two masters worked together. Overall, the session produced a rather mediocre album, but the version of "Indian Summer"— recorded on the singer's fifty-second birthday—reveals Sinatra at the top of his form. More than one critic has called it a masterpiece. Indeed, Nelson Riddle, the singer's longtime arranger (a job here taken by Billy May), once claimed it was his favorite Sinatra arrangement, calling it the "only chart he wished he had written."[4] Part of Sinatra's genius lay in his ability to make even the most mundane lyrics sound like the most powerful words ever uttered, a trait fully on display for "Indian Summer." With Sinatra at the mike, one feels the loneliness of regret, especially as he reaches for the high notes to mournfully proclaim, "You're the ghost of a romance in June," only to then return to the low tenor to trace that ghost "Going astray, fading too soon." The slow, mature evocation of loss grows stronger still when Johnny Hodges, the heart and soul of Ellington's horns, blows a light bluesy solo on the alto sax. It is a stunning performance, one worthy of the many accolades it has received.[5] In such hands, Indian summer seems the most genuinely sad time of the year.

In her 1956 best-selling novel *Peyton Place*, Grace Metalious replaced Sinatra's ache with a foreboding season looming just below New England's contented sense of itself. As I mentioned in the introduction, the novel opens with a startling line: "Indian summer is like a woman. Ripe, hotly passionate, but fickle, she comes and goes as she pleases so that one is never sure whether she will come at all, nor for how long she will stay."[6] As the novel's many readers instantly recognized, Metalious unmasks the dirty secrets of small-town New England. Though pleasantly situated, Peyton Place is not a pleasant town to live in, particularly for Selena Cross, the young woman who must endure the violence of her stepfather's assaults. But it was not just the incestuous sexual violence that made this novel seem so salacious. As Ardis Cameron notes, *Peyton Place* most unnerved proper readers for its frank depiction of female sexual agency. Much to the shock of Eishenower-era Americans, Metalious "positioned women at the center of sexual relations, politicizing both the female body and attempts to control it."[7] Indian summer contributed to this celebration of the female erotic. "Like a laughing, lovely woman," Metalious writes in the novel's second paragraph, the season "came and spread herself over the countryside and made everything hurtfully beautiful to the eye." Such a statement brings us to an imaginative realm that would have made the fastidious Thoreau shiver. At once voluptuous and dangerous, Metalious's version of Indian summer draws equally from the wells of beauty and pain.

Metalious added a new wrinkle to the old notion of Indian summer deceit. Like Dickinson, she understood that the season's darker possibilities remained hidden to those too easily blinded by "the second sun." Peyton Place's older residents "know sorrowfully that Indian summer is a sham to be met with hard-eyed cynicism." It promises continued life only to take it away. But whereas Dickinson seemed intent simply to uncover the seasonal fraud, Metalious invokes its trickery to reveal the "ripe, passionate energies" that lurk within her fictional town.[8] Never coquettish, her version of the season acts with all the wiles at her (and Metalious deliberately employs the feminine) disposal. Metalious's Indian summer opening, then, signals the start of the refreshing fidelity that so many 1950s American readers found enthralling in the novel. Indian summer is not the true deceiver in either Peyton Place or *Peyton Place*. Rather, the lies are told by those who would believe that such towns could ever be truly idyllic in the first place. Indeed, the presence of lecherous stepfathers, patricidal daughters, and secret abortions renders this fictional village the polar opposite of the equally fictional stable towns so essential to the New England ideal. And so when Indian Summer erotically presents herself to the northern New England town of Peyton Place, the secrets of the town begin to ooze out.

Toward the end of the twentieth century some of America's better poets managed to keep Indian summer imagery usefully alive, although even here they mined poetic territory that others had previously explored.[9] My favorite is Maxine Kumin's 1992 "Indian Summer," a poem that begins with the year's "last grasshoppers taxiing / like wingless aircraft down some eternal runway." Like Dickinson before her, Kumin finds the departure of insects just after the season's warmth to be eerily disquieting. In the third stanza the speaker describes watching her brother sleep after they have returned from a grievous family ordeal:

> We have come back from burying a sister.
> He is not given to my several panics.
> When he drove too fast swerving across the
> clacking lane dividers to take advantage of
> an illusory gap in the highway's steady flow,
> I gasped. He was oblivious to my terror.

With Kumin we see and hear once again the deep-seated isolation presented by Dickinson. As the speaker watches her brother this Indian summer afternoon, the two siblings do not speak. She braces herself by thinking "of the house of our childhood."[10] Like Dickinson, Kumin senses the season's lonely tugs of regrets, the beautiful but isolating frames that the late-year sunlight and warmth construct.

Though its heyday was clearly in the nineteenth century, we do not have to look far to find twentieth-century constructions of Indian summer. Rock singers, poets, and novelists all have found creative energy in the season's elegiac qualities. Likewise, nearly every part of the country hosts an Indian summer festival in the fall, usually by bringing together musical groups and artists to help celebrate the end of the local harvest. Native Americans have also found the season's name an appropriate title for cultural festivals.[11]

Despite its continued popularity, an ever increasing conceptual looseness marks most twentieth-century literary and artistic gestures toward the season. It can mean all things to all people, even more so than it did in the nineteenth century. Indeed, there always loomed the possibility that Indian summer terminology could be used for just about anything, especially once advertisers figured out how to market Indian summer products. Perhaps the preeminent example of this looseness is the "Indian Summer" fragrance currently hawked on the Internet by Priscilla Presley, Elvis's widow. According to the company website, Indian Summer perfume "is for the one who loves what is original and natural," who "breathes the golden light of the Indian Summer sun." Such slogans are designed to appeal to virtually anyone, and indeed I suspect few potential purchasers of this or any other perfume—a distinctly nonnatural substance—would ever admit to *not* loving what is original and natural. The banality of the campaign becomes even more clear when the website designers specifically identify the target group for Indian Summer perfume as "Women who are down to earth, know what they want, look for balance between family, profession, friends, and ego, are quality and price conscious, enjoy life, are attracted to nature *and have an affinity to Priscilla Presley*" (emphasis added).[12] I'm not sure if this final qualifier broadens or restricts the fragrance's appeal. I am sure, however, that a perfume that marketers target for fans of Elvis's widow takes us a long way from the sacrificial language of Dickinson and the transcendental musings of Thoreau.

New England, too, has seen its Indian summer become a marketer's dream, particularly in the tourist trade. As I mentioned in chapter 2, early-nineteenth-century gazetteers often extended the duration of Indian summer to a period lasting six weeks, a seemingly endless interlude for travelers in search of scenery. Today, Internet websites promote the region with similar appeals to the season's beauty. One German site, for example, entices would-be visitors to Vermont by calling Indian summer the "high point of the year" for which reservations must be made in a timely manner.[13] On this and other similar sites, gorgeous images of New England scenery beckon tourists to come to the region during Indian summer. The technology may have changed since the days of the nineteenth-century gazetteers, but the message remains the same: New England's Indian summer can make tourists of us all.

I do not want to suggest, however, that either Priscilla Presley's perfume or the touristic Indian summer represent a fall from the true version of the season. As I have suggested throughout this book, there never has been a true Indian summer. Virtually from the moment the term entered the American vernacular it functioned as a seasonal Rorschach test. Commentators stared at the sudden beauty and saw in it what they were prepared to see. Some found sentiment, some lamented Indians, while still others saw a way to make a buck. One could make of it what one wished.

And yet, I am not entirely satisfied with such an explanation, as it risks obscuring the obvious beauty of Indian summer beneath layers of cultural analysis. To be sure, Indian summer has always functioned as a constructed time of year, as a collection of metaphors that could be applied to several aspects of American life. In saying this, however, we risk losing sight of the glorious immediacy of an Indian summer afternoon. Try as I may to understand how and why the season assumed the meanings that it did, I must initially confront the beauty that naturally presents itself on the first Indian summer days in the fall.

Such beauty arrives every year on the urban campus where I teach in Boston, when on a perfect Indian summer day students and faculty alike can barely collect their things before they sprint out of class. To stay indoors on such a day seems a sin. If I am lucky enough to be in a less developed section of New England, the same primeval urge to slough off my professional concerns and wallow in the present takes hold. I come to understand completely the momentary reverie Thoreau enjoyed when he briefly broke from his surveying one Indian summer day in 1851. The faces at farm stands, in village squares, and on hilly paths all confirm the central paradox I discovered while writing this book: To write about Indian summer during an Indian summer spell is well-nigh impossible. We must take notes and then write during other times of the year. And so, on this spring afternoon I recall in my mind's eye the warm light and anxious joy of my wedding day, a day that sent me down my Indian summer path. On an Indian summer day one might stay inside to write about the season's constructed cultural history. But to be outside is the most natural thing in the world.

Notes

Introduction (pp. 1–10)

1. Lawrence Buell, *The Environmental Imagination: Thoreau, Nature Writing, and the Formation of American Culture* (Cambridge, Mass.: Belknap Press of Harvard University Press, 1995), 228.

2. Arden Reed, *Romantic Weather: The Climates of Coleridge and Baudelaire* (Hanover, N.H.: University Press of New England, 1983), 14. My understanding of the "logos of meteors" in this and subsequent chapters owes much to Reed's work. See especially pp. 3–77.

3. I am grateful to Barry Keim, the New Hampshire state meteorologist and a professor of meteorology at the University of New Hampshire, for explaining this process to me over the phone and through several email exchanges. For a well-written account of Indian summer weather see David Ludlum, *The American Weather Book* (Boston: Houghton Mifflin, 1982), 228–29.

4. Albert Matthews first pointed out this historical anomaly in a remarkable two-part 1902 article, "The Term Indian Summer," *Monthly Weather Review* 30 (January 1902), 19–28, and (February 1902), 69–78.

5. Grace Metalious, *Peyton Place* (Boston: Northeastern University Press, 1999), 1.

6. Sarah Whitman, "A Day of the Indian Summer," in *The Rhode-Island Book: Selections in Prose and Verse, from the Writings of Rhode Island Citizens* (Providence, 1841), 142.

7. Philip Booth, "Vermont: Indian Summer," in *Relations: New and Selected Poems* (New York: Viking Press, 1986), 7. Special thanks to the poet for granting me permission to quote from his poem.

8. The number included here and elsewhere in this study refers to the numbers assigned by R. W. Franklin in his 1998 edition of *Dickinson's Poems* (Cambridge,

Mass.: Belknap Press of Harvard University Press, 1998). Franklin's numbers differ slightly from the Johnson numbers, which had been standard since the late 1950s.

9. Donald Hall, *Seasons at Eagle Pond* (New York: Ticknor and Fields, 1987), 86.

10. Henry David Thoreau, *Journal*, vol. 5, Patrick F. O'Connell, ed. (Princeton, N.J.: Princeton University Press, 1997), 400. Princeton University Press is currently reissuing definitive versions of Thoreau's *Journal* to replace the edition issued at the beginning of the twentieth century. The project is ongoing. I use Arabic numbers to distinguish the Princeton volumes from the older version, which carry Roman numerals. My preference throughout this study is for the modern edition.

11. Ralph Waldo Emerson, "Nature," in *Essays: Second Series, Collected Works of Ralph Waldo Emerson*, Alfred R. Ferguson and Jean Ferguson Carr, eds. (Cambridge, Mass.: Belknap Press of Harvard University Press, 1983), 99.

12. Henry David Thoreau, *Journal* IX (Boston: Houghton Mifflin, 1906), 108.

13. *Glossary of Weather and Climate, with Related Oceanic and Hydraulic Terms*, Ira W. Greer, ed. (Boston: American Meteorological Society, 1996), 122.

14. Flagg discusses Indian summer and frost in *The Woods and By-Ways of New England* (Boston, 1872), 319. Thoreau was quite loose with his definition of Indian summer. He records Indian summer weather throughout the fall, both before and after killing frosts.

15. Henry David Thoreau, "Autumnal Tints," in *The Natural History Essays* (Salt Lake City: Peregrine Smith Books, 1980), 138.

16. Emerson, *Works*, vol. 1, Alfred R. Ferguson, ed. (Cambridge, Mass.: Belknap Press of Harvard University Press, 1971), 19.

17. Matthews, "The Term Indian Summer."

1. The Birth of a Season (pp. 11–28)

1. Thoreau, *Journal* VI (Boston: Houghton Mifflin, 1906), 85.

2. Pliny the Elder, *Natural History*, Book II (Cambridge, Mass.: Harvard University Press, 1958), 265.

3. For St. Demetrius' feast see George A. Megas, *Greek Calendar Customs* (Athens, Greece: Press and Information Department, Prime Minister's Office, 1958), 19. I am grateful to my colleague Wendy Larson for alerting me to this citation. References to other Indian summer precursors can be found in several books of weather proverbs. George Lyman Kittridge discusses them all in *The Old Farmer and His Almanac* (Boston: William Ware, 1904), 190–99.

4. *Poetical Works of John Greenleaf Whittier* (Boston, 1888), 420.

5. *Henry VI, Part One* (I, ii, 131); *Henry IV, Part One* (I, ii, 171–72). Kittridge discusses these Shakespearean references in *The Old Farmer and His Almanac*, 193–

94. Kittridge also mentions the "Old Woman's Summer" of Russian, German, and Dutch folklore.

6. Albert Matthews, "The Term Indian Summer," *Monthly Weather Review* 30 (January 1902), 19–21.

7. Petr Kalm, *Travels in North America*, vol. 1 (New York: Dover Press, 1937), 619.

8. See the on-line version of the *Oxford English Dictionary* at http://dictionary.oed.com.

9. Hector St. John de Crevecoeur, "A Snow Storm as it affects the American Farmer," in *Sketches of Eighteenth-Century America*, Ralph H. Gabriel and Stanley T. Williams, eds. (New York: Benjamin Bloom, 1972), 41. I have selected this translation because it is the easiest to read. For a more accurate version that leaves Crevecoeur's odd spelling and rough English syntax in place, see *More Letters of an American Farmer*, Dennis D. Moore, ed. (Athens: University of Georgia Press, 1995), 143.

10. Moore discusses the publishing history of the several essays not included in the original *Letters of an American Farmer* in the introduction to *More Letters of an American Farmer*.

11. Harmar's journal quoted in Josiah Morrow, "Indian Summer," *Monthly Weather Review* 39 (March 1911), 469. For Harmar's campaign see Andrew R. L. Clayton, *Frontier Indiana* (Bloomington: Indiana University Press, 1996), 98–138.

12. Ebenezer Denny, *The Military Journal of Ebenezer Denny* (Philadelphia, 1860), 402.

13. Alan Nevins discusses the rise of British writing about America in *America Through British Eyes* (New York: Oxford University Press, 1948), 4–14.

14. Henry Bradshaw Fearon, *Sketches of America: A Narrative of a Journal of Five Thousand Miles Through the Eastern and Western States of America*, reprinted in *Early Western Travels, 1748–1846*, vol. 12, Rebuen Gold Thwaites, ed. (Cleveland: Arthur H. Clark, 1904), 369.

15. Quoted in Matthews, "The Term Indian Summer," 23, 24. The veracity of Ashe's account was questioned almost as soon as it was published. See Francis H. Herrick, "Thomas Ashe and the Authenticity of His Travels in America," *Mississippi Valley Historical Review* 13 (June 1926), 50–57.

16. William Faux, *Memorable Days* (1823), reprinted in *Early Western Travels*, Thwaites, ed., 1:223–24.

17. Henry B. Wonham, "In the Name of Wonder: The Emergence of Tall Narrative in American Writing," *American Quarterly* 41 (June 1989), 288.

18. James Kirke Paulding, *John Bull in America; or, The New Munchhausen* (New York, 1825), 128, 129. For Paulding's role in the paper wars, see Larry J. Reynolds, *James Kirke Paulding* (Boston, Twayne Publishing, 1979), 61.

19. Kalm, *Travels in North America*, 1:276–77. The literature on eighteenth-

century concern about climate and health is extensive. See especially Karen Ordahl Kupperman, "Fear of Hot Climates in the Anglo-American Colonial Experience," *William and Mary Quarterly*, 3rd series, 41 (1984), 213–40; and Gilbert Chinard, "Eighteenth-Century Theories on America as a Human Habitat," *Proceedings of the American Philosophical Society* 91 (1947), 27–57.

20. John Beale Davidge, *A Treatise on the Autumnal Endemial Epidemick of Tropical Climates* (Baltimore, 1798), 1.

21. William Priest, *Travels in the United States* (1802), quoted in Matthews, "The Term Indian Summer," 22. For a history of yellow fever in Philadelphia see J. M. Powell, *Bring out Your Dead: The Great Plague of Yellow Fever in Philadelphia in 1793*, 1949 (Philadelphia: University of Pennsylvania Press, 1993).

22. Eleanor R. Long, "How the Dog Got Its Days: A Skeptical Inquiry into Traditional Star and Weather Lore," *Western Folklore* 43 (October 1984), 256–64.

23. Mason Cogswell, "Sketch of the History of the Weather and Disease at Hartford, During the Winter and Spring of 1798, *Medical Repository* ii (1798), 299; Shadrach Ricketson, "Observations on the Weather and Diseases in the Autumn of 1808, in the City of New York," *Medical Repository* 6, second hexade (1809), 187. Matthews quotes both Cogswell and Ricketson in "The Term Indian Summer," 22–23. For Cogswell's role in the history of early American journalism, see James H. Cassedy, "The Flourishing Character of Early American Medical Journalism, 1797–1860," *Journal of the History of Medicine and Allied Sciences* 38 (April 1983), 135–50.

24. Daniel Drake, *Natural History and Statistical View; or, Picture of Cincinnati* (Cincinnati, 1818), 110. For Drake's several contributions to the development of western American medicine see *Physician to the West: Selected Writings of Daniel Drake on Science and Society*, Zane L. Miller and Henry D. Shapiro, eds. (Lexington: University of Kentucky Press, 1970). The preface provides a concise overview of Drake's efforts to explain the western climate both to Americans on the eastern seaboard and to Europeans.

25. Frances Trollope, *Domestic Manners of the Americans* (London: George Routledge and Sons, 1927), 264–65.

26. Quoted in the introduction to *Early Western Travels*, Thwaites, ed., 11:14.

27. Adlard Welby, *A Visit to North America and the English Settlements in Illinois, with a Winter Residence in Philadelphia*, in *Early Western Travels*, Thwaites, ed., 12: 271.

28. Quoted in Matthews, "The Term Indian Summer," 26.

29. John Bradbury, *Travels in the Interior of America in the Years 1809, 1810, and 1811, Including a Description of Upper Louisiana, Together with the States of Ohio, Kentucky, Indiana, and Tennessee, with Illinois and Western Territories, and Containing Remarks and Observations Useful to Persons Emigrating to Those Countries*, reprinted in *Early Western Travels*, Thwaites, ed., 5:254. For biographical information concerning Bradbury see Rodney H. True, "A Sketch of the Life of John Bradbury,

Including His Unpublished Correspondence with Thomas Jefferson," *Proceedings of the American Philosophical Society* 68 (1929), 133–50.

30. *Journal*, XI:230.

31. Gregory H. Nobles, "Breaking into the Backcountry: New Approaches to the Early American Frontier," *William and Mary Quarterly*, 3rd series, 46 (October 1989), 649.

32. Susan Fenimore Cooper, *Rural Hours* (Syracuse, N.Y.: Syracuse University Press, 1968), 229.

33. Cooper, *Rural Hours*, 228. For Cropsey in England, see *Art Journal* (September 1857), 173, and the Newington-Cropsey Foundation Object Research File. Other passages in this paragraph are quoted in Matthews, "The Term Indian Summer," 27, 73.

2. Science and Sentiment (pp. 29–48)

1. Ralph Waldo Emerson, "Circles," in *Selections from Ralph Waldo Emerson*, Stephen E. Whicher, ed. (Boston: Houghton Mifflin, 1960), 172.

2. Marjorie Hope Nicholson, *Mountain Gloom and Mountain Glory: The Development of the Aesthetics of the Infinite* (Ithaca, N.Y.: Cornell University Press, 1959), 49–50.

3. Stephen J. Pyne, *How the Canyon Became Grand* (New York: Viking, 1998), 1–30.

4. For a thorough discussion of the complex overlap of nature and culture in New England see Kent C. Ryden, *Landscape with Figures: Nature and Culture in New England* (Iowa City: University of Iowa Press, 2001). Ryden's final chapter is especially relevant to this paragraph.

5. Stephen Nissenbaum, *The Battle for Christmas* (New York: Alfred A. Knopf, 1997), 49–85.

6. Elizabeth Peck, "The Making of the Domestic Occasion: The History of Thanksgiving in the United States," *Journal of Social History* 32 (1998–99), 773–89.

7. Hobsbawm discusses invented traditions in the introduction to *The Invention of Tradition*, Eric Hobsbawm and Terrence Ranger, eds. (Cambridge: Cambridge University Press, 1983). For kilt wearing see Hugh Trevor-Roper, "The Invention of Tradition: The Highland Tradition in Scotland," 13–41 in the same volume.

8. Gene Bluestein, *Poplore* (Amherst: University of Massachusetts Press, 1994), 8.

9. H. G Spafford, *Gazetteer of the State of New York* (New York, 1813) 14; John Farmer and Jacob Moore, *Gazetteer of the State of New Hampshire* (Concord, N.H., 1823), 9. Albert Matthews quotes these two gazetteers in "The Term Indian Summer," *Monthly Weather Review* 30 (January 1902), 24, 27. For the rise of tourism see Dona Brown, *Inventing New England: Regional Tourism in the Nineteenth Cen-*

tury (Washington, D.C.: Smithsonian Institution Press, 1995). Chapters 1 and 2 are particularly relevant for my discussion of Indian summer.

10. Alexander Wilson, "The Foresters: A Description of a Pedestrian Journey to the Falls of Niagara," in *The Poems and Literary Prose of Alexander Wilson* (Philadelphia, 1876), 113.

11. Mary W. Bowden discusses the conventional aspects of Freneau's seasonal poetry in *Philip Freneau* (Boston: Twayne Publishing, 1976), 145.

12. Philip Freneau, "The Seasons Moralized," in *The Poems of Philip Freneau* vol. 2 (Princeton, N.J.: Princeton Historical Society, 1902), 282, and "October's Address" vol. 3 (1907), 273. "October's Address" appeared in an 1815 collection of Freneau's work that included poems written between 1797 and 1815. Lewis Leary suggests that most of the poems in the collection were previously unpublished and that Freneau brought them to the public for the first time in 1815. See Leary's introduction to Freneau's *A Collection of Poems on American Affairs, and a Variety of Other Subjects, Chiefly Moral and Political* (New York: Scholars' Facsimiles Reprints, 1976), v.

13. Robert Ferguson discusses the roots of this tradition in *Law and Letters in American Culture* (Cambridge, Mass.: Harvard University Press, 1984), 199–205.

14. John Greenleaf Whittier, *The Literary Remains of John G. C. Brainard* (Hartford, 1832), 14, 20. For biographical information see Evert A. and George L. Duyckinck, *The Cyclopedia of American Literature*, vol. 1 (Philadelphia, 1880), 966–97.

15. *Poems of John Brainard* (Hartford, 1841), 97–98.

16. William Thompson Bacon, *Poems* (Boston, 1837), 67.

17. A large number of Indian summer poems appeared in magazines during the 1830s and 1840s. Those mentioned in this paragraph can be found in *Arthur's Magazine* 1 (November 1844), 219; *The Corsair* 1 (October 12, 1839), 497; *Michigan Farmer and Western Agriculturalist* 7 (December 1, 1849), 363; *Zodiac* 1 (1835), 69; and *Selections from the American Poets, by William Cullen Bryant* (New York, 1860), 102.

18. Ronald J. Zboray, "Antebellum Reading and the Ironies of Technological Innovation," *American Quarterly* 40 (1988), 76. Zborary's article discusses the cultural implications of the industrialization of printing in detail. See especially pp. 71–74 for the impact of new technologies. A less probing but still useful analysis can also be found in Helmut Lehman-Haupt, *The Book in America: A History of the Making and Selling of Books in the United States* (New York: R. R. Bowker, 1952), 77–78.

19. *Harper's New Monthly Magazine* 7 (1853), 842.

20. James Dixon, "Indian Summer," in *Poets of Connecticut* (New York, 1864), 437.

21. "Indian Summer," in *Lucy Larcom's Poems* (Boston, 1868), 46. The poem first appeared in an 1857 edition of the antislavery newspaper the *National Era*.

22. Dixon, "Indian Summer," 437. Barbara Rotundo discusses the rural ceme-

tery movement in "Mount Auburn: Fortunate Coincidences and an Ideal Solution," *Journal of Garden History* 4 (July–September 1984), 255–66.

23. Lawrence Buell discusses the implications of the neoclassical legacy in early American Romantic poetry in *New England Literary Culture, from Revolution to Renaissance* (Cambridge: Cambridge University Press, 1986), 283–85.

24. The earliest almanac reference to Indian summer that I have seen is in *Cramer's Pittsburgh Alamanack, for 1812* (Pittsburgh, 1811), 15.

25. Indian summer poems can be found in *The New England Farmer* 18 (October 31, 1838), 136; *New England Farmer* 19 (October 30, 1839), 124; *Farmer's Cabinet and American Herd-Book* 9 (October 1844), 314–15; *Michigan Farmer and Western Agriculturist* 7 (December 1, 1849), 363; and the *Boston Cultivator* 11 (November 2, 1840), 4. For the importance of agricultural journals, see Tamara Plakins Thornton, *Cultivating Gentleman: The Meaning of Country Life Among the Boston Elite, 1785–1860* (New Haven, Conn.: Yale University Press, 1989).

26. Arden Reed, *Romantic Weather: The Climates of Coleridge and Baudelaire* (Hanover, N.H.: University Press of New England, 1983), 1–14.

27. William Tudor, *Letter on the Eastern States* (Boston, 1821), 312; *United States Magazine and Democratic Review* 3 (1838), 154; Henry David Thoreau, *Journal* XII (Boston: Houghton Mifflin, 1906), 449. Matthews includes the references to Tudor and the *Democratic Review* in "The Term Indian Summer," 24.

28. Washington Irving, "A Tour of the Prairies," in *The Crayon Miscellany*, Dalhai Kirby Terrell, ed. (Boston: Twayne Publishing, 1979), 61.

29. Shepard Kreech III, *The Ecological Indian: Myth and History* (New York: W. W. Norton, 1999), 112–13. See also William Cronon, *Changes in the Land: Indians, Colonists, and the Ecology of New England* (New York: Hill and Wang, 1983), 47–51.

30. Zadock Thompson, "Smoky Atmosphere and Indian Summer," *Green Mountain Repository* 1 (October 1831), 217. Thompson repeated this same theory in his *Natural History of Vermont* (Burlington, 1842). For the role of aerosols see Peter J. Marchand, *Autumn: A Season of Change* (Hanover, N.H.: University Press of New England, 2000), 125.

31. Nathaniel Hawthorne, "Snow-flakes," in *Twice-Told Tales* (Columbus: Ohio State University Press, 1974), 343.

32. Samuel Taylor Coleridge, "Frost at Midnight," in *Oxford Authors: Samuel Taylor Coleridge* (Oxford: Oxford University Press, 1985), 87.

33. *Knickerbocker* 46 (December 1855).

34. William Talbot, "*Indian Summer* by Jasper F. Cropsey," *Bulletin of the Detroit Institute of Art* 58 (1980), 151–52.

35. Jasper Cropsey, "Up Among the Clouds," *The Crayon* 2 (August 8, 1855), 79.

36. See the *American Journal of Science and Arts* 18 (July 1830), 66; 27 (1834–35), 140–147; 30 (1836), 8–13. For Silliman's important role in the development of American science journalism see John F. Fulton and Elizabeth Thomson, *Benjamin*

Silliman: Pathfinder in American Science (New York: Henry Schuman, 1947), 117–29.

37. "Remarks on Indian Summers," *American Journal of Science and Arts* 30 (1836), 8–13.

38. Laura Dassow Walls, "Textbooks and Texts from the Brooks: Inventing Scientific Authority in America," *American Quarterly* 49 (March 1997), 1–5.

39. Wilson Flagg, *Studies in the Field and Forest* (Boston, 1857), 285–86; *The Woods and By-Ways of New England* (Boston, 1872), 316.

40. Flagg, *Studies in the Field and Forest*, 289.

41. Nathaniel Hawthorne, *The Scarlet Letter* (Boston: Riverside Edition, 1960), 34.

3. Fighting Words (pp. 49–72)

1. Henry David Thoreau, *Journal*, vol. 2, Robert Sattelmeyer, ed. (Princeton:, N.J.: Princeton University Press, 1984) 38.

2. Michael Rogin, *Fathers and Children: Andrew Jackson and the Subjugation of the American Indian* (New York: Alfred A. Knopf, 1975), 4.

3. Henry David Thoreau, *The Maine Woods* (Boston: Houghton Mifflin, 1906), 151.

4. H. L. Mencken, *The American Language Supplement* 1 (New York: Alfred A. Knopf, 1945), 181.

5. William Tudor, "An Address Delivered to the Phi Beta Kappa Society," *North American Review* 2 (1815), 15.

6. The best modern treatment of this dynamic is in Robert K. Berkhofer, Jr.s', *The White Man's Indian: Images of the American Indian from Columbus to the Present* (New York: Alfred A. Knopf, 1978), 90–91. Roy Harvey Pearce's work on this subject remains invaluable. See *Savagism and Civilization: A Study of the Indian and the American Mind* (Baltimore: The Johns Hopkins University Press, 1965), 72–88.

7. James Fenimore Cooper, *The Last of the Mohicans* (New York: Signet Classics, 1962), 415.

8. Caroline L. Karcher, introduction to Child's *Hobomok and Other Writings on Indians* (New Brunswick, N.J.: Rutgers University Press, 1986), xxii. The previous two paragraphs draw on chapter 1 of Karcher's biography of Child, *The First Woman in the Republic: A Cultural Biography of Lydia Maria Child* (Durham, N.C.: Duke University Press, 1994). See especially pp. 19–37.

9. C. F. Volney, *A View of the Soil and Climates of the United States of America*, C. B. Brown, trans. (Philadelphia, 1804), 210; Zadock Thompson, *A Natural History of Vermont* (Burlington, 1842), 16. Albert Matthews mentions both Volney and

Thompson in "The Term Indian Summer," *Monthly Weather Review* 30 (January 1902), 20, 26.

10. William Cronon, *Changes in the Land: Indians, Colonists, and the Ecology of New England* (New York: Hill and Wang, 1983), 45. Cronon draws on research indicating that Squanto probably learned how to fertilize with fish while held captive in England prior to the arrival of the Pilgrims.

11. "Essay on the Indian Summers," *American Journal of Science and Arts*, 27 (1834–35), 140.

12. *Harper's* editor George Curtis recalls Webster making such claims in *Harper's Magazine* 30 (December 1864), 124–25.

13. Matthews dismisses the contentions of Thompson and Brown along these lines in "The Term Indian Summer," 76.

14. Reprinted in Samuel Kercheval's *History of the Valley of Virginia*, 1833 (Strasburg, Va., 1973), 211. Kercheval's reprint has become the standard edition of Doddridge's history.

15. Patrick M. Malone, *The Skulking Way of War: Technology and Tactics Among the New England Indians* (Baltimore: The Johns Hopkins University Press, 1991), 26–27.

16. Quoted in *Early American Proverbs and Proverbial Phrases*, Bartlett Jere Whiting, ed. (Cambridge, Mass.: Belknap Press of Harvard University Press, 1977), 233. For discussion of the origin of "Indian giving" see Wilbur R. Jacobs, *Wilderness Politics and Indian Gifts: The Northern Colonial Frontier, 1748–1763* (Lincoln: University of Nebraska Press, 1950), 11–18; and Richard White, *The Middle Ground: Indians, Empires, and Republics in the Great Lakes Region, 1650–1815* (New York: Cambridge University Press, 1991), 94–104. I am grateful to Professor Colin Calloway of Dartmouth College for pointing out the role of gift giving in native culture.

17. Daniel J. Boorstin, *The Americans: The Colonial Experience* (New York: Random House, 1958), 342.

18. Daniel K. Richter, *Facing East from Indian Country: A Native History of Early America* (Cambridge, Mass.: Harvard University Press, 2001), 184–236. See also Michael N. McConnell, *A Country Between: The Upper Ohio Valley and Its Peoples, 1724–1774* (Lincoln: University of Nebraska Press, 1992), 238–54.

19. Elizabeth A. Perkins, *Border Life: Experience and Memory in the Revolutionary Ohio Valley* (Chapel Hill: University of North Carolina Press, 1998), 156, 159.

20. Jill Lepore, *The Name of War: King Philip's War and the Origins of American Identity* (New York: Alfred A. Knopf, 1998), 191–226. See also Donna K. Akers, "Removing the Heart of the Choctaw People: Indian Removal from a Native Perspective," *American Indian Culture and Research Journal* 23 (1999), 63–76.

21. Lepore, *The Name of War*, 193.

22. James Freeman, *Sermons on Particular Occasions* (Boston, 1821), 174–179. See also Matthews, "The Term Indian Summer" (February 1902), 73.

23. *American Journal of Science and Arts*, 27 (1834–35), 140; George Ticknor, *The Life of William Prescott* (Boston, 1864), 380. These references appear in Matthews, "The Term Indian Summer."

24. Roger Williams, *A Key to the Language of America*, 1643 (Providence: Rhode Island and Providence Plantation Tercentenary Commission, 1936). For Cautantowwit's place in Narraganset culture see William Scranton Simmons, *Cautantowwit's House: An Indian Burial Ground on the Island of Conanicut in Narragansett Bay* (Providence: Brown University Press, 1970), and *Spirit of the New England Tribes* (Hanover, N.H.: University Press of New England, 1986), 38–39. For the absence of pre-Freeman references to Cautantowwit and Indian summer, see Matthews, "The Term Indian Summer," 36–37.

25. Frank G. Speck, "Penobscot Tales and Religious Beliefs," *The Journal of American Folk-Lore* 48 (January–March 1935), 1, 22, 95–96. I am grateful to Joseph Bruchac for alerting me to Speck's work and for the time he spent answering my questions on the phone.

26. Joseph Bruchac, "How Indian Summer Came to Be," in *The Faithful Hunter: Abenaki Stories* (Greenfield Center, N.Y.: Greenfield Review Press, 1988), 59, 61.

27. William M. Clements, "Schoolcraft as Textmaker," *Journal of American Folklore* 103 (1990), 177. Richard G. Bremer summarizes criticisms to Schoolcraft's methodologies in *Indian Agent and Wilderness Scholar: The Life of Henry Rowe Schoolcraft* (Mount Pleasant, Mich.: Central Michigan University, 1987), 250–51. Biographical information concerning Schoolcraft is from Bremer.

28. Henry Rowe Schoolcraft, *Algic Researches: Comprising Inquiries Respecting the Mental Characteristics of the North American Indians* (New York, 1839), 214–215. See also Matthews, "The Term Indian Summer," 76.

29. *Ojibwa Narratives of Charles and Charlotte Kawbawgam and Jacques LePique, 1883–1895*, compiled by Homer H. Kidder, Arthur P. Bourgeois, ed. (Detroit: Wayne State University Press, 1994), 31.

30. Peter Jones, *History of the Ojibway Indians* (London, 1861), 35. Matthews dismisses Jones, unfairly I believe, for writing only to white readers. "The Term Indian Summer," 77.

31. Robert E. Bieder discusses Schoolcraft's views of Indian psychology in "Anthropology and the History of the American Indian," *American Quarterly* 33 (1981), 309–26, and "The Representations of Indian Bodies in Nineteenth-Century Anthropology," *American Indian Quarterly* 20 (1996), 165–179.

32. Donald B. Smith, *Sacred Feathers: The Reverend Peter Jones (Kahkewaquonaby) and the Mississauga Indians* (Lincoln: University of Nebraska Press, 1987), 249. For an especially strong critique of Jones see Gerald Vizenor, *The People Named*

the Chippewa: Narrative Histories (Minneapolis: University of Minnesota Press, 1984), 72.

33. Donald L. Fixico discusses these questions in "Ethics in Writing American Indian History," in *Natives and Academics: Research and Writing About American Indians* (Lincoln: University of Nebraska Press, 1998), 84–89. See also Barry O'Connell's introduction to William Apess's *On Our Own Ground: The Complete Writings of William Apess, a Pequot* (Amherst: University of Massachusetts Press, 1992), xl–xli.

34. Brian Dipple, *The Vanishing American: White Attitudes and U.S. Indian Policy* (Middletown, Conn.: Wesleyan University Press, 1982), 12–31.

35. Quoted in Ila Weiss, *Poetic Landscape: The Art and Experience of Sanford Gifford* (Newark: University of Delaware Press, 1987), 91. Weiss discusses Gifford's several Indian summer scenes on pp. 221–23.

36. William Cullen Bryant, *Poems*, vol. 1 (New York, 1854), 119, 122, 123. Dipple discusses the naturalizing of Indian decline in *The Vanishing American*, 9–10.

37. *Life of Henry Wadsworth Longfellow*, vol. 2, Samuel Longfellow, ed. (Boston, 1886), 250–251.

38. Newton Arvin, *Longfellow: His Life and Work* (Boston: Little Brown, 1962), 136–72.

39. Henry Wadsworth Longfellow, *Complete Poetical Works of Henry Wadsworth Longfellow* (Boston, 1893), 118.

40. Nathaniel Parker Willis, "The Cherokee's Threat," in *Prose Works of Nathaniel Parker Willis* (Philadelphia, 1850, 376; William Ellery Channing, "Wachuset," in *The Collected Poems of William Ellery Channing* (Gainesville, Fla: Scholars' Facsimiles Reprints, 1967), 255.

41. *Chicago Tribune*, September 27, 1909.

42. Josiah Canning, "The Indian Gone!" in *Poems* (Greenfield, Mass., 1838). Canning fancied himself a true New England agrarian. In addition to his Indian summer poem, his collection contains several verses about rural life in the region's western edge.

43. Quoted in Matthews, "The Term Indian Summer," 25–26.

44. Edwin C. Martin, *Our Own Weather: A Simple Account of Its Curious Forms, Its Wide Travels and Its Notable Effects* (New York: Harper & Brothers, 1913), 157.

4. Indian Summer and the Creation of New England (pp. 73–96)

1. Grace Metalious, *Peyton Place* (Boston: Northeastern University Press, 1999), 1–2.

2. A. Cash Koeninger, "Climate and Southern Distinctiveness," *Journal of Southern History* 54 (1988), 21; Stephen P. Knadler, "Francis Parkman's Ethnography

of the Brahmin Caste and the History of the Conspiracy of Pontiac," *American Literature* 65 (June 1993), 215–38.

3. William Tudor, "An Address delivered to the Phi Beta Kappa Society," *North American Review* 3 (November 1815), 29.

4. Daniel S. Curtiss, *Western Portraiture, and Emigrants' Guide: A Description of Wisconsin, Illinois, and Iowa; with Remarks on Minnesota and Other Territories* (New York, 1852), 242. John Pendleton Kennedy's brief Indian summer statement occurs in the 1832 novel *The Swallow Barn*. I am grateful to Dan Philippon on the University of Minnesota for alerting me to the Poe reference.

5. Bernard Mergen, *Snow in America* (Washington, D.C.: Smithsonian Institution Press, 1997), 4; Kent C. Ryden, *Landscape with Figures: Nature and Culture in New England* (Iowa City: University of Iowa Press, 2001), 261–62.

6. Ryden, *Landscape with Figures*, 246.

7. William Tudor, *Letters on the Eastern States* (Boston, 1821), 312; *United States Magazine and Democratic Review* 3 (1838), 153. Albert Matthews includes these two references in "The Term Indian Summer," *Monthly Weather Review* 30 (January 1902), 24, 26.

8. Frances Osgood, *The Poetry of Flowers* (New York, 1841), 216.

9. Stephen Nissenbaum, "New England as Region and Nation," in *All Over the Map: Rethinking American Regions*, Edward L. Ayers, Patricia Nelson Limerick, Stephen Nissenbaum, and Peter Oruf, eds. (Baltimore: The Johns Hopkins University Press, 1996), 40.

10. Joseph A. Conforti, *Imagining New England: Explorations of Regional Identity from the Pilgrims to the Mid–Twentieth Century* (Chapel Hill: University of North Carolina Press, 2001), 79–122.

11. For discussion of the difficulty American poets faced when adopting English conventions see Eugene L. Huddleston, "Topographical Poetry in the Early National Era," *American Literature* 38 (November 1966), 303–22. Peter M. Briggs discusses how one early national poet worked to overcome British conventions in "Timothy Dwight 'Composes' a Landscape for New England," *American Quarterly* 40 (September 1988), 359–77.

12. Sarah Josepha Hale, *Northwood, or North and South*, 1827 (New York: Johnson Reprint Corporation, 1970), 42.

13. Newton Arvin, *Longfellow: His Life and Work* (Boston: Little Brown, 1962), 45–62.

14. Arvin, *Longfellow*, 39–40.

15. Lawrence Thompson, *Young Longfellow* (New York: Octagon 400ks, 1969), 131–46.

16. *The Works of Henry Wadsworth Longfellow*, vol. 3 (New York: Davio Press, 1909), 175.

17. *Poetical Works of Henry Wadsworth Longfellow*, vol. 2 (Boston, 1896), 29.

18. Oliver Wendell Holmes, *Else Venner* (Boston, 1891), 3.

19. For an overview of Brahmin culture see Paul Goodman, "Ethics and Enterprise: The Values of a Boston Elite, 1800–1860," *American Quarterly* 16 (fall 1966), 437–51; and Ronald Story, "Class and Culture in Boston: The Athenaeum, 1807–1860," *American Quarterly* 27 (May 1975), 178–99.

20. Ellery Sedgwick, *The Atlantic Monthly, 1857–1909: Yankee Humanism at High Tide and Ebb* (Amherst: University of Massachusetts Press, 1994), 21–43. Newton Arvin maps the decline of Longfellow's critical stock in the epilogue to his 1962 biography, *Longfellow*, 318–27. Longfellow's sinking reputation matched that of his Brahmin colleagues.

21. The most thorough biography of Lowell is Martin Duberman's *James Russell Lowell* (Boston: Houghton Mifflin, 1966). For Lowell's place in Brahmin culture see pp. 182–97.

22. James Russell Lowell, "An Indian Summer Reverie," in *The Complete Writings of James Russell Lowell*, vol. 9 (Cambridge, 1878), 192–93. The full poem runs on pp. 191–202.

23. Lowell, "An Indian Summer Reverie," 201, 202.

24. D. H. Lawrence, *Studies in Classic American Literature*, 1923 (New York: Viking Press, 1968), 54.

25. Lowell, *Complete Writings*, 1:20, 28. For the Brahmins' continuing hold on cultural and economic power at midcentury, see Goodman, "Ethics and Enterprise," 437–38.

26. Quoted in Stephen P. Knadler, "Francis Parkman's Ethnography of the Brahmin Class and the History of the Conspiracy of Pontiac," *American Literature* 65 (June 1993), 223.

27. Oliver Wendell Holmes, *Complete Poems* (Boston: 1878), 1–2. Holmes's early years and initial poetic efforts are discussed in Edwin P. Hoyt, *The Improper Bostonian: Dr. Oliver Wendell Holmes* (New York: William Morrow, 1979), 17–38.

28. Holmes, "The Seasons," in *Pages from an Old Volume of Life* (Boston, 1899), 166.

29. I am thinking here most specifically of Michael Wigglesworth's *Day of Doom*.

30. For discussion of how this dynamic unfolded in the mid–nineteenth century, see George B. Forgie, *Patricide in the House Divided: A Psychological Interpretation of the Age of Lincoln* (New York: W. W. Norton, 1979), 13–53.

31. Holmes, *The Guardian Angel* (Boston, 1891), 163, 164, 165. Matthews, in "The Term Indian Summer," mentions the scenic description that runs through this passage without commenting on Holmes's use of an Indian summer day as the setting for a thwarted sexual assault.

32. David Hackett Fischer, *Growing Old in America* (New York: Oxford University Press, 1979), 121–22.

33. Kate Sanborn, *Indian Summer Calendar* (Hartford, Conn.: Case, Lockwood & Brainard, 1904), 7–8.

34. Kenneth S. Lynn, *William Dean Howells: An American Life* (New York: Harcourt Brace Jovanovich, 1970), 89–109.

35. William Dean Howells, *Indian Summer*, 1886 (Bloomington: Indiana University Press, 1971), 56, 198, 280.

36. *New York Review of Books*, February 1, 1990, 14.

37. Howells, *Indian Summer*, 128.

38. Van Wyck Brooks, *New England: Indian Summer* (New York: E. P. Dutton, 1940), 330. Henry Adams, *Education of Henry Adams* (Boston: Houghton Mifflin, 1973), 362.

39. *Crayon* 2 (November 21, 1855), 329.

40. Bela Hubbard, *Memorials of a Half-Century: Account of Climate, Plants and History of Michigan* (New York, 1887), 558. Hubbard's quote has been mistakenly used to bolster arguments that seventeenth-century New Englanders routinely spoke of Indian summer. In an otherwise outstanding book on the natural history of autumn, for instance, Peter Marchand attributes this passage to William Hubbard, a seventeenth-century Puritan minister. The quote clearly comes from Bela Hubbard's book, however. Peter J. Marchand, *Autumn: A Season of Change* (Hanover, N.H.: University Press of New England, 2000), 122–23.

41. Karen Ordahl Kupperman, "The Puzzle of the American Climate in the Early Colonial Period," *American Historical Review* 87 (December 1982), 1262–89.

42. Eric Hobsbaum, *The Invention of Tradition*, Hobsbaum and Terrence Ranger, eds. (Cambridge, Mass.: Cambridge University Press, 1983), 1.

43. See Michael Kammen, *Mystic Chords of Memory: The Transformation of Tradition in American Culture* (New York: Alfred A, Knopf, 1991), 63–90.

44. Conforti, *Imagining New England*, 171–96.

45. *Litchfield Centennial Celebration, Held at Litchfield, Connecticut, 13 and 14 August, 1851* (Hartford, 1851), 29; John Greenleaf Whittier, *Poems*, vol. 1 (Boston, 1892), 203.

46. *Crayon* 2 (November 21, 1855), 329.

47. My understanding of how Stowe mined the New England past has been greatly influenced by Stephen Nissenbaum's "New England as Region and Nation," 43–46. Nissenbaum outlines several areas where early-nineteenth-century New England iconography depended upon an assumed connection to the region's past.

48. Harriet Beecher Stowe, *Oldtown Folks* (New York: AMS Press, 1967) xiii, 385–86.

49. M. J. Bowden, "The Invention of American Tradition," *Journal of Historical Geography* 18 (1992), 3–12.

50. Nissenbaum, "New England as Region and Nation," 43–46.

51. Lowell, "An Indian Summer Reverie," 200.

52. For the invention of village mythology see Joseph S. Wood, *The New England Village* (Baltimore: The Johns Hopkins University Press, 1997), 162. Wood's first chapter and pp. 135–50 also provide interesting discussion of how villages emerged as cultural icons.

53. Barry Keim, a professor of meteorology at the University of New Hampshire and the New Hampshire state climatologist, collected these statistics as part of his ongoing analysis of historical changes in New England's growing season. He kindly shared them with me in personal conversation.

54. Nissenbaum discusses the geographical movement of the image of the "real New England" in "New England as Region and Nation," 39.

55. Ryden, *Landscape with Figures*, 204.

5. With Faith as in Spring (pp. 97–125)

1. Henry David Thoreau, *Journal* IX (Boston: Houghton Mifflin, 1906), 91. Princeton University Press is currently reissuing authoritative editions of Thoreau's *Journal*. When possible, I refer to the modern versions. The 1906 editions carry Roman numerals for volume numbers, while the Princeton volumes use Arabic numbers.

2. "Autumnal Tints," in *The Natural History Essays* (Salt Lake City: Peregrine Smith Books, 1980), 158.

3. The definitive study of seasonal imagery in Thoreau is Richard Lebeaux's *Thoreau's Seasons* (Amherst: University of Massachusetts Press, 1984). See also Scott Slovic, *Seeking Awareness in American Nature Writing* (Salt Lake City: University of Utah Press, 1992), 21–32.

4. William Howarth, *Book of Concord: Thoreau's Life as a Writer* (New York: Viking Press, 1982), 165. Howarth discusses Thoreau's fascination with autumn on pp. 162–89. See also Lebeaux, *Thoreau's Seasons*, 293–332.

5. For Thoreau's use of seasons as a test of the doctrine of correspondence see Slovic, *Seeking Awareness in American Nature Writing*, 29–31. Lebeaux nicely articulates Thoreau's overall seasonal sense in *Thoreau's Seasons*. Chapter 4, "Seedtime," and chapter 5, "Second Spring," particularly enhanced my understanding.

6. Lawrence Buell, *The Environmental Imagination: Thoreau, Nature Writing, and the Formation of the American Literary Canon* (Cambridge, Mass.: Belknap Press of Harvard University Press, 1995), 242–43.

7. *A Week on the Concord and Merrimack Rivers* (Orleans, Mass.: Parnassus Imprints, 1987), 63.

8. Robert F. Sayre, *Thoreau and the American Indian* (Princeton, N.J.: Princeton University Press, 1977), 101–22; Richard Fleck, *The Indians of Thoreau* (Albuquerque, 1974), 2.

9. Ning Yu, "Thoreau's Critique of the Pastoral in *A Week*," *Nineteenth-Century*

Literature 51 (December 1996), 305–10. *A Week on the Concord and Merrimack Rivers* reveals Thoreau's deep interest in the present appearance of the landscape as well as its historic uses. As he describes his journey through the Merrimack Valley, he moves from the history of Indian settlements to the several modern textile mills powered by the river's falls.

10. Walter Harding, *Days of Henry Thoreau: A Biography* (Princeton, N.J.: Princeton University Press, 1982), 243–46. Harding's book remains the definitive biography of Thoreau.

11. H. Daniel Peck, *Thoreau's Morning Work: Memory and Perception in "A Week on the Concord and Merrimack Rivers," "The Journal," and "Walden"* (New Haven, Conn.: Yale University Press, 1990), 44. Peck's discussion on pp. 39–49 was particularly useful for helping me see how Indian summer fits into Thoreau's journal practice. Also helpful was Joan Burbick, *Thoreau's Alternative History: Changing Perspectives on Nature, Culture, and Language* (Philadelphia: University of Pennsylvania Press, 1987), 35–47.

12. Burbick, *Thoreau's Alternative History*, 35, 37.

13. The specific changes of Thoreau's journal technique for these months are outlined in the historical introduction to Thoreau's *Journal*, vol. 3, Elizabeth Hall Witherell and John C. Broderick, eds. (Princeton, N.J.: Princeton University Press, 1991). See especially pp. 488–92. For Thoreau's trip to Canada see Harding, *Days*, 279–83.

14. "Walking," in *The Natural History Essays*, 95.

15. For Thoreau's surveying skills see Harding, *Days*, 274–77.

16. *Hamlet*, I, iv, 53. Upon seeing the Ghost of Hamlet Senior for the first time, Hamlet asks,

> What may this mean,
> That thou, dead corse, again in complete steel,
> Revisits thus the glimpses of the moon,
> Making night hideous; and we fools of nature
> So horridly to shake our disposition
> With thoughts beyond the reaches of our souls?
> (I, iv, 51–56).

17. *Journals and Miscellaneous Notebooks of Ralph Waldo Emerson*, vol. 2 (Cambridge, Mass.: Harvard University Press), 400.

18. The best account of the strains in the Emerson-Thoreau friendship is Harmon Smith's *My Friend, My Friend: The Story of Thoreau's Relationship with Emerson* (Amherst: University of Massachusetts Press, 1999), 129–43.

19. John Conron, " 'Bright American Rivers': The Luminist Landscapes of Thoreau's *A Week on the Concord and Merrimack Rivers*," *American Quarterly* 32 (1980), 146. See also Conron's book *American Picturesque* (University Park: The Pennsylvania State University Press, 2000), 289–306.

20. Barbara Novak, "On Defining Luminism," in *American Light: The Luminist Movement, 1850–1875,* John Wilmerding, ed. (Princeton, N.J.: Princeton University Press, 1989), 24.

21. Elana Weiss, *Poetic Landscape: The Art and Experience of Sanford R. Gifford* (Newark: University of Delaware Press, 1987), 18, 19.

22. Quoted in Conron, "Bright American Rivers," 166.

23. Robert D. Richardson, *Henry Thoreau: A Life of the Mind* (Berkeley: University of California Press, 1986), 259–66. See also Conron, *American Picturesque,* 291.

24. Richard Schneider, "Thoreau and Nineteenth-Century American Landscape Painting," *ESQ: A Journal of the American Renaissance* 31 (1985), 67.

25. Lebeaux, *Thoreau's Seasons,* 2.

26. Joseph Wood Krutch, *Henry David Thoreau* (Westport, Conn.: Greenwood Press, 194), 143. Thoreau's struggles with bird identification are discussed in Richard Fleck, "The Bird Journal of Sophia, John and Henry David Thoreau," *Bulletin of Research in the Humanities* 87 (1986–87), 489–508.

27. Jones Very, *Complete Poems of Jones Very,* Helen R. Deese, ed. (Athens: University of Georgia Press, 1993), 341. Thoreau, *A Week,* 442.

28. *A Week,* 44.

29. For the use of witch hazel by eighteenth-century New Englanders see Alan Taylor, "The Early Republic's Supernatural Economy: Treasure Seeking in the American Northeast, 1780–1830," *American Quarterly* 38 (1986), 10.

30. Laura Dassow Walls, *Seeing New Worlds: Henry David Thoreau and Nineteenth-Century Natural History* (Madison: University of Wisconsin Press, 1995), 147. Walls's discussion of Thoreau's scientific practice was tremendously helpful to my understanding of how he pursued his researches into the natural world. See especially pp. 134–57.

31. Rod and Ken Preston-Mahfam, *Spiders of the World* (London: Blandford, 1999), 99–101.

32. *Works of Jonathan Edwards: Scientific and Philosophical Writings,* Wallace E. Anderson, ed. (New Haven, Conn.: Yale University Press, 1980), 164. Gilbert White, *The Natural History and Antiquities of Selborne* (London, 1875), 213.

33. Kirby and Spence, *Introduction to Entomology* (London, 1817), 341.

34. "Autumnal Tints," 158.

35. Walls, *Seeing New Worlds,* 183.

36. Harding, *Days,* 416–21.

37. Thoreau's calendar manuscripts for April, May, June, and November are in the Pierpont Morgan Library in New York. Peck, *Thoreau's Morning Work,* 47–48; and Howarth, *Book of Concord,* 176–77, enriched my understanding of how the project fits into Thoreau's late thinking.

38. Harding, *Days,* 438. My discussion in this paragraph on Thoreau's reading of Darwin's *Origin of Species* and its influence on his conception of tree succession,

including the example of oak and pine trees, relies on Harding, *Days*, 438–40, and Walls, *Seeing New Worlds*, 194–99.

39. Robert D. Richardson, Jr., introduction to Thoreau's *Faith in a Seed*, Bradley P. Dean, ed. (Washington, D.C.: Island Press, 1993), 13. Richardson's introduction provides a concise discussion of Thoreau's aims for his seed dispersal research.

40. The initial *Journal* entry is at XI: 338; the slightly revised version is *Faith in a Seed*, 80–81.

41. *Journal*, V:457.

42. Harding, *Days*, 442–67.

6. Emily Dickinson and Indian Summer (pp. 126–55)

1. Ernest Sandeen, "Delight Deferred by Retrospect: Emily Dickinson's Late-Summer Poems," *New England Quarterly* 40 (1967), 486.

2. Richard Sewall discusses Dickinson's reading Longfellow's novel *Kavanagh* in *The Life of Emily Dickinson* (New York: Farrar, Straus and Giroux, 1974), 163–65 and 683–88.

3. *Letters of Emily Dickinson*, vol. 2, Thomas H. Johnson, ed. (Cambridge, Mass.: Belknap Press of Harvard University Press, 1958), 463.

4. For accounts of Dickinson and Indian summer see Charles R. Anderson, *Emily Dickinson's Poetry: Stairway of Surprise* (New York: Holt, Rinehart and Winston, 1960), 145–55; Cynthia Griffin Wolff, *Emily Dickinson* (Reading, Mass.: Addison-Wesley, 1986), 307–11; Timothy Morris, "The Development of Dickinson's Style," *American Literature* 60 (1988), 36–40; and Sandeen, "Delight Deferred," 483–500.

5. The number in parenthesis (F 122) refers to the number provided by R. W. Franklin's edition of *Dickinson's Poems* (Cambridge, Mass.: Belknap Press of Harvard University Press, 1998). Franklin's numbers differ slightly from the numbers assigned by Thomas Johnson in his 1958 edition of Dickinson's poems.

6. Lawrence Buell makes this point about Longfellow's "Aftermath" in *The Environmental Imagination: Thoreau, Nature Writing, and the Formation of American Culture* (Cambridge, Mass.: Belknap Press of Harvard University Press, 1995), 109–10.

7. Thoreau, "Autumnal Tints," in *The Natural History Essays* (Salt Lake City: Peregrine Smith Books, 1980), 174.

8. Some feminist scholars have identified Dickinson's characteristic evasiveness with a gender-specific decision to forgo a conventional public voice—which, as a middle-class woman residing in stately Amherst was largely cut off to her—in favor of the more daring interior explorations that her poems chart. See Suzanne Juhasz,

The Undiscovered Continent: Emily Dickinson and the Space of the Mind (Bloomington: University of Indiana Press, 1983), 4–14. We may also attribute part of this silence to what Lawrence Buell has identified as the "absent center" of much nineteenth-century American verse. Citing examples from Emerson, Whittier, and Dickinson, Buell argues that such poems invoke a "general strategy of contemplating or rationalizing the elusiveness or loss of some ideal from a present position of spiritual barrenness." Lawrence Buell, *New England Literary Culture: From Revolution Through Renaissance* (Cambridge: Cambridge University Press, 1986), 124.

9. Comparisons of mid-nineteenth-century Amherst temperatures with those of the rest of the century can be found in Raymond S. Bradley, Jon K. Eischeid, and Philip T. Ives, *The Climate of Amherst, Massachusetts, 1835–1985*, (Amherst, Mass.: Amherst College Department of Geology and Geography, 1987), 49–53.

10. These quotes appear on the first page of the *Hampshire and Franklin Express* or the *Springfield Republican* for the dates listed in the paragraph.

11. Morris discusses Dickinson's early meter and rhyme schemes in "The Development of Dickinson's Style," 30–32.

12. I am grateful to my Boston University colleague William E. (Ted) Davis for sharing his deep knowledge of birds with me. Professor Davis is a Fellow of the American Ornithologists Union and a past president of the Wilson Ornithological Society.

13. Wolff, *Emily Dickinson*, 307.

14. A vast body of scholarship has been amassed around this poem. Particularly useful are Wolff, *Emily Dickinson*, 309–10; Morris, "The Development of Dickinson's Style," 36–37; Sandeen, "Delight Deterred," 488–89. See also Jane Donahue Eberwein, "Emily Dickinson and the Calvinist Tradition," *ESQ: A Journal of the American Renaissance* 33 (2nd quarter, 1987), 99–100.

15. Eberwein, "Emily Dickinson and the Calvinist Tradition," 90–91.

16. Wolff, *Emily Dickinson*, 143. My understanding of Dickinson's struggles with orthodoxy in this paragraph draws heavily on Wolff's biography. For Amherst revivals see pp. 66–67. For detailed discussion of the poet's religious questions see pp. 260–365.

17. Wolff, *Emily Dickinson*, 309.

18. Betty L. Mitchell traces the range of responses in "Massachusetts Reacts to John Brown's Raid," *Civil War History* 19 (March 1973), 65–79.

19. Quoted in Shira Wolosky, *Emily Dickinson: A Voice of War* (New Haven, Conn.: Yale University Press, 1984), 69.

20. Sewall, *The Life of Emily Dickinson*, 466.

21. These quotes are taken from page-one articles in the *Springfield Republican* on the cited dates.

22. *Springfield Republican*, December 2, 1859.

23. Karen Dandurand, "New Dickinson Civil War Publications," *American Literature* 56 (March 1984), 23–24. My summary of this episode is drawn from Dandurand's entire article, pp. 17–27.

24. Martha Nell Smith, *Rowing in Eden: Rereading Emily Dickinson* (Austin: University of Texas Press, 1992), 181.

25. Dandurand, "New Dickinson Civil War Publications," 23.

26. Christopher Kent Wilson, "Winslow Homer's *The Veteran in a New Field*: A Study of the Harvest Metaphor and Popular Culture," *American Art Journal* 17 (1985), 16. Wilson discusses Bushnell and Lincoln on pp. 3–4.

27. Quoted in Wilson, "Winslow Homer's *The Veteran in a New Field*," 17. The poem, "The Only Son," appeared in *Harper's Weekly* 7 (October 31, 1863), 702.

28. Henry Howard Brownell, "The Battle Summers," in *War Lyrics and Other Poems* (Boston, 1866), 39.

29. Mary Clemmer Ames, "Indian Summer in Virginia," in *Outlines of Men, Women, and Things* (New York, 1873), 37–42.

30. Dickinson was long assumed to have little to say about the Civil War. Recent scholarship, however, has demonstrated the many ways the carnage affected her both personally and poetically. See especially Wolosky, *Emily Dickinson: A Voice of War*.

31. Wolff, *Emily Dickinson*, 62. Wolff discusses the impact of Amherst religious life on Dickinson's development as a poet in pp. 62–75.

32. Wolff, *Emily Dickinson*, 78–79, 428–29.

33. Sewall, *The Life of Emily Dickinson*, 338, 343.

34. Jack L. Capps, *Emily Dickinson's Reading, 1836–1886* (Cambridge, Mass.: Harvard University Press, 1966), 128.

35. Barton Levi St. Armand, *Emily Dickinson and Her Culture: The Soul's Society* (Cambridge: Cambridge University Press, 1984), 190.

36. Ellery Sedgwick, *The Atlantic Monthly, 1857–1909: Yankee Humanism at High Tide and Ebb* (Amherst: University of Massachusetts Press, 1994), 3–10.

37. The Higginson essays quoted in this paragraph are most accessible in his collection *Out-Door Papers* (Boston, 1871).

38. Quoted in Capps, *Emily Dickinson's Reading*, 137.

39. *Springfield Republican*, September 15, 1850, p. 4; October 16, 1860, and November 3, 1860, p. 2.

40. *Springfield Republican*, November 10, 1860.

41. David S. Reynolds, *Beneath the American Renaissance: The Subversive Imagination in the Age of Emerson and Melville* (New York: Alfred A. Knopf, 1988), 7.

42. Sandeen, "Delight Deterred," 488.

43. Morris, "The Development of Dickinson's Style," 38. Morris's cogent and insightful reading of the poem informs much of this paragraph. My analysis differs from his in one important way, however. He goes on to suggest that Dickinson's

preference lay in the second June, in the Indian summer (39). In several of her Indian summer poems this is the case, but I find this one more ambiguous.

44. The poem appeared in the *Springfield Republican*, September 28, 1861, p. 6. Capps lists a copy of Bryant's complete poems in his survey of the Dickinson family library in *Emily Dickinson's Reading*. For the circumstances of Bryant's initial composition see Charles H. Brown, *William Cullen Bryant* (New York: Charles Scribner's Sons, 1971), 192–93. For Thoreau and the blue gentian see *Journals*, XI:183.

45. William Cullen Bryant, *Poems* vol. 2 (New York, 1854), 17.

46. For an excellent discussion of Dickinson's botanical knowledge see Elizabeth A. Petrino, *Emily Dickinson and Her Contemporaries: Woman's Verse in America, 1820–1885* (Hanover, N.H.: University Press of New England, 1998) 129–60.

47. Petrino, *Emily Dickinson and Her Contemporaries*, 152.

48. *Letters of Emily Dickinson*, Thomas H. Johnson, ed., 2: 444.

49. Vincent G. Delthier, *Crickets and Katydids, Concerts and Solos* (Cambridge, Mass.: Harvard University Press, 1992), 110, 111.

50. Frank D. Rashid, "Emily Dickinson's Voice of Endings," *ESQ: A Journal of the American Renaissance* 31 (1985), 26.

51. Wolff, *Emily Dickinson*, 312.

52. Wolff, *Emily Dickinson*, 310.

53. Rashid, "Emily Dickinson's Voice of Endings," 32.

54. R. W. Franklin identifies the various recipients in *Poems of Emily Dickinson: Variorum Edition*, vol. 2 (Cambridge, Mass.: The Belknap Press of Harvard University Press, 1998), 831–35.

7. Coda (pp. 156–63)

1. Martha Gilbert Dickinson, "Indian Summer," *New England Magazine* 23 (October 1897), 212.

2. *Century Illustrated Monthly Magazine* 71 (November 1905), 21.

3. "Indian Summer," by Al Dubin and Victor Herbert, © 1919, 1939 (Copyrights renewed), Warner Bros. Inc. All rights reserved. Used by permission. Phil Furia discusses Dubin's film lyrics in *The Poets of Tin Pan Alley: A History of America's Great Lyricists* (New York: Oxford University Press, 1990), 237.

4. Quoted in Will Friedwald, *Sinatra: The Song Is You: A Singer's Art* (New York: De Capo Press, 1997), 308.

5. The session is described in Leonard Mustazza, *Ol' Blue Eyes: A Frank Sinatra Encyclopedia* (Westport, Conn.: Greenwood Press, 1998), 68.

6. Grace Metalious, *Peyton Place* (Boston: Northeastern University Press, 1999), 1.

7. Cameron writes this on p. xiv of the introduction to the 1999 edition of

Peyton Place cited in note 6. Cameron's essay provides a thorough discussion of the cultural background surrounding Metalious's novel.

8. Metalious, *Peyton Place*, 1.

9. See, for example, Lewis Turco, "Sestina in Indian Summer," *The Southern Review* 26 (winter 1990), 223–24.

10. Maxine Kumin, "Indian Summer," in *Looking for Luck* (New York: W. W. Norton, 1992), 87. The poem first appeared in *American Poetry Review* 21 (January/February 1992), 43. The poem is quoted with the kind permission of W. W. Norton & Company.

11. A short list of rock 'n' roll artists who have written Indian summer songs include Van Morrison, The Doors, U2, and Roy Orbison. Among the states that hold Indian summer festivals are Ohio, Georgia, and Pennsylvania. These are usually weekend-long events held along scenic riverways or in large urban parks. Every September, Indian Summer Festivals, Inc., hosts a celebration of Native American culture in Wisconsin.

12. www.arinanoasis.com/prisicilla 4/25/02.

13. www.ferweh-online.de/Reiseberichte/USA.Vermont. The quote in this paragraph is a translation from the German text. 4/25/02.

Index